D0856872

Noises in the Blood

Noises in the Blood

Orality, Gender, and the "Vulgar" Body of Jamaican Popular Culture

CAROLYN COOPER

Duke University Press
Durham 1995

First U.S. Edition, Duke University Press, 1995
Originally published by Macmillan Press Ltd, 1993

Printed in the United States of America on acid-free paper ∞
Library of Congress Cataloging-in-Publication Data appear on the last printed page of this book.

For my sister, Donnette, who insisted
and for Ben, who inveigled

Contents

	Preface: Informing cultural studies: a politics of betrayal?	*ix*
	Acknowledgments	*xiii*
	Introduction: Oral/sexual discourse in Jamaican popular culture	1
1	'Me know no law, me know no sin': transgressive identities and the voice of innocence: the historical context	19
2	'Culture an tradition an birthright': proverb as metaphor in the poetry of Louise Bennett	37
3	That cunny Jamma oman: representations of female sensibility in the poetry of Louise Bennett	47
4	Words unbroken by the beat: the performance poetry of Jean Binta Breeze and Mikey Smith	68
5	Writing oral history: Sistren Theatre Collective's *Lionheart Gal*	87
6	Country come to town: Michael Thelwell's *The Harder They Come*	96
7	Chanting down Babylon: Bob Marley's song as literary text	117
8	Slackness hiding from culture: erotic play in the dancehall	136
9	From 'centre' to 'margin': turning history upside down	174
	Appendix 1: Proverbs from Louise Bennett	200
	Appendix 2: Jamaican proverbs: a gender perspective	202
	Bibliography	205
	Index	210

Preface: Informing Cultural Studies
A Politics of Betrayal?

Black identity is not simply a social and political category to be used or abandoned according to the extent to which the rhetoric that supports and legitimises it is persuasive or institutionally powerful. Whatever the radical constructionists may say, it is lived as a coherent (if not always stable) experiential sense of self. Though it is often felt to be natural and spontaneous, it remains the outcome of practical activity: language, gesture, bodily significations, desires.

Paul Gilroy, *The Black Atlantic*

In a troubled voice, my grandmother asked me the last time I saw her before she died, "How can you live so far away from your people?" In her mind, "my people" were not synonymous with a mass of black people, but with particular black folks that one is connected to by ties of blood and fellowship, the folks with whom we share a history, the folks who talk our talk (the patois of our region), who know our background and our ways. Her comment silenced me. I felt a pain in my heart as though I had been pierced by a sharp blade. My grandmother's words were like that; they felt to me like little knives. My silent response was tacit agreement that only misguided confused folks would live away from their people, their own.

bell hooks, 'Third World Diva Girls'

Wi no infaama, infamieshan wi no gi
If a man a moles mi an mi famili
Mi naa ron fi poliis ar sikuoriti
Mi uda chek fi mi ruud bwai kompini

[We are not informers, we don't give information
If someone is molesting me and my family
I wouldn't run to the police or the security forces
I would rather call on my rude boy posse]

Shabba Ranks, 'Rude Boy,' *X-Tra Naked*

The undermining of the 'informer' that is such a pronounced feature of current Jamaican dancehall music defines a culture-specific genealogy for my self-reflexive analysis of the function of cultural criticism as a politics of betrayal. As a cultural critic I am aware that my location at the crossroads—as an intermediary between competing discourses—makes me vulnerable to border clashes.[1] The 'border clash,' yet another frequent theme in dancehall music, encompasses the clashing of bordering communities, rival gangs, rival sound systems, and female rivals (wife and matey) competing for the attention of shared male lovers. At the same time it more broadly images the hostile interfacing of ideological systems that coexist in Jamaican society and in the reluctant host societies to which Jamaicans constantly migrate.

Attempts to study the nature of these border clashes can result in an alternately frustrating and liberating sense that the slippery text continuously eludes the grasp of the critic. It is not simply that the products of the popular imagination, by their very nature, keep changing rapidly. It is also that dynamic processes of cultural production that are designed purely for experiential pleasure become subject to a disempowering discourse that can appear to reduce live(d) art forms to stripped-down, boxed-in, museum pieces. Indeed, I argue in the penultimate chapter, 'Slackness Hiding from Culture: Erotic Play in the Dancehall,' that subjection to analysis is yet another form of containment; a clear sign that 'High Culture' is successfully appropriating the 'low' in an act of restrictive scholarship.

From an African-American perspective, bell hooks defines the problem thus:

> Cultural studies could easily become the space for the informers: those folks who appear to be allied with the disadvantaged, the oppressed, who are either spies or there to mediate between the forces of domination and its victims.[2]

I offer these essays on Jamaican popular culture not as the published travelogue of a spy in enemy country; or the medi(t)ation of a paid informer. Rather, these essays are a message from an insider, transmitting a 'bottoms-up' history of working-class resistance in Jamaica.

In Jamaican folklore the 'vulgar' image of the bottom as a site of anticolonialist resistance is most dramatically realised in the assertion that the historical Nanny, the powerful female leader of the Maroons, used her bottom to deflect the bullets of British soldiers. In a metaphorical representation of this myth, Kamau Brathwaite argues that "[t]here is no way that Nanny could have turned her back & done what they say she did. But she could have turned her back, lifted her skirt, & *displayed the derriere as a symbol of derision & abuse* which is a very common feature of 'the culture', as you know. . . ."[3] I propose that this legendary instance of female 'bottom power' must be related to the much more sexualised representation of the potent female bottom in contemporary Jamaican dancehall culture.

These noises in the blood articulate a body of knowledge that is often devalued both at home and abroad. The negative image of working-class Jamaican 'yardie' culture that prevails at home is magnified in the stereotype of Jamaican 'posse' culture that prevails abroad.

The process of migration does facilitate the cutting and mixing of old aesthetic forms and stereotypes to accommodate new sociopolitical realities. For example, Paul Gilroy offers a summary of his argument in chapter 1 of *The Black Atlantic* that

> hip-hop culture grew out of the cross-fertilization of African-American vernacular cultures with their Caribbean equivalents rather than springing fully formed from the entrails of the blues. The immediate catalyst for its development was the relocation of Clive "Kool DJ Herc" Campbell from Kingston to 168th Street in the Bronx. The syncretic dynamics of the form were complicated further by a distinctly Hispanic input into and appropriation of the break dance moves which helped to define the style in its early stages. But hip-hop was not just the product of these different, though converging, black cultural traditions. The centrality of "the break" within it, and the subsequent refinement of cutting and mixing techniques through digital sampling which took the form far beyond the competence of hands on turntables, mean that the aesthetic rules which govern it are premised on a dialectic of rescuing appropriation and recombination which creates special pleasures and is not limited to the technological complex in which it originated.[4]

The arts of cross-fertilisation are multifarious. The beginnings of ska—the precursor of rock-steady, reggae, and now ragga/dancehall—are located as much in the blues as in indigenous Jamaican mento musical forms. Imported African-American music informed the evolution of Jamaican popular music just as exported DJ-ing allowed recombinant possibilities. Family ties are complicated by the crossing and recrossing of cultural blood lines as illustrated in the success of Snow, the culturally 'black'/white Canadian DJ, whose 'Informer' somewhat ironically defines his role as trangressive interlocutor. In 1993, Snow's 'Informer' and Shaggy's 'Oh Carolina' made history: for the first time, two reggae songs were simultaneously number one on both the Billboard Hot 100 chart and the British Pop chart, respectively.

Snow's 'Informer' illustrates the metaphorical remastering that digital sampling propagates. In the cut and mix of sophisticated technological reconfigurations, the noises in the blood become world-beat music, appropriatable *ad infinitum*. Nevertheless, the counter-colonising, international spread of reggae as "classical" popular music, heard in every capital of the world (and in small villages), can also be reconceptualised as a compelling argument in favour of the cultural politics of high-tech miscegenation.

The word and the beat are the subjects of this study of Jamaican popular culture. In Gilroy's terms, "language, gesture, bodily significations, desires" constitute the critical corpus—not the metastatic body as mummified museum corpse. Performance poetry, popular song, and autobiographical and biographical narrative are the informing texts. As informer, I invite readers to participate in a 'border clash,' a crossing of the conventional boundaries of family; a reconfiguration of the 'ties of blood and fellowship.' This is not a betrayal of the disalienating vision of bell hooks's grandmother and all those 'folks with whom we share a history, the folks who talk our talk (the patois of our region), who know our background and our ways.'

The technology of the word, both oral and scribal—those noises in the blood and the reverberating echoes in the bone—facilitates dialogue within a rehumanised community that includes the posses, the informers, the police, the security forces and even the former owners of the plantation that was and is the Americas. Informing becomes a gateway to understanding the insurgent culture of maroonage that is the shared heritage of diasporic Africans in the black Atlantic/Caribbean.[5]

Notes

1 See, for example, the uses of the trope of the border in Iain Chambers, *Border Dialogues: Journeys in Postmodernism* (Routledge: London, 1990); and Stanley Aronowitz and Henry A. Giroux, "Border Pedagogy in the Age of Postmodernism" in *Postmodern Education: Politics, Culture, and Social Criticism* (Minneapolis: University of Minnesota Press, 1991).

2 bell hooks, *Yearning: Race, Gender, and Cultural Politics* (Boston: South End Press, 1990) p. 9.

3 Kamau Brathwaite, "Nanny, Palmares and the Caribbean Maroon Connexion" in E. Kofi Agorsah, ed. *Maroon Heritage: Archaeological Ethnographic and Historical Perspectives* (Barbados, Jamaica, Trinidad and Tobago: Canoe Press, The University of the West Indies, 1994) p. 126.

4 Paul Gilroy, *The Black Atlantic: Modernity and Double Consciousness* (Cambridge: Harvard University Press, 1993) pp. 103–4.

5 For an "archipelagic middle zone" review of *The Black Atlantic* see Norval (Nadi) Edwards, "Roots, and Some Routes Not Taken: A Caribcentric Reading of *The Black Atlantic*," *Found Object*, Fall 1994.

Acknowledgements

This book is the result of a series of negotiations: with my students in West Indian literature at the University of the West Indies, on whom I tested many of the ideas presented here; with my colleagues in the Faculty of Arts and General (Interdisciplinary) Studies, whom I brazenly forced into reading the manuscript in various stages of evolution; with my collaborators in Women and Development Studies in the wider University community, who have helped me refine a gender perspective on Jamaican popular culture; with the 'massive' Jamaican street culture that I have used to 'big up' my academic research.

I must name Mervyn Morris and Nadi Edwards, with whom I work in the Department of English at Mona, both of whom have contributed in great measure to the development of this project. Mervyn, my former teacher, and Nadi, my former student, have helped me define my own work as issuing from a kind of Legba-like crossroads dialectic of africanist/post-modernist discourse. Mervyn's pioneering work on Louise Bennett, and his on-going research in 'performance poetry' – I am indebted to him for that coinage – liberated the territory of popular culture for academic exploration. Nadi's generous sharing of his work on ethnopoetics and literary theory has helped me establish areas of difference and similarity between my own work and the more self-consciously theoretical research in popular culture that proceeds from the margins of Western academia. I particularly appreciated access to Nadi's extensive library – his trailerload of books – that have the same amplitude and currency as Shabba Ranks' trailerload a girls.

I must also name my mother and first teacher, Modesta Riley Cooper, who dragged me off to primary school with her when I was 3 – largely because I was giving so much trouble at home; and my substitute mother, Mrs Ivy Pryce – Lady P – whose witticisms and plain insights, issuing from the 'unschooled' wisdom of largely oral Jamaicans, have continually guided my research. I have tested many of my ideas on her for an authoritative 'folk' perspective. Lady P is an ideal 'informant', inter-actively structuring the development of the project.

I am indebted to the British Council for a Commonwealth Academic Staff fellowship which allowed me a year's leave from teaching to do much of the recent work for this book. As Visiting Scholar in the Centre of West

African Studies at the University of Birmingham, I had the pleasure of working with Stewart Brown (my nominal supervisor) and Karin Barber, who generously read various drafts of chapters that vaguely related to her own work. I must thank Marlene Wray, formerly of the Centre, and now liberated from the despotic rule of low-level bureaucracy, for patiently showing me how to use the Centre's Macintosh computer.

While on fellowship leave, I had the opportunity to present papers on several occasions: at a joint Cultural Studies/Centre of West African Studies seminar at Birmingham University, on Louise Bennett's poetry; at the 1989 conference on 'African Discourse' of the embryonic Oxford School of African Studies, where I presented a paper on spirit possession as trope in Erna Brodber's *Myal*; at the 12th annual conference of the German-Speaking Countries on the New Literatures in English, Giessen, where I presented the earliest version of the chapter on the lyrics of the DJs; at the annual meeting of the (British) Society for Caribbean Studies, where I presented a later version of that paper; at the Silver Jubilee Conference of the Association for Commonwealth Literature and Language Studies, University of Kent, where I presented the paper on the work of the performance poets, Jean Breeze and Mikey Smith; at a conference on Rastafari, organised by Barry Chevannes at the Institute of Social Studies, The Hague, where I presented a recontexualised version of the paper on Bob Marley's lyrics. I am grateful to the various audiences whose responses to these essays, presented as works-in-progress at academic conferences, have helped shape their final form.

I am grateful to *Kunapipi*, for permission to reprint 'Writing Oral History: Sistren Theatre Collective's *Lionheart Gal*'; to *Wasafiri* for permission to reprint 'Words unbroken by the beat: the performance poetry of Jean Binta Breeze and Mikey Smith'; and most of all to *Jamaica Journal* for publishing, in the first place, the early essays: 'Proverb as Metaphor' and 'Female Sensibility in the Poetry of Louise Bennett'; and 'Bob Marley's Song as Literary Text'. I am equally grateful to the *Journal* for permission to reprint these essays, and the more recent 'Slackness hiding from culture: erotic play in the dancehall'.

The inversion of the high/low–universal/local hierarchy that is an important theme of this study is markedly demonstrated in the order of publication of these essays, the majority of which were first published locally. In the global economics of the university, locally published research does not have the same authority and value as that published in 'international' journals. But since centres and margins keep shifting, and every scholar's local journal is some other scholar's international journal – *Jamaica Journal*, like reggae music, is certainly international – I am pleased that the publication of this book reverses the usual order of privilege of the local and the international.

The author and publishers are grateful to Sangster's (In Jamaica) for permission to quote poems by Louise Bennett, and to Polygram and EMI Music Publishing for permission to quote lyrics by Bob Marley.

The Marley lyrics are 1) © 1974, Cayman Music, Inc., USA. Reproduced by permission of Cayman Music Inc./EMI Tunes plc, London WC2H 0EA; and 2) © 1975 Cayman Music Inc., USA. Reproduced by permission of Cayman Music Inc./EMI Tunes plc, London WC2H 0EA.

The extracts in Chapter 5 from *Lionheart Gal* are reprinted by permission of Honor Ford Smith and Sistren Theatre Collective; first published in 1986 by The Women's Press Ltd, 34 Great Sutton Street, London EC1V 0DX, and in 1987 by Sister Vision Black and Women of Colour Press, PO Box 217, Station E, Toronto, Ontario M6H 3C2.

The publishers have made every effort to contact other copyright holders. If any feel that they have been overlooked, they should contact The Macmillan Press Ltd, who will be pleased to come to an arrangement at the earliest possible time.

Introduction: Oral/sexual discourse in Jamaican popular culture

'I dont know much 'bout book, but I tell you what me fren, I is a man wid a terrible long head, I can tell you, and de man dat want fe mek me a fool, mek him come.' Old John.

Quoted in Henry G. Murray, *Manners and Customs of the Country a Generation Ago: Tom Kittle's Wake*

'Kishee says to be a Griot, I must have no doubt when a knowledge comes to me like an echo in the bone or a noise in the blood.'

Vic Reid, *Nanny Town*

'Now I'd like to describe for you some of the characteristics of our nation language. First of all, it is from, as I've said, an oral tradition. The poetry, the culture itself, exists not in a dictionary but in the tradition of the spoken word. It is based as much on sound as it is on song. That is to say, the noise that it makes is part of the meaning, and if you ignore the noise (or what you would *think* of as noise, shall I say) then you lose part of the meaning. When it is written, you lose the sound or the noise, and therefore you lose part of the meaning. Which is, again, why I have to have a tape recorder for this presentation. I want you to get the sound of it, rather than the sight of it.

Edward Kamau Brathwaite, *History of the Voice*

The linguistic trap
(dominance)
. . .
The oral – the written
(the release of inhibitions)

Edouard Glissant, *Caribbean Discourse*

> 'Well, you know what dey say "uh white man and uh nigger woman is de freest thing on earth." Dey do as dey please.'
>
> Zora Neale Hurston, *Their Eyes Were Watching God*

> 'One must assume the feminine role deliberately, which means already to convert a form of subordination into an affirmation, and thus to begin to thwart it.'
>
> Luce Irigaray, *This Sex Which Is Not One*

The six epigraphs that frame these essays on Jamaican popular culture define the shifting boundaries of the critical terrain. The primary project of *Noises in the Blood* is to examine the seemingly oppositional ideology of 'long head' and 'book' as expressed in the statement attributed to Old John in Henry G. Murray's *Manners and Customs of the Country a Generation Ago: Tom Kittle's Wake*: '"I dont know much 'bout book, but I tell you what me fren, I is a man wid a terrible long head, I can tell you, and de man dat want fe mek me a fool, mek him come."' 'The Writer and the Oral Tradition in Jamaica', the original sub-title of this collection of essays, similarly articulates a dialectical relationship between oral and scribal discourse; though it seems to assume the primacy of the writer's reformulation of Afro-Jamaican oral texts and devices in Western literary forms, the original sub-title with its conjunctive 'and' allows for both the relative autonomy of oral texts existing independently of a tradition of writing, and the interdependence of the scribal and the oral traditions. In this spirit of 'intertextuality', the epigraph from Edouard Glissant's litany of 'Cultural Identity' simply juxtaposes 'the written' and 'the oral', the egalitarian dash signalling openness/closure, 'the release of inhibitions' and liberation from the dominance of '[t]he linguistic trap'.

The oral tradition in Jamaica is conceived as a broad repertoire of themes and cultural practices, as well as a more narrow taxonomy of verbal techniques. The thematic repertoire includes diverse cultural beliefs/practices such as religion – obeah, myal, ettu, revival, kumina, spirit-possession; entertainment/socialisation practices – children's games, story-telling rituals, tea-meetings and social dance, for example. The verbal techniques include the compressed allusiveness of proverb, the enigmatic indirection of riddle and the antiphonal repetitions of oral narration which recur as set linguistic formulations in folk-tale, legend, song-text and performance poetry. Jamaican, the preferred language of orality, assumes the burdens of the social stigmatisation to which the practitioners of afrocentric ideology in Jamaica are continually subjected. Upward social mobility in Jamaica requires the shedding of the old skin of early socialisation: mother tongue, mother culture, mother wit – the feminised discourse of voice, identity and native knowledge.

The written texts originally selected to illustrate the antagonism/complementarity of long head and book in twentieth-century Jamaican literature/popular culture were, firstly, novels: Herbert DeLisser's *Jane's Career;* Claude McKay's *Banana Bottom*; Erna Brodber's *Jane and Louisa Will Soon Come Home* and *Myal;* Vic Reid's *Nanny Town.* Each of these experiments in form inscribes the Jamaican attempt to 'colonise' a western literary form, the novel, adapting the conventions of the genre to accommodate orality. For example, Erna Brodber's narrative method exemplifies the interpenetration of scribal and oral literary forms: a modernist, stream-of-consciousness narrative voice holds easy dialogue with the traditional teller of tales, the transmitter of anansi story, proverb, folk song and dance. The casual centrality of the 'supernatural' in Brodber's fiction is also an excellent example of the writer's adaptation of marginalised thematic concepts from the oral tradition which she legitimises in the very process of 'writing them up'. But if the oral, broadly defined, does achieve 'status' once it appears in written form, it nevertheless contaminates the written as subversive praxis. What Brodber actually writes in *Myal* is an alternative curriculum that challenges the process of zombification whereby the colonised/educated mind assumes the convenient state of living dead, easily manipulable. Long head and (certain kinds of) book function in clear opposition in this novel. But the qualifying kind of book makes all the difference. In the words of Brodber's Mr. Dan, who is redeemed in *her* book from the false fictions of eurocentric primary school texts for Caribbean children:

> My people have been separated from themselves, White Hen, by several means, one of them being the printed word and the ideas it carries. Now we have people who are about to see through that. And who are these people, White Hen? People who are familiar with the print and the language of the print. Our people are now beginning to see how it and they themselves have been used against us. Now, White Hen, now, we have people who can and are willing to correct images from the inside, destroy what should be destroyed, replace it with what it should be replaced and put us back together, give us back ourselves with which to chart our course to go where we want to go.[1]

In Glissant's terms the linguistic trap is not just zombification but it is also the smugness of Old John's self-protective dismissal of (all) book.

In its use of the Jamaicanism 'a knowledge', the epigraph from Vic Reid's *Nanny Town,* points to the cultural relativism of knowledge as quantifiable commodity. One culture's 'knowledge' is another's 'noise'. The metonymy of bone and blood embodies the text, the marrow of literary tradition assuming a particularised cultural character. The artist as *griot* transmits a body of knowledge that is the accreted wisdom of generations. The emotive trope of blood and bone connotes what may be constructed as 'racist' assumptions about biologically-determined culture, if the label is applied by the alienating Other. Assumed by the in-group, this figure of speech denotes a genealogy of ideas, a blood-line of beliefs and practices that are transmitted in the body, in oral discourse; for example, marronage, that tradition of resistance science that establishes an alternative psychic space both within and beyond the boundaries of the enslaving plantation. Further, Vic Reid's *Nanny Town,* with its use of the *griot* as narrator clearly tests the boundaries of the oral and the scribal, operating as it does on the edge of speech and writing, to cite Glissant again.

The poetry of Louise Bennett, Mikey Smith and Jean Binta Breeze represents a further stage along the scribal/oral continuum. Explicitly performance texts, these poems, though composed with clear reference to both oral and scribal literary traditions, are actualised in contexts of more-than-verbal production. Though the poem (as script) may be available in print, the performance itself cannot be printed. Audio-visual technology, rather than the printed word, best records the total theatre that is performance poetry.

Sistren Theatre Collective's *Lionheart Gal* and Michael Thelwell's novelisation of the film *The Harder They Come* are included as doubly engaging examples of transitional narrative forms. As fictionalised (auto)biography both narratives explore the relationship between identity and the explicatory ordering of the life story; as scribalised oral forms they raise theoretical issues about marginality and the boundaries of voice and print. Both works, focusing in large measure on the impact of migration from rural Jamaica to the concrete jungle of Kingston, are centrally concerned with a collision of values that tests the authority of the oral tradition. On issues of gender and social order the brash revisionism of the ghetto youth's cries for social justice challenges the wisdom of the conservative peasant culture.

The lyrics of the reggae musician and the DJ, related in performance terms to the poetry of Bennett, Breeze and Smith constitute the fourth group of texts to be examined. The least scribal of the texts under consideration, they become the most de-contexualised in the kind of close verbal/textual reading to which they are subjected here. The cautionary Brathwaite epigraph from *History of the Voice* draws deliberate attention to the sound and not simply the sight of the text. The basic limitation of this sighted focus on lyrics is that relatively little attention is given to analysis of the non-verbal elements of production and performance: melody, rhythm, the body in dance and the dancefloor itself as a space of spectacle and display. Relatively little attention is paid to the institutions of music production or to assessing the degree to which modes of production and performance reinforce or undermine the power relations identified at play in the lyrics. But the value of the analysis of disembodied lyrics is that the 'noise' of the reggae musician and the DJ is heard as intelligible and worthy of serious critical attention.

The power of Bob Marley's lyrics has been universally acclaimed. Singing in a language close to the English end of the linguistic continuum in Jamaica, but with clearly *rootsical* vibes, Marley sold himself internationally. The efficient marketing strategies of the Island Records empire made Bob Marley a superstar. Raw talent would not have been enough without the operations of international capital. Indeed, Bob Marley was not a better singer than Peter Tosh or Bunny Wailer; he was an opportunist, in the best sense of that word. The lyrics of the DJs in the present sample cannot be favourably compared to Bob Marley's, with the striking exception of Lloyd Lovindeer's. They nevertheless deserve attention because of their massive appeal. Their 'noise' can be simply dismissed as yet another example of the increasing vulgarity of both rural and urban life in Jamaica. Or, it can be recognised as a profoundly malicious cry to upset the existing social order. Night noises that pollute middle-class neighbourhoods, disturbing a neighbour's sleep, are a threatening challenge to those uneasily awake in comfortable beds. In the words of Bob Marley's 'Bad Card' from his *Uprising* album:

> You a go tired fi see mi face
> Can't get mi out of the race
> Oh man you said I'm in your place
> And then you draw bad card
> A make you draw bad card
> . . .
> I want to disturb my neighbour
> Cause I'm feeling so right
> I want to turn up my disco
> Blow them to full watts tonight
> Ina rub-a-dub style

This is the politics of noise. The literal reference to megawattage noise also evokes, however unintentionally, the Watts 'riots'/uprisings and the blowing-up of placid assumptions about the appropriate place/space for the insurgent African in the diaspora.

A problem surfaced as I tried to determine the sequence in which these essays should be ordered for publication. I wanted to begin chronologically with DeLisser's *Jane's Career*, the first West Indian novel in which the 'dialect'-speaking[2] character is the central consciousness. But I intuitively knew that since the tradition of the spoken word preceded the scribal there was another kind of logic that was requiring me to begin with the noises of *neo-oral* verbal creativity. I wanted Bennett to come before DeLisser. Further, the title chosen for the yet unwritten essay on *Jane's Career,* 'Throwing Words', a Jamaicanism for the sly act of casting aspersions without naming the object of abuse, voices an ideological problem with DeLisser's representation of Jane's career which made me unwilling to give him primacy of place: DeLisser's instinct is essentially satirical. Knowledge of Jamaican and facility in its use do not necessarily extend to shared sympathies with its habitual speakers. Boundaries of colour, class and gender seem to define the limits of DeLisser's conception of Jane's career. Her middle-class ambitions are derided as the fanciful vulgarity of her group. The fact that Jane does 'rise' in the little world of urban hurry-come-ups in Kingston is itself evidence of the triviality of that world.

In addition, I somewhat illogically wanted to preserve the arbitrary order of the actual evolution of the essays. The order of writing reflects the loose nature of this project which was not originally conceived as a book. It grew organically. The present Chapter 2 was written for the 21st Anniversary Symposium on the Cultural Heritage of Jamaica, convened in 1983 by the African Caribbean Institute of Jamaica/Folklore Studies Committee; in 1984/85 there followed the present Chapter 3 on 'Female sensibility in the poetry of Louise Bennett', which developed out of a lecture to a class in West Indian Literature; and then also in 1985, 'Afro-Jamaican Foklore Elements in Brodber's *Jane and Louisa Will Soon Come Home*'; and, finally, in 1986, 'Chanting Down Babylon' (now Chapter 7). It only then occurred to me that I had the core of an extended study of oral/scribal discourse in Jamaican literature.

I have resisted the temptation to rewrite these early essays, but a few essential changes have been necessary. When, for example, in the essay on Bob Marley's lyrics, I wrote somewhat dismissively of the 'inscrutable art of the DJ', I did not anticipate that I would later penetrate the lyrics in such excruciating detail: the crosses of the new convert. These early essays are much less discursive than the later ones; the subversive ideological implications of the early work were somewhat repressed by the nature of the critical discourse employed. The mode was formalist, close-reading.

The problem of ordering has been solved by separating the essays into two strands: one that focuses on the largely scribal end of the continuum, ('literature') the other on the primarily oral ('popular culture'). The former grouping, widened to include other written texts, will be the subject of another project. I present here the latter grouping of essays: performance poetry: Louise Bennett, Mikey Smith and Jean Breeze; auto/biographical narrative: Sistren Theatre Collective's *Lionheart Gal* and Michael Thelwell's novelisation of *The Harder They Come;* popular song: the anonymous, eighteenth-century 'Me Know No Law, Me Know No Sin', other pre-twentieth-century texts, the lyrics of Bob Marley and the DJs.

The tidiness of this arrangement raises other problems, oversimplifying as it does the full complexity of the oral/scribal literary continuum in Jamaica. It perpetuates the prejudice that oral texts are unlettered country cousins of a more legitimate body of texts that is 'literature'; they become distant relatives, not immediate family. Nevertheless, the focus on the noises of Jamaican popular culture facilitates the elaboration of a transgressive subtext that emerges from the primary study of orality: the engenderment of a subversive discourse of marginality and vulgarity.

The epigraph from Zora Neale Hurston's *Their Eyes Were Watching God* introduces the gender-specific dimensions of this study of Jamaican oral texts. It is evoked also to confirm precise continuities between Jamaican and African–American female culture, and modes of literary reproduction. The hierarchical gender relations between (white) men and (black) women are reproduced in the patriarchal discourse of master texts conspiring to exclude secondaried female 'minor' forms from the (scribal) literary canon. Feminised literary forms such as letters, diaries and the literature of romance have had the same relationship to the 'Great Tradition' as marginalised oral texts: beyond the pale.

But Hurston's use of African–American proverb, 'uh white man and uh nigger woman is de freest thing on earth', denotes a subversive freedom in the condition of marginality akin to the 'real' political power of the male authority figures at the centre of discourse. Though the proverb's silence on white women and black men seems to suggest that they are conjoined in powerlessness, this is only half the truth. The white woman often enjoys the vicarious power of consorting with the great. The black man, in whose mouth the proverb is put in Hurston's novel, is not himself entirely innocent of sexual politics; he often enjoys the vicarious power of consorting with the lesser great. Like all proverbs this one speaks its limited truth with epigrammatic authority. The blood knowledge of the proverb encapsulates the theoretical elaborations of Irigarian feminist polemics: 'One must assume the feminine role deliberately, which means already to convert a form of subordination into an affirmation, and thus to begin to thwart it.'

These six prefatory statements are intended, finally, to demarcate the fluid boundaries of an open-ended project: oral/sexual discourse in Jamaican popular culture. The revised sub-title of *Noises in the Blood – Orality, Gender and the 'Vulgar' Body of Jamaican Popular Culture* – denotes an ideological shift of emphasis to foreground both text (orality) and fully emergent sub-text (gender). The sub-title also amplifies the figure of the body, intimating the openness of the dilatory text to promiscuous turns of meaning. Sexual punning on orality – a vulgar trope – is at the root of this transgressive discourse on marginality, identity and voice.

Indeed, the 'vulgarity' of the vulgar must itself be contested. The *OED* defines the vulgar as '[h]aving a common and offensively mean character; coarsely commonplace; lacking in refinement or good taste. 1643. Now the only sense in ordinary colloq. use.' This conception of the vulgar seems to originate in a fear of the coarse texture of the (feminised) body and the baseness of the flesh that must be made subject to the refining influence of magisterial 'good taste': not eating the fruit of the knowledge of good and evil.

Despite the orality of the trope of taste – '[t]he sense of touch, feeling (with the hands, etc.); . . . [t]he act of tasting or perceiving the flavour of a thing with the organ of taste' (*OED*) – one senses a cerebral, lineal–scribal imperative that narrowly circumscribes the meaning of 'taste': 'the faculty of perceiving and enjoying what is excellent in art, literature, and the like 1671' (*OED*). Taste becomes aesthetics, the criticism of taste. This abstracting body/mind shift in the definition of taste has precise ideological implications for the playful exploration of the body of Jamaican popular culture that is the subject of this study.

The pejoration of 'the vulgar' – the people, the language and the corpus of culture produced – marks the high/low-euro/afrocentric cultural divide that is encoded in the Jamaican body politic. From the relative neutrality of the Latin *vulgus*, 'the common people', the vulgar becomes 'coarsely commonplace.' The vulgate – '[o]f language or speech: Ordinary, vernacular. Now arch. 1513' (*OED*) – becomes the sign of illiteracy. The vulgar body of knowledge produced by the people – '[c]ommon or customary in respect of the use or understanding of language, words or ideas 1553. . . . [c]ommonly current or prevalent, generally or widely disseminated, as a matter of knowledge, assertion, or opinion 1549' (*OED*) – is devalued. In all domains, the 'vulgar' is that which can be traced to "Africa"; the 'refined' is that which can be traced to "Europe". (The quotation marks are intended to foreground the constructed nature of this ideology of essential cultural difference). In the domain of language and verbal creativity, English is 'refined' and Jamaican is 'vulgar'; oral texts are 'vulgar'; written texts are 'refined'.

Reclaiming the old vulgarity (and legitimacy) of a democratising ideology of popular taste, these essays argue for a much looser, more inclusive definition of what constitutes 'good taste' and, by extension, the critical 'faculty of perceiving and enjoying what is excellent in art, literature, and the like'. This revisionist project thus redefines the appropriate subjects of scholarship. But these essays simultaneously, and somewhat subversively, argue against the academy as the exclusive locus of intellectual enquiry. Both the creators and consumers of popular culture in Jamaica (for example, the spontaneous film critics in every cinema), continuously engage in what may be termed 'low theory' – an ongoing critique of mass entertainment.[3]

The subjects of this study are, for the most part, bastard oral texts – literary jackets.[4] These vulgar products of illicit procreation may be conceived – in poor taste – as perverse invasions of the tightly-closed orifices of the Great Tradition. They require that the 'greatness' of tradition itself become subject to the vulgarising redefinitions of *popular* 'good taste'. Though the promiscuous dilations of the critical text need to be contained within limits of respectablility, the ordering imperative of academic propriety does not entirely silence the cunning language of subversive noises in the blood.

Focusing on both oral and oral/scribal texts, the chapters which follow trace the bloodline of this heritage of transgressive innocence in twentieth-century Jamaican popular culture. Louise Bennett's crafty women who speak in proverb and affirm their claim to an oral legacy of 'culture an' tradition an' birthright' are close kin to the speaker in 'Me Know No Law, Me Know No Sin'. Like Bennett, Jean Breeze and Mikey Smith employ a broad repertoire of techniques from Jamaican orature to write and perform a script of cultural resistance to the hegemony of anglocentrism. Rehabilitating the pejorated 'bare foot' language that Jamaican is still dismissed as in the late twentieth century, these talented writer/performers challenge the smug equivalence of class/language/intelligence so zealously espoused by the uncunningly ignorant.[5]

Sistren's lionhearted women who learn how to *play fool fi ketch wise* dramatise the subtleties of transmitting a politicised tradition of subversive ignorance across gender, race and class boundaries. By contrast, headstrong Ivan of *The Harder They Come*, perceived as a victim of obeah, is consumed with that *rhygin* revolutionary energy which manifests itself as a simple imperative: down with the oppressors. In his rejection of the ambiguous morality of the folk culture, emblematised in the 'problem tale' which he discounts as a 'woman story', Ivan sets himself up for disaster. Dependence on overt aggression, rather than native wit, precipitates his demise.

Bob Marley's chant against Babylon, like the rebellious lyrics of the reggae cowboy, Ivan, challenges the political ideology of the ruling elite. But Marley has become a symbol of non-partisan revolutionary consciousness in Jamaica largely because his message of social change is mediated by the cunning language of Rastafari.[6] In its subversion of the semantics of English, the language of Rastafari attempts covertly to undermine the power of Babylon; it reveals the wisdom of Jah in largely mystical terms. Using biblical symbolism and the indirection of Jamaican proverb, Marley's chant contains the revolutionary threat in the redemptive vison: 'We no know how we and dem a go work it out'. In Rastafari reasoning there is a clear separation of 'Church' and State, of political power and moral authority: 'we and dem'. What is lawful for Babylon is often sinful for Rastafari, and vice versa. For example the use of kaya, the 'holy herb', prescribed by Rastafari for vision, is proscribed by Babylon as a mind-altering 'illegal drug'. Thus the language of Babylon as the vehicle of its suspect law must be deconstructed. To truly overstand[7] Babylon is to sight the danger of passively standing under the doubtful protection of its law.

The peripheral positioning of woman in Rastafari is a provocative issue in the analysis of Marley's lyrics. Transgressive Woman, synonymous with Babylon as whore, becomes an alluring entrapper, seducing the Rastaman from the path of righteousness. But woman is a necessary evil. The other side of the woman as whore equation is woman as the Church, the fallen bride of Christ in need of redemption. In an oral critique of the gender double-standard in Rastafari, Maureen Rowe, herself a Rastawoman, notes somewhat wryly that

> Once redeemed, the Rastawoman becomes Queen/Empress, occupying a pedestal which precludes sexuality. She is separated from her sexual nature and becomes almost a religious icon and cultural role model. This makes it possible for the Rastaman to have at least two women, one fulfilling bodily/sexual needs and the other cultural/spiritual. The rigid dress code prescribed for the Queen contrasts radically with the flexibility allowed the Other Woman: for example, long, loose skirts that conceal the body versus fashionably tight jeans that reveal all.[8]

This ambivalent representation of woman in Rastafari, an extreme manifestation of the duplicitous gender ideology that pervades Jamaican society, is ultimately derived, via Victorian England, from Judaeo-Christian theology. Writing on rhetoric, gender and property in Renaissance literature and beyond, Patricia Parker provides a reversible reading of the promiscuously dilated body of woman that can easily be transferred to the Jamaican context:

> The Church figured as female is that other redeemed harlot who in the space between the First and Second Coming of another Joshua, Christ . . . expands or dilates in order, so to speak, to take in more members, before that ultimate apocalyptic end. One of the iconographic embodiments of this female figure – ambiguously recalling both Mary the Mother and the harlot Mary Magdalene – is the figure most often called *Mater Misericordiae* and pictured as

> opening her cloak wide enough to encompass the gathered members of the Church or the Body of Christ.[9]

Transgressive Woman is Slackness personified, embodying the porous openings in the oral text.

Analysis of the lyrics of the DJs completes the genealogical review. In 'Slackness hiding from culture: erotic play in the dancehall' the metaphor of Slackness/Culture is used to investigate how the 'high/low' cultural divide that is endemic to Jamaican society is (re)produced in the hierarchical relations of gender and sexuality that pervade the dancehall. Though the denigration of 'slackness' seems to determine the concomitant denigration of female sexuality, this feminisation of slackness in the dancehall can also be read in a radically different way as an innocently transgressive celebration of freedom from sin and law. Liberated from the repressive respectability of a conservative gender ideology of female property and propriety, these women lay proper claim to the control of their own bodies. Further, the seemingly oppressive macho DJ ethic must itself be problematised as a function of the oppressive class relations which produce what may be defined as a 'diminished masculinity'.

Situating the DJ's performance within a neo-African folk aesthetic confirms its subordinate position in the hierarchy of 'high' and 'low' culture in Jamaica. But, as I attempt to demonstrate in the concluding chapter, 'From "centre" to "margin": turning history upside down', hierarchy inversion is an important project of these low culture texts. What is true of the DJs' lyrics is essentially true of the work of all of the performers who are the subjects of this study, with the possible exception of Michael Thelwell whose fictional biography of the legendary reggae rebel/hero, Ivanhoe Martin, alias Rhygin, loudly proclaims its scribal pedigree. Thelwell's novelisation of the movie *The Harder They Come* is the most self-consciously scribal of the texts analysed; nevertheless, in some purist circles, his clearly 'committed' afrocentric politics would itself call into question his literary credentials. The pioneering work of Louise Bennett, and now more so 'dub/performance' poetry, are both located on the fringes of literary respectability.[10] The 'lifestories' of the women of the Sistren Theatre Collective are autobiography, a marginalised literary form. Popular song is not generally acknowledged as 'serious' literature, though the recent publication of the *Voiceprint* anthology of Caribbean 'oral and related poetry',[11] which includes two of Bob Marley's songs and several calypsos, does canonise excommunicated oral texts, the sur/round becoming centre.

The Slackness/Culture dialectic also has a precisely linguistic character. Jamaican, the language of popular culture, is the inferiorised language of performance, not the preferred language of academic discourse. In my own analysis of these largely oral texts I have become sensitive to the massive shift of register between the voice of the text and the language of analysis. Thus, in my critique of *Lionheart Gal* I was moved to experiment with Jamaican as a language of academic discourse. That essay deviates quite dramatically from conventional literary/linguistic practice. There is a clear linguistic fissure in the scholarly text which, somewhat paradoxically, attempts to cross the divide between Slackness and Culture, between Jamaican and English, between the oral and scribal traditions. In an act of scholarly transgression I, too, declare my innocence of sin and law.

The writing system used for Jamaican in the essay on *Lionheart Gal* also marks a departure from conventional wisdom. Popular orthographies for Jamaican depend exclusively on English orthography: colonialism inscribed. With varying degrees of skill, amateur linguists adapt the notoriously irregular writing system of English to suit the sounds of Jamaican. This dependence on English orthography has decided advantages for readers already literate in English; they know the spelling conventions. Although there is often wide variation in the representation of sounds in the individualised systems of each writer, readers can usually figure out what the symbols mean. The common English orthography base makes the idiosyncratic systems mutually intelligible. In his essay, 'Printing the Performance', Mervyn Morris (the editor of Louise Bennett's *Selected Poems*, Mikey Smith's *It a Come* and Jean Breeze's *Riddym Ravings*), gives the commonsense rationale for the writer's choice of an English-looking orthography for Jamaican:

> But, anxious not to be rejected unread, most of us have chosen compromise. The most common (if inconsistent) approach is to write the vernacular for the eye accustomed to standard English, but with various alterations signalling creole.[12]

For the *Lionheart Gal* critique I have chosen the writing system developed specifically for Jamaican by the linguist Frederic Cassidy who collaborated with Robert LePage in writing the *Dictionary of Jamaican English*. For the lyrics of Bob Marley I have used a modified version of Garth White's English-oriented transcription; for the lyrics of the DJs I have used a rather loose orthography – in the spirit of compromise. The virtue of the Cassidy system is its internal consistency, one symbol or pair of symbols always representing the same sound.[13] But the very regularity of this writing system (its good sense in purely linguistic terms) constitutes its major drawback for readers literate in English. The words on the page look strange; they don't 'sound' like they would in English. The symbols, though largely based on the conventions of English orthography, form words that are excised of idiosyncrasies, those etymological oddities that bear the imprint of the history of a language and make it look and feel 'natural'. The

Cassidy writing system seems to reinforce the negative perception of Jamaican as an unnatural, mangled tongue. It becomes an emotional and ideological matter, not a purely technical problem.

For potential readers of Jamaican who are not literate in English, the consistency of the Cassidy system is advantageous. Vernacular literacy can be acquired in a coherent system unmarred by frustrating 'exceptions' to every rule. Access to literacy, not necessarily literacy in English, is thus facilitated. Conversely, the reader who is already literate in English is forced to temporarily surrender the privileges of literacy. This loss of status does level new and old illiterates, narrowing the social distance between 'privileged' and 'non-privileged' groups. Literates in English become the slow learners they often assume non-literate Jamaican speakers to be. They are forced to revert to the child-like state of dependence on 'reading and spelling', that tedious process in the early learning of a writing system when the symbols on the page have to be vocalised before their meanings can be understood. Sophisticated readers gradually learn how to eliminate voicing and move directly from sight to sense, from anxiety to control. If literacy deprivileges the orality of language, literacy in English, in this context, deprivileges not only Jamaican but the orthography that revalorises the language as autonomous system.

The marginalised Cassidy orthography, if not immediately accessible to the eye of literates in English, is nevertheless open to the ear of receptive readers. In a clear case of hierarchy inversion, Mr Andrew Sewell, the man who delivers the mail in my neighbourhood, having read (and understood) a newspaper article written in the Cassidy system – unlike the eminent jurist Morris Cargill who c/wouldn't, in his own words, 'make head or tail of the maze of phonetics' – goes straight to the heart of the matter: 'It ful di spies af owa rial Afrikan langgwij': 'It fills the space of our real African language.' The very strangeness of the orthography restores to Jamaican its integrity; it gives the language and its speakers presence. A political issue. Mr Sewell's 'ful', the preferred Jamaican equivalent of the English 'fill', fulfils an expectation of completion and closure in the transfer of culture across the Atlantic; fulling up the void of that 'deep amnesiac blow'[14] that was the Middle Passage – to cite the early Derek Walcott.

Not surprisingly, these essays on Jamaican popular culture have their genesis in my 1977 doctoral dissertation, '"A Different Rage": An Analysis of the Works of Derek Walcott, 1948-76.' They can be seen as a mirror image of the much earlier work; a transgressive reversal of ideological positions. In my study of Walcott's poetry and plays I clearly recognised the poetry:drama :: intellectual:folk :: English:Creole :: modernist:neo-African :: scribal:oral dialectic in Caribbean literature. In a sense, I have gone down in academic life since that thesis. The study of poetry, and in particular that of Derek Walcott, Nobel Laureate, our most distinguished 'international' writer, is the top end of the literary market (except for the rarefied air of literary theory.) To turn from mainstream, Establishment Walcott to peripheral, insular Jamaican popular culture is to risk 'folking up' one's criticism.[15] Worse, to 'criticize' primary texts as though they were written to be read by non-specialists in literary theory is plain heresy.

Stephen Slemon and Helen Tiffin, in their 'Introduction' to *After Europe: Critical Theory and Post-Colonial Writing*, observe the operation of a new imperialism of 'theory' that colonises not only displaced 'primary' literary texts, but also criticism itself:

> Under the hegemony of Anglo-American 'theoretical' methodology, we now read critical texts – we probably even write them – from the footnotes backwards; and the paradoxical result is that even as the theoretically vigilant critical work establishes its autonomous grounding by ploughing under the now debunked thematics of the *literary* text, it also initiates an astonishingly filiative network of semantic and citational obedience towards the master-texts and master codes of 'theory' itself. One of the most ironic developments of what began as revolutionary scepticism has been the production of an institutionalised army of ridiculously credulous readers – 'critics' who systematically shut out the world in order to practice what Frank Lentriccia accurately depicts as a textual form of interior decoration.[16]

These disobedient essays on Jamaican popular culture proceed from a basic conviction that literature and criticism have less to do with sophistry and more with illuminating the lives of 'real people' and the fictions we inhabit: the thematics of the literary text have not been entirely debunked.

The multi-functional meaning of afrocentric literature is underscored by Micere Mugo in her essay 'The Relationship between African and African–American Literature as Utilitarian Art: A Theoretical Formulation':

> Among Africans on the continent and in the diaspora, literature has always projected itself as interdisciplinary in personality, cutting across such fields as anthropology, history, religion, philosophy and education. I would boldly describe authentic African literature, written or verbal, as a utilitarian art form. Historically, literature has been part of our people's culturalization and socialization processes. Literature has also been used by generations as a weapon of struggle against negative forces in life that have sought to stifle our people's imagination. This is the sociology of our literary heritage.[17]

This is not to deny the slipperiness of language, and the dizzying divide between the signifier and the signified. Rather, it is to recognise that in neo-colonial societies such as ours, the very acknowledgement of certain distinctly Jamaican 'noises' as 'art' implies a transgressive ideological position that redefines the boundaries of the permissible, legitimising vagrant texts that both restructure the canon and challenge the very notion of canonicity. For the law is often fixed in print and the canon, even as musical composition, requires strict imitation of the same subject.

Somewhat paradoxically, in the new decentring orthodoxies, previously marginalised oral texts that have only recently become canonisable (and have not had time to enjoy their new 'literary' status) become subject to debunking along with all the old master texts. Or they become symbols of the endless deferral of meaning that is all literature. In the latter case one has to be careful that one is not simply celebrating the 'noble savage' who stumbles on post-modernism having by-passed civilisation. The ultimate post-colonial fiction is the tale of the native emperor's new clothes, the naked truth of the text parading in the elaborate dress of theory.

Despite the egalitarian neologism, most of us 'post-colonials' know that all post-colonials are not created equal. Some post-colonials are more out-posted than others. Our literatures can become appropriated by totalising literary theories that reduce all 'post-colonial' literatures to the common bond(age) of the great – however deconstructed – European tradition. There are endless interrogations of the text and the prisoner on the stand is always the native. The very idea of 'national' literatures is passé. That old fiction of literature as the product of an age, the ethos of a people, is subsumed in the new reductive fiction of literature as pathology – metastasis beyond remission. Mervyn Alleyne, writing in *Roots of Jamaican Culture*, notes that '[c]ultural forms can become so transformed across the generations that they sometimes appear as imperfect or pathological manifestations of forms belonging to some other culture'.[18] Transformation across cultural traditions exacerbates the degenerative process.

Choosing to raise the subversive question 'Is the Post- in Postmodernism the Post- in Postcolonial?,' Kwame Anthony Appiah somewhat paradoxically contests the continuing otherness of the African (at home and abroad), in the meeting of the double colonialisms of post-modernism and post-colonialism itself – while simultaneously re-encoding the signs of 'unimaginable' difference:

> The role that Africa, like the rest of the Third World, plays for Euro-American modernism – like its better-documented significance for modernist art – must be distinguished from the role postmodernism might play in the Third World; what that might be it is, I think, too early to tell. What happens will happen not

> because we pronounce on the matter in theory, but will happen out of the changing everyday practices of African cultural life.
>
> For all the while, in Africa's cultures, there are those who will not see themselves as Other. Despite the overwhelming reality of economic decline; despite unimaginable poverty; despite wars, malnutrition, disease, and political instability, African cultural productivity grows apace: popular literatures, oral narrative and poetry, dance, drama, music, and visual art all thrive. The contemporary cultural production of many African societies, and the many traditions whose evidences so vigorously remain, is an antidote to the dark vision of the postcolonial novelist.[19]

In the spirit of post-post-coloniality I offer these essays as strong (mis)readings of culture-specific, Jamaican fictions.

Notes

1 Erna Brodber, *Myal* (London: New Beacon Books, 1988), pp. 110–11. 'Myal': 'cf Hausa *maye*, 1. Sorcerer, wizard; 2. Intoxication; Return. (All of these senses are present in the Jamaican use of the word.). . . . In recent use in AFRICAN and similar cults: formal possession by the spirit of a dead ancestor, and the dance done under possession', *Dictionary of Jamaican English*. Myal is the complement of obeah which is defined thus in the *Dictionary of Jamaican English*: 'the derivation is prob multiple – cf Efik *ubio*, 'a thing or mixture of things, put in the ground, as a charm to cause sickness or death' (OED); also the base of Twi *-bayifo*, witch, wizard, sorcerer. . . . The practice of malignant magic as widely known in Jamaica. Its origins are African; in practice it has never been clearly distinguished from MYAL: though the latter was supposedly curative of the ills caused by the former, both have shared the same methods to a great extent (MYAL with some admixture of elements derived from Christianity).' An alternative etymology for myal – which admits moral ambivalence – is provided by the linguist Hazel Carter in personal communication with Maureen Warner-Lewis, March 1985: '*mayal* < *Mayaala*, Kikongo, "person/thing exercising control."' In 'Masks of the Devil: Caribbean Images of Perverse Energy', unpublished conference paper, UWI, St Augustine, 1991, Warner-Lewis argues that the universe is governed by opposing energy flows, one, which is creative/sustaining ('good'), the other, destructive/negating ('evil'). The myal/obeah dichotomy seems to have its genesis in an afrocentric cosmology where good and evil, though distinguishable, are derived from a common energy source.

2 The Jamaican language has several names in Jamaica: *patois* alternates in popular usage with *dialect*, which has been superseded (in the academy) by *Jamaican Creole* or the more generic (pan-Caribbean) *Creole* – for good linguistic reasons. A more recent term is, simply, *Jamaican* which I prefer because it moves towards settling the issue of the status of the language as the legitimate expression of the ethos of a people. I use *Jamaican*, *Jamaican Creole*

and *Creole* interchangeably, especially in contexts where ambiguity might arise in the use of *Jamaican* as noun or adjective.

3 I take the term 'low theory' from Andrew Ross, *No Respect: Intellectuals and Popular Culture* (New York: Routledge, 1989), p. 234 where Ross attributes the term to Simon Firth: 'Simon Firth has drawn attention to what he calls "low theory" – the choices, reasons and arguments over interpretation which all consumers of popular culture engage in.' The academic theorisation of popular culture, he points out, has resulted in the exclusion, ironically, of the popular consumers themselves. See his Introduction to Craig MacGregor, *Pop Goes the Culture* (London: Pluto Press, 1984), p. 6, and also 'Hearing Secret Harmonies', in *High Theory/Low Culture*, p. 57.

4 In Jamaica a 'jacket' is a child whose mother deceitfully assigns paternity to her primary sexual partner who accepts the child as his. The Trinidadian equivalent is a 'ready-made shirt'.

5 John Hearne, 'Patois – a Barefoot Language', *Sunday Gleaner*, 25 November 1990, p. 7A. John Hearne did make a public retraction of his inflammatory comments in a subsequent column, after having received from his students at the University a respectable Jamaican translation of what he considered 'difficult' modern English prose; see also Morris Cargill, 'Corruption of Language is no Cultural Heritage', *Sunday Gleaner*, 29 October 1989, p. 8A. My response to Cargill, 'Cho! Misa Cargill, Riispek Juu', *Sunday Gleaner*, 5 November 1989, p. 8A, received widespread attention largely because I used the Cassidy orthography for Jamaican. Cargill's dismissively paternalistic 'response' is quoted here in full: 'I am sorry, by the way, that I cannot respond to the piece in the *Gleaner* of Sunday, November 5, by Dr. Carolyn Cooper as I cannot make head or tail of the maze of phonetics. But I am glad she is happy in whatever it is she does, and I am sure she is a very clever girl.' *Sunday Gleaner*, 12 November 1989, p. 8A.

6 For the authoritative (scholarly) account of the language of Rastafari, see Velma Pollard, 'The Social History of Dread Talk' in Lawrence D. Carrington (ed.), *Studies in Caribbean Language* (School of Education: UWI, St Augustine, Trinidad, 1983), pp. 46–62.

7 Rastafarian inversion of 'understand'.

8 Telephone interview, February 1991. For an earlier statement (in need of updating), see her essay 'The Woman in Rastafari', *Caribbean Quarterly* 26.4 (1980): pp. 13–21, from which I quote in Chapter 7.

9 Patricia Parker, *Literary Fat Ladies: Rhetoric, Gender, Property* (London: Methuen, 1987), p. 9. The Jamaican equivalent of this (sexual) dilatoriness is 'slackness', the preferred term for Standard English 'looseness'.

10 Time and the scholarly work of, first, Mervyn Morris and others, have now made Louise Bennett's performance poetry respectable. The early scepticism about the 'literary' value of Bennett's work is echoed in contemporary valuations of dub poetry such as Victor Chang's review of Christian Habekost's presumably indiscriminate selection/editing of *Dub Poetry: 19 Poets from England and Jamaica* (Michael Schwinn: Neustadt, 1986): 'Thus, while dub poetry covers a range of topics, its tonal range as represented here is essentially limited: protesting, threatening, accusatory. And we need to recognize this.' Chang proceeds to generalise: 'I am not saying that this poetry does not have its value or that it should be like traditonal poetry. I merely want to suggest that we cannot often expect any subtlety of approach, anything that is inward-looking,

musing, quiet, reflective, tender, delicate, registering a complexity of position or feeling. . . . And for those who value and want more than the broad effects, the clout on the head, the deafening roar, the enraged shout this poetry is just not enough.' *Jamaica Journal* 21.3 (1988): p. 50.

11 Stewart Brown, Mervyn Morris, Gordon Rohlehr (eds), *Voiceprint* (London: Longman, 1989). An entry on Bob Marley has been commissioned for the Routledge *Encyclopaedia of Commonwealth Writers.*

12 Mervyn Morris, 'Printing the Performance', *Jamaica Journal* 23.1 (1990): p. 22

13 For a full account of the historical phonology of Jamaican see Cassidy and LePage (eds), *Dictionary of Jamaican English* (Cambridge: Cambridge University Press, 1967); 2nd edn, 1980, xxxvi–1xiv.

14 Derek Walcott, 'Laventville' in *The Castaway* (London: Jonathan Cape, 1965), p. 35.

15 An irreverent pun used by Kenneth Ramchand in the discussion period of a session of the 1971 conference of the Association of Commonwealth Literature and Language Studies, held in Jamaica, to distinguish himself from nativist critics like (Edward) Kamau Brathwaite. In an unpublished May 1991 public lecture, 'West Indian Literature in the Nineties: Blowing Up the Canon,' to mark 21 years of the teaching of the course in West Indian Literature at UWI, which he initiated, Ramchand illustrated the necessity of folking up one's criticism.

16 Stephen Slemon and Helen Tiffin (eds), *After Europe* (Mundelstrup, Denmark: Dangaroo Press, 1989) pp. x–xi.

17 Micere Mugo, 'The Relationship between African and African–American Literature as Utilitarian Art: A Theoretical Formulation', in Joseph E. Harris (ed.), *Global Dimensions of the African Diaspora* (Washington, DC: Howard University Press, 1982), p. 89.

18 Mervyn Alleyne, *Roots of Jamaican Culture* (London: Karia Press/Pluto Press, 1988), p. 1.

19 Kwame Anthony Appiah, 'Is the Post- in Postmodernism the Post- in Postcolonial?', *Critical Inquiry*, 17.2 (1991): p. 356.

CHAPTER 1

'Me know no law, me know no sin': transgressive identities and the voice of innocence: the historical context

Me know no law, me know no sin

Altho' a slave me is born and bred,
My skin is black, not yellow:
I often sold my maiden head
To many a handsome fellow.

My massa keep me once, for true,
And gave me clothes, wid busses:
Fine muslin coats, wid bitty too,
To gain my sweet embraces.

When pickinniny him come black
My massa starve and fum me;
He tear the coat from off my back,
And naked him did strip me.

Him turn me out into the field,
Wid hoe, the ground to clear-o;
Me take pickinniny on my back,
And work him te-me weary.

Him, Obisha, him de come one night,
And give me gown and busses;
Him get one pickinniny, white!
Almost as white as missess.

Then missess fum me wid long switch,
And say him da for massa;
My massa curse her, 'lying bitch!'
And tell her, 'buss my rassa!'

Me fum'd when me no condescend:
Me fum'd too if me do it;
Me no have no one for 'tand my friend,
So me am for'cd to do it.

Me know no law, me know no sin,
Me is just what ebba them make me;
This is the way dem bring me in;
So God nor devil take me![1]

'Me Know No Law, Me Know No Sin', an eighteenth-century Jamaican popular song recorded in print by the bookkeeper, J. B. Moreton in his *West India Customs and Manners,* is an appropriate introduction to this collection of essays on orality, gender and the 'vulgar' body of Jamaican popular culture. Reproduced in the recent V*oices in Exile: Jamaican Texts of the 18th and 19th Centuries,* this song-text exemplifies in the very process of its transmission the interrogations of oral/scribal discourse in the body of *oraliterature*[2] that is the subject of this study. 'Me Know No Law, Me Know No Sin' also illustrates the correlation of issues of orality and gender, and the confluence of these with issues of language, class, 'race'[3] and nation. The feminisation of oral discourse engenders parallel hierarchies of marginality and subversion: Jamaican:English :: folk:'ristocrat :: oral:scribal :: female:male. Moreton, '[a]pparently a non-native of Jamaica',[4] includes this female-centred song in a collection of observations on 'customs and manners' the title of which encodes the perspective of anthropologist/voyeur in quest of exotica. The *vo/localised* text, refracted through the multiple densities of the scribal sensibility of the non-native, white, male, recorder, becomes subject to transformation.

Of Moreton's rendering of 'Me Know No Law, Me Know No Sin' D'Costa and Lalla note that 'the systems of Jamaican Creole and Standard English mingle in Moreton's version as if to satisfy the more anglicized audience of the writer. The English meter of the poem promotes interference from the standard language.'[5] A fragment of this song which seems to have been very popular is also reproduced 45 years later in Michael Scott's *Tom Cringle's Log,*[6] an acknowledged fiction. Scott, himself an expatriate recorder of West Indian customs and manners, presents a version of the song in which there is more English interference (in lexicon, grammar and syntax) than in Moreton's, as illustrated in the passages below.

MORETON: Him, Obisha, him de come one night,
And give me gown and busses;
Him get one pickinniny, white!
Almost as white as misses.

Then misses fum me wid long switch,
And say him da for massa;
My massa curse her, 'lying bitch!'
And tell her, 'buss my rassa!'

SCOTT: Young hofficer come home at night
Him give me ring and kisses
Nine months, one picaninny white
Him white almost like missis.
But missis fum my back wid switch,
Him say de shild for massa;
But massa say him —

This truncation of the verse which erases the switch/bitch, massa/rassa rhymes is yet another deformation of the text to accommodate the supposedly delicate sensibilities of the British reader to whom the narrator apologises for including the verse at all: 'I was turning to go to sleep again, when a female, in a small suppressed voice, sung the following snatch of a vulgar Port Royal ditty, which I scarcely forgive myself for introducing here to polite society.'[7] The pornographic impulse to simultaneously expose and conceal the pruriently exotic facts of native life is barely suppressed. Travel-writing of this age is essentially a colonising fiction, civilising savage landscapes – but only so far. Domesticating difference by making the strange intimately 'familiar' and acceptable, the travel-writer feeds the eroticised *conquistador* fantasies of the *voy(ag)eur*/reader safe at home, and tames the feminised, alien landscape. Ernest Rhys, in his 'Introduction' to Scott's fiction, recommends it thus: '*Tom Cringle's Log* is so true to its subject that when one puts it down, the West Indies have become a region familiar as Strathclyde'.[8] A dubious distinction.

The narrator explains away the fracture in the song-text thus: 'The singer broke off suddenly, as if disturbed by the approach of some one.'[9] In the written narrative it is the woman's husband who intrudes, asking foolish questions which she quickly dismisses. In a nativist re-reading of the imperial sub-text of *Tom Cringle's Log,* the break conveniently emblematises the penetration of the discursive terrain of the Caribbean ur-text – the woman's space – by the conquering master text.

Similarly, Moreton, who seems to have fancied himself as something of a poet – his compositions are liberally sprinked throughout *West India Customs and Manners* – may have 'improved' the original 'Me Know No Law, Me Know No Sin' from mere song to 'poem',[10] the context of performance thus shifting from oral to scribal discourse and the weight of the language from Jamaican to English. Commenting in general on the mode and mood of Jamaican songs, Moreton notes that '[w]hen working, though at the hardest labour, they are commonly singing; and though their songs have neither rhime nor measure, yet many are witty and pathetic. I have often laughed heartily, and have been as often struck with deep melancholly (sic) at their songs.'[11] Moreton, who may have attempted to give rhime and measure to the song, introduces the transposed text thus: 'I shall annex the song of a young woman . . . : – it is in the negroe dialect, and is no less true than curious.'[12] Though 'annex' primarily means 'append' we may speculate that the imperial resonances of appropriation are perhaps signalled in Moreton's curious truth.

But the transformation of the song into written text seems largely cosmetic: English grammar and metre are imposed on the Jamaican text but the essential meaning of the song – its subversively vulgar intention – seems to have escaped intact. In the absence of the audio-visual technologies that can now record purely oral discourse without the interpolation of patronising anglo-scribal editorialising, any record at all, however vagrant, is valuable. Thus D'Costa and Lalla affirm that '[e]ven in the novels and travelogues written by white visitors survive echoes of the voices of those who, having neither quill nor printing press, left the mark of their exile upon the minds of white observers.'[13]

As written text, 'Me Know No Law, Me Know No Sin' is preserved and regenerated through the combined efforts of the curious outsider and the scholarly indigenous participant–observer. The perspectives of tourist and native share a rare point of convergence. As oral text the song functions as a trope of orality itself: the oral text that is not successfully transmitted orally becomes extinct, or so it seems. But the multiplicity of versions of the oral text embodies the multifariousness of oral transmission. There is no single, definitive text; the text is made on each occasion of its verbalisation. Thus the text, and its meanings are constantly made anew even when the mute 'form' of the text appears to be extinct. In late twentieth-century Jamaica we may not be able to readily identify a 'vulgar Port Royal ditty' named 'Me Know No Law, Me Know No Sin'; but we can trace its genealogy in that vibrant tradition of contemporary Jamaican dancehall music in which women, in the spirit of the *persona* of that song, vigorously celebrate their freedom from the constraints of law and sin: echoes in the native bone.

'Me Know No Law, Me Know No Sin' is a relatively early literary expression of those often subversive noises in the blood that articulate the preoccupations of a people and define the particular cultural contexts of their verbal creativity. The official, written histories of enslavement, voicelessness and erasure that seem to have absolute authority in neo-colonial societies such as Jamaica are continually contested by alternate oral discourses that reclaim the self and empower the speaker. In the case of the *persona* of this song the issues of gender, race, class and voice intersect: the transgressive black woman, bearer of the composite burden of master, overseer and mistress, is triply oppressed – or so it seems. Reduced to the function of mere sex object, she signifies both the dehumanisation of the black person and the disempowerment of woman in a slave society.

But kisses go by favour and in the inverted hierarchies of her deformed society the black woman is often the preferred sex object. 'The Sable Venus – An Ode', recorded in Bryan Edwards' *The History, Civil and Commercial, of the British Colonies in the West Indies*[14] is a sentimental apostrophe to the idealised, interchangeable black woman:

> O Sable Queen! thy mild domain
> I seek, and court thy gentle reign,
> So soothing, soft and sweet
> Where meeting love, sincere delight,
> Fond pleasure, ready joys invite.
> And unbrought raptures meet.
>
> Do thou in gentle Phibia smile,
> In artful Benneba beguile
> In wanton Mimba pout
> In sprightly Cuba's eyes look gay
> Or grave in sober Quasheba
> I still shall find thee out.[15]

Despite the prevailing tone of supplication the insistent final line above seems more rapacious threat than chivalric promise. With no apparent irony, Barbara Bush comments thus on this hyperbolic ode in *Slave Women in Caribbean Society 1650-1838*:

> The 'Sable Queen' was one of the more pleasant contemporary images of the black woman. Part of white male mythology, it reflected a common and often near-obsessional interest in the 'exotic charms' of African womanhood. Not all European impressions of the black woman were so favourable. The plantocracy ascribed to her two distinct and, in many senses, contradictory functions. Whereas the male slave was valued solely for the economic contribution he made to the plantation, the woman was expected to perform both sexual as well as economic duties. Childbearing fell into the former area, but also sexual duties performed for white masters.[16]

Michael Scott's 1833 *Tom Cringle's Log* records a John Canoe/Jonkonnu song that traces Massa Buccra's gradual path from the soft, silken dove of his white love, to the brown girl, and, ultimately, we may presume, to the black devil herself:[17]

Massa Buccra lob for see
Bullock caper like monkee –
Dance, and shump and poke him toe,
Like one humane person – just so.

But Massa Buccra have white love,
Soft and silken like one dove.
To brown girl – him barely shivel! –
To black girl – ho, Lord, de Devil!

But when him once two tree year here,
Him tink white lady wery great boder;
De coloured peoples, never fear,
Ah, him lob him de morest nor any oder.

But top – one time had fever catch him,
Coloured peoples kindly watch him -
In sick-room, nurse voice like music -
From him hand taste sweet de physic.

So alway come – in two tree year,
And so wid you, massa – never fear -
Brown girl for cook – for wife – for nurse,
Buccra lady – poo – no wort a curse.[18]

This Jonkonnu song, fascinating in its nativist account of Massa's prurient love of the near-human bullock capering like monkee, turns the masquerade into a metaphor of transgressive sexuality. The newly-arrived white man in the tropics brings with him the border-crossing meanings of the masquerade as it functioned in England. In *Masquerade and Civilization: The Carnivalesque in Eighteenth-Century English Culture and Fiction*, Terry Castle confirms that

> Not surprisingly, English masqueraders typically impersonated members of national or ethnic groups with fashionably romantic associations. The fascination with exotic peoples was often indistinguishable from a fascination with their clothes; those groups considered most excitingly foreign in the eighteenth century were invariably those with the most unusual costumes. The spirit of Orientalism suffused masquerade representation: Persians, Chinese, and Turks remained exemplary subjects for sumptuous reconstruction throughout the century. American Indians, Polynesian islanders, Siberian Kamchatkas, 'blackamores,' and other supposedly savage races also offered interesting possibilities for impersonation. . . .

> A primitive ethnography is at work here; one should not be surprised at its crudeness. A similar impulse informed the masquerade itself. Granted, one might see in foreign costume a mere displacement of imperialist fantasy; the popularity of the masquerade coincided after all with the expansion of British imperialism, and the symbolic joining of races could conceivably be construed as a kind of perverse allusion to empire. Yet at a deeper level, such travesties were also an act of homage – to otherness itself. Stereotypical and innaccurate (sic) though they often were, exotic costumes marked out a kind of symbolic interpenetration with difference – an almost erotic commingling with the alien. Mimicry became a form of psychological recognition, a way of embracing, quite literally, the unfamiliar. The collective result was a utopian projection: the masquerade's visionary 'Congress of Nations' – the image of global conviviality – was indisputably a thing of fleeting, hallucinatory beauty.[19]

This beauty is disputable. The (sexual) congress of nations in the Caribbean was quite literal, as the Jonkonnu song illustrates. This almost erotic commingling of the English with the alien often reflected the racial/sexual politics of the times: exploitation of the savage native. The celebration of sexuality and death/life rites of passage that is naturalised in native masquerades like Jonkonnu, assumes pathological proportions when appropriated for entertainment by the slumming tourist/visitor.[20]

Edward Long, in his *History of Jamaica*, notes that the Jonkonnu masquerader, 'carrying a wooden sword in his hand, is followed with a numerous crowd of drunken women, who refresh him frequently with a sup of aniseed-water whilst he dances at every door, bellowing out *John Connu!* with great vehemence.'[21] In a malodorous account of these carnivalesque Jonkonnu festivities, Edward Long exposes his fearful fascination with the contaminated body of the feminised Other. This dilatory passage, with its ridiculed aetiological tale, is a 'complication of stinks', worthy of full quotation:

> These exercises, although very delightful to themselves, are not so to the generality of the white spectators, on account of the ill smell which copiously transudes on such occasions; which is rather a complication of stinks, than any one in particular, and so rank and powerful, as totally to overcome those who have any delicacy in the frame of their nostrils. The Blacks of Affric assign a ridiculous cause for the smell peculiar to the goat; and with equal propriety they may well apply it to themselves. They say, 'that, in the early ages of mankind, there was a she-divinity, who

> used to besmear her person with a fragrant ointment, that excited the emulation of the goats, and made them resolve to petition her, to give them a copy of her receipt for making it, or at least a small sample of it. The goddess, incensed at their presumption, thought of a method to be revenged, under the appearance of granting their request. Instead of the sweet ointment, she presented them with a box of a very foetid mixture, with which they immediately fell to bedaubing themselves. The stench of it was communicated to their posterity; and to this day, they remain ignorant of the trick put upon them, but value themselves on possessing the genuine perfume; and are so anxious to preserve it undiminished, that they very carefully avoid rain, and every thing that might possibly impair the delicious odour.'
>
> This rancid exhalation, for which so many of the Negroes are remarkable, does not seem to proceed from uncleanliness, nor the quality of their diet. I remember a lady, whose waiting-maid, a young Negroe girl, had it to a very disagreeable excess. As she was a favourite servant, her mistress took great pains, and the girl herself spared none, to get rid of it. With this view, she constantly bathed her body twice a day, and abstained wholly from salt-fish, and all sorts of rank food. But the attempt was similar to washing the Black-a-moor white; and after a long course of endeavours to no purpose, her mistress found that there was no remedy but to change her for another attendant, somewhat less odoriferous.[22]

We may reasonably assume from this passage that Edward Long is one of those refined souls who have much delicacy in the frame of their nostrils, and would thus be easily overcome by such powerful animal smells. But the seductive fall is as complicated as the compound stink itself. As Stallybrass and White state epigrammatically in their conclusion to *The Politics And Poetics of Transgression*, 'disgust always bears the imprint of desire':

> It has been argued that 'the demarcating imperative' divides up human and non-human, society and nature, 'on the basis of the simple logic of excluding filth'. . . . Differentiation, in other words, is dependent upon disgust. The division of the social into high and low, the polite and the vulgar, simultaneously maps out divisions between the civilized and the grotesque body, between author and hack, between social purity and social hybridization. These divisions, as we have argued, cut across the social formation, topography and the body, in such a way that subject identity cannot be considered independently of these domains. The bourgeois subject continuously defined and re-defined itself through

> the exclusion of what it marked out as 'low' – as dirty, repulsive, noisy, contaminating. The low was internalized under the sign of negation and disgust.[23]

In the hierarchy-inverted world of sexual fantasy, the 'rancid exhalation' that forces the Mistress to dismiss her favourite servant, becomes the 'genuine perfume' of the African 'she-divinity' that draws Massa Buccra from the bothersome purity of his worthless lady's bed.

Barbara Bush, highlighting the white man's internalisation of the low, as seen in the disgust/desire conflict between his public statements on black women and his private behaviour, argues that '[d]espite the unflattering picture painted by white men, in practice the physical appearance of black women failed to repel them sexually. Few men, however, openly admitted to their attractions for and relationships with slave women.'[24] Bush elaborates:

> By the late eighteenth century, the black and, even more so, the coloured woman was well established, in the eyes of the white man, in her role as concubine. According to plantocratic commentators like Bryan Edwards slave women were free of any restrictive moral codes, 'refused to confine themselves to a single connexion with the other sex' and boldly disposed themselves sexually 'according to their own will and pleasure'. Thomas Atwood declared that marriage among slaves was unstable, the more so because it was 'common for women to leave their husbands for others'; slave women were prostitutes who submitted to white men for money or clothes and likewise sold their own daughters for 'a moderate sum'. . . .
>
> Edward Long fulminated about the conniving and licentious ways of the black woman while Emma Carmichael, writing in the penultimate years of slavery, blamed the moral ruin of white men in the West Indies upon the seductive capabilities of the black woman. Although the latter writer, as a white woman, was undoubtedly personally hostile, a marked tendency did exist, on the part of white men, to transfer the blame for their sexual improprieties on to the 'forwardness' of black women and thus exonerate themselves.[25]

'De Black Man's Lub Song', described by its anonymous author as 'Caricature and Verse', and quite obviously not the work of a Black Man, is an illuminating text that suggests, inversely, the masked white male's perception of sexual politics in West Indian slave society. The Black man goes 'home' to Scotland to seek a wife, but is immediately repelled:

> I'm de Genman called Reform 'Bill,'
> Come home from all de way, Ma'am,
> To take myself to wife from Scotch,
> Spite let dem do or say, Ma'am;
> Dey tel me lass here bery cheap –
> De market glut – got for catch in heap,
> So first me land, me quickly leap,
> To catch first Miss – but 'stead of kiss,
> Catch'd stroke of fis' – as large as dis,
> Closed up my lights of day, Ma'am –

The black man has presumed too much; the reform bill does not absolutely revise sexual politics or other property rights:

> I tought de ack dat gets my name,
> Had made de prop'ty all de same,
> For Black – for White – for Blind, for Lame –
> And dat a Clause, among dem laws
> Gave strong man cause, to pounce hims paws
> On ebery ting he see, Ma'am –

Unlike Mrs Carmichael's morally ruined white man, this black man has no desire for the devilish black woman. He offers to be the grand protector of the white woman, if she will flee with him to 'Mancipation Isles:'

> In Porto Ric, one gets so sick
> Of look on debil face, Ma'am,
> For Misses dere all Nigger are,
> And fat is all de grace, Ma'am,
> Den, here at feet of you I lie,
> To say I'll lub you eberly,
> And I hab brought tree dozen eye,
> Of sheep to throw, my lub to show,
> For dat you so, on me may throw,
> An sheepis eye of grace, Ma'am.

> Den come from Scotlum's thistle hills,
> And from old Englum flee, Ma'am,
> And go to 'Mancipation Isles,
> Far, far upon de sea, Ma'am,
> Dere de plantain's flagrant shade we'll seek,
> On leaf you lay you butus cheek,
> Eat melons – l'orange – all de week,

Black miss when spy, will passion fly,
But nebber cry, – till deaph will I
Your grand purtector be Ma'am.[26]

The voyeuristic black miss, seen through the eyes of the white man's masquerade, is reduced to a fury of jealous passion.

The placement of the Sable Venus thus becomes ambiguous. Is she simply a helpless victim in a racist/sexist society, or does she exercise some complex measure of control over her own sexuality, that of the black man and of Massa? In the very first verse of 'Me Know No Law, Me Know No Sin' the woman (artful, beguiling Benneba, perhaps?) flaunts her cunning ability to capitalise on her body – selling her 'maiden head' several times over '[t]o many a handsome fellow'. The qualifying '[a]ltho' a slave me is born and bred' declares her refusal to be commodified by anybody but herself. She may be a legal 'slave' but she is free nevertheless to exploit her status as commodity in the sexual marketplace. She is able to seduce gullible men into purchasing a non-existent product, not her body, but the illusion of virginity and first conquest of undiscovered territory; the imperial myth (dis)embodied.

In a language of feigned innocence this woman assumes the lisping guile of Anansi to declare her ignorance of (and therefore freedom from) the bonds of law and sin.[27] Not to know is to be innocent of responsibility. Verbal cunning – that dubious not-knowing echoed in the no/know homonym – thus voices the essentially subversive relationship of the enslaved black woman to the dominant social/moral order. Indeed, she is apparently not at all ignorant of the complicated advantages of marginality: to transgress is to go beyond the enslaving boundaries that delimit her person and her place. Transgression thus becomes the acknowledgement of a rehumanised identity. Role-playing as a strategy for survival may perhaps be detected in another song sung by women that is also recorded by Moreton: 'Tajo! My Mackey Massa!' (Here there appears to be less interference in the recorded text than in 'Me Know No Law, Me Know No Sin.') 'Mackey massa', defined in the *Dictionary of Jamaican English* as 'a phrase showing submission and respect' signifies the woman's deferential *persona*. 'Tajo', defined as '[a]n exclamation of excitement and enjoyment' verbalises her apparently exuberant response to the ministrations of Mackey Massa:

Tajo, tajo, tajo! tajo, my mackey massa!
O! laud, O! tajo, tajo, tajo!
You work him, mackey massa!
You sweet me, mackey massa!
A little more, my mackey massa!

Tajo, tajo, tajo! my mackey massa!
O! laud, O! tajo, tajo, tajo!
I'll please my mackey massa!
I'll jig to mackey massa!
I'll sweet my mackey massa![28]

These protestations seem somewhat excessive. Indeed, the marked You/I pronoun divide of verses one and two, paralleling the present/future tense shift suggests, perhaps, the woman's quite conscious expectation of a precise division of sexual labour with foreseeable benefits. Her job is to feed the ego of Mackey Massa by proclaiming his sexual skill in loud 'tajo'. His job is to continue to favour her by allowing her to keep the work.

For there are no guarantees in this job market, especially when the woman reserves the right to play the field. The speaker of 'Me Know No Law, Me Know No Sin' reports the absolute reversal of fortune when the child she ostensibly bears her white massa is unequivocally black:

When pickinniny him come black
My massa starve and fum me;
He tear the coat from off my back,
And naked him did strip me.

Him turn me out into the field,
Wid hoe, the ground to clear-o;
Me take pickinniny on my back,
And work him te-me weary.

In his gloss on the song, Moreton, sympathising somewhat with the unlucky woman, mocks the vanity of the cuckold:

> Some masters and overseers, of jealous pimping dispositions, flog, and otherwise ill treat their black wenches, when they chance to get black children. I have often been diverted, and laughed heartily, when a raw, infatuated gaukey, or a doating, debilitated debauchee has been disappointed, after all his endearing fondness and amorous exertions, with his soft slobber-chop bundle, to get a black, instead of an olive babe.[29]

Despite his punitive actions, the Mackey Massa of 'Me Know No Law, Me No Know Sin' seems somewhat divided in loyalty. When the black woman later bears a child '[a]llmost as white as misses' – presumably for the overseer who has replaced Massa as the source of 'gown and busses' – she is victimised by her vindictive Misses who reasonably assumes that this child is Massa's. Massa, the 'doating, debilitated debauchee,' it would appear, responds to his wife's accusations with aggressive verbal (not physical) abuse: 'My massa curse her, "lying bitch!"/ And tell her, 'buss my rassa!"' The song seems to turn quite humorously/sadly on this ambiguous 'buss.' For 'buss' is primarily 'kiss' in the give and take of the black woman's opportunistic mating with master, overseer and unidentified baby-fathers:[30]

> My massa keep me once, for true,
> And give me clothes, wid busses:
> Fine muslin coats, wid bitty too,
> To gain my sweet embraces.

But in the construction 'buss my rassa' – 'kiss my arse' – 'buss' becomes a term of abuse directed by Massa at his railing wife. In a citation on 'buss' the *Shorter Oxford English Dictionary* provides a serendipitous gloss on this song in a quote from Herrick: 'We busse our wantons, but our wives we kisse.' Here, both wife (who seems to have been neither kissed nor bussed), and wanton (who seems to have kissed and bussed too much) are levelled in Massa's indiscriminate contempt.[31]

Further, 'bus' is defined in the *Dictionary of Jamaican English* as '[a] sound imitating the effect of something falling with a dull thud; hence something disappointing, an occurence that fails to come up to expectation'. In addition, D'Costa and Lalla in their gloss on 'buss' as verb define it thus: 'To punch, strike, kick; to burst, break open. Possibly < burst. In expression "buss you rass" (vulgarism), signifying "to kick your arse".'[32] The kiss/kick pun on 'buss' thus encodes the reversibility of pain and pleasure – and of roles – in the complicated power games between massa, wife and wanton. For though the grammar of the line 'And tell her, "buss my rassa!"'logically indicates that it is Massa's nonchalant rassa that is to be kissed by his wife, we intuitively know that the sexual politics of this confrontation also dictates that Massa authorise his wife to kick the black woman's all-too-ready rassa. Having kissed arse the doubly-abused black woman is forced to concede the disadvantages of her bargaining position.

In the final two stanzas of the song there is thus pathos, not just defiance, in the woman's recognition of her precarious tenure:

> Me fum'd when me no condescend:
> Me fum'd too if me do it;
> Me no have no one for 'tand my friend,
> So me am forc'd to do it.

But the suspicion of duplicity lingers. The subdued, friendless black woman, forced to perform according to script – 'Me is just what ebba them make me' – is a potentially tragic figure, doubly masking the pain of alienation in the passive gesture of contrition and the aggressive posture of revolt: 'This is the way dem bring me in;/ So God nor devil take me!' Stripped of her temporary privileges as Massa's favourite, the woman assumes a 'poor me gal'[33] pose to elicit sympathy. Though she represents herself as ultimately friendless, and alone, there did exist in her society large numbers of women who shared similar survival strategies in a sisterhood of transgressive innocence. The exigences of their circumstances required that they exploit the sexual weaknesses of their masters for their own benefit. Indeed, Moreton notes that on the death of many a Massa-benefactor, and in the absence of any protection for such 'wantons' who were themselves property, these women often banded together to engage in surreptitious seizure of a measure of security:

> As soon as the breath is out of a white man, his favourite black or mongrel wench, assisted by her female friends, who are always ready and expert on such occasions, will, if not prevented by some sensible sharp white person, plunder and make away with as much of the moveable property of the deceased as possible: such as cash, furniture, apparel etc. etc.[34]

There is a Jamaican proverb that pointedly legitimises this kind of reparative behaviour: 'Thief from thief Massa God laugh.' Retributive justice is divinely sanctioned in good humour.

The tragic condition of the exploited black woman thus shades into comedy/farce. This reversibility of psychological states is expressed proverbially in Jamaican popular culture as the regenerative capacity to take *bad tings make joke*. Therapeutic masking. The repertoire of cunning strategies employed by black women was shared with black men. 'The Runaway', recorded in Matthew G. Lewis's *Journal of a West India Proprietor*, tells the story of Peter, who enticed by a 'lilly white girl,' runs away and is forced to beg pardon of his Massa. His flattering appeal to Missy helps reinstate him:

> 'Missy, you cheeks so red, so white;
> Missy, you eyes like diamond shine!
> Missy you Massa's sole delight,
> And Lilly Sally, him was mine!
> Him say – "Come, Peter, mid me go!" –
> Could me refuse him? Could me say "no"? –
> Poor Peter – "no" him could no say!
> So Peter, Peter ran away!'
>
> Him Missy him pray; him Massa so kind
> Was moved by him prayer, and to Peter him say:
> "Well, boy, for this once I forgive you! – but mind!
> With the buckra girls you now more go away!

Though fair without, they're foul within;
Their heart is black, though white their skin.
Then Peter, Peter with me stay;
Peter no more run away![35]

The song presents yet another appearance/reality inversion, the deceptive white woman playing the black woman's role of seductress to her naive black male other. Once Peter's stolen money is spent, he is abandoned:

Peter, him Massa thief – Oh fye!
Missy Sally, him say him do so.
Him money spent, Sally bid him bye,
And from Peter away him go;
Fye, Missy Sally, fye on you!
Poor Blacky Peter what him do?
Oh! Peter, Peter was a sad boy;
Peter was a runaway![36]

Lewis's representation of the Jamaican language in his *Journal*, warrants the following comment from D'Costa and Lalla: 'As a newcomer to Jamaica, Lewis had to acquire Jamaican Creole and obviously found the language difficult to produce. His reluctance to set it down verbatim may arise simply from not knowing it well enough or from literary habit and prejudice against such a socially condemned vernacular.'[37]

Song, itself, functions as a complex mechanism for containing and displacing aggression. In circumstances where the enslaved could not realise their basic desires, they were forced to sublimate their hostility in song. Edward Long observes that:

> They have good ears for music; and their songs, as they call them, are generally *impromptus*, without the least particle of poetry, or poetic images, of which they seem to have no idea. The tunes consist of a *solo* part, which we may style the recitative, the key of which is frequently varied; and this is accompanied with a full or general chorus. Some of them are not deficient in melody; although the tone of voice is, for the most part, rather flat and melancholy. Instead of choosing panegyric for their subject-matter, they generally prefer one of derision, and not infrequently at the expence of the overseer, if he happens to be near, and listening: this only serves to add a poignancy to their satire, and heightens the fun.[38]

'If Me Want fe Go in a Ebo' is a good example of a derisive song that throws words at whoever has curtailed freedoms that the absent Massa might have allowed. The song, recorded in Moreton's *West India Customs and Manners,* illustrates the creolisation of desire in the movement from 'Ebo' to 'Kingston':

> If me want for go in a Ebo,
> Me can't go there!
> Since dem tief me from a Guinea,
> Me can't go there!
>
> If me want for go in a Congo,
> Me can't go there!
> Since dem tief me from my tatta,
> Me can't go there!
>
> If me want for go in a Kingston,
> Me can't go there!
> Since massa go in a England,
> Me can't go there.[39]

The chapters which follow trace the liberating path of Jamaican popular culture as it sustains the perennial desire to retrace the routes of Caribbean culture in the lost homelands of Ebo, Guinea and Congo; the evolution of Jamaican popular culture also illustrates the creolisation process – the making of a distinctly *Jamaican* cultural identity.

Notes

1 Presumably 'anonymous', appearing in J. B. Moreton, *West India Customs and Manners*, 2nd edn (London: J. Parsons, 1793), p. 153. Cited in Jean D'Costa and Barbara Lalla (eds), *Voices in Exile: Jamaican Texts of the 18th and 19th Centuries* (Tuscaloosa: University of Alabama Press, 1989), pp. 13–14.
2 This coinage is intended to suggest the oral/scribal literary continuum in Jamaica.
3 For a lucid discussion of the problematics of 'race' as a 'meaningful category in the study of literature and the shaping of critical theory', see Henry Louis Gates, Jr 'Writing "Race" and the Difference It Makes' in Henry Louis Gates, Jr (ed), *Race, Writing and Difference* (Chicago: University of Chicago Press, 1985, 1986), pp. 1–20.
4 D'Costa and Lalla, *Voices in Exile*, p. 12.
5 Ibid., pp. 130–31. It is the constraints of rhyme, not metre, that account for the English interference. Thus the pluralisation of 'busses' to rhyme with 'missess.'
6 Michael Scott, *Tom Cringle's Log*, 1838; rpt (London: Everyman's Library, No. 710, 1938), p. 179.
7 Ibid., p. 179.
8 Ibid., p. viii.
9 Ibid., p. 179.
10 D'Costa and Lalla themselves use the term 'poem' for the song in the passage cited above.

11 Moreton, *West India Customs and Manners*, p. 152.
12 Ibid., p. 154.
13 D'Costa and Lalla, *Voices in Exile*, p. 8.
14 Bryan Edwards, *The History, Civil and Commercial of the British Colonies in the West Indies* (London, 1801, 5 vols), II, p. 28.
15 Cited (as 'anonymous' after Edwards) in Barbara Bush, *Slave Women in Caribbean Society 1650–1838* (London: James Currey; Kingston: Heinemann; Bloomington: Indiana University Press, 1990), p. 11. Edward Brathwaite in 'Creative Literature of the British West Indies during the period of Slavery', *Savacou* 1.1 (1970): p. 50, attributes the poem to Rev. Isaac Teale – without supporting documentation in the essay. I am indebted to Dr Claudette Williams, Department of Spanish, UWI, Mona (whose unpublished doctoral dissertation is on 'Images of Black and Mulatto Women in Spanish Caribbean Poetry: Discourse and Ideology', Stanford University, 1986), for the Teale refinement of the reference.
16 Bush, *Slave Women*, op. cit.
17 'John Canoe' is defined in the *Dictionary of Jamaican English* as 'The Leader and chief dancer of a troop of negro dancers. He wears an elaborate horned mask or head-dress, which by the end of the 18th and early 19th cents, had developed into or been replaced by the representation of an estate house, houseboat, or the like (never a canoe). The celebration takes place during the Christmas holidays, the John Canoe leading the other masqueraders in procession singing and dancing, with drums and noisy "music", and asking for contributions from bystanders and householders.' The alternate spellings indicate the English/West African eytmologies of the word. John Rashford notes in 'Plants, Spirits and the Meaning of "John" in Jamaica', *Jamaica Journal* 17.2 (1984): p. 62, that 'objects named "John" are often associated in Jamaica with the world of spirits'.
18 Quoted in *Voices in Exile*, p. 54. Note that in Jamaican, 'him' is both male and female.
19 Terry Castle, *Masquerade and Civilization: The Carnivalesque in Eighteenth-Century English Culture and Fiction* (Stanford, CA.: Stanford University Press, 1986), pp. 60–2.
20 This argument is extended in the concluding chapter of this study where I examine Jamaica Kincaid's representation of the problematic relationship between native and visitor in the tourist industry – *A Small Place*; and in the experience of Caribbean migration – *Lucy*.
21 Edward Long, *The History of Jamaica*, 1774; rpt (London: Frank Cass, 1970, Vol. II), p. 424.
22 Ibid., pp. 425–6.
23 Peter Stallybrass and Allon White, *The Politics and Poetics of Transgression* (Ithaca, New York: Cornell University Press, 1986), p. 191.
24 Barbara Bush, *Slave Women in Caribbean Society 1650–1838*, p. 17. A notable exception is Thomas Thistlewood, whose diary lavishly documents his numerous encounters with black women and his long-term relationship with one Phibbah. See Douglas Hall (ed.), *In Miserable Slavery: Thomas Thistlewood in Jamaica, 1750–86* (London: Macmillan, 1989). Hall observes that 'Thistlewood noted his sexual occasions in such Latin as he remembered', p. 23. This linguistic transfer of 'illicit' sexuality to a dead/scholarly language may very well be yet another example of hierarchy inversion.

25 Barbara Bush, *Slave Women in Caribbean Society 1650–1838*, pp. 17–18.
26 Cited in *Voices in Exile*, pp. 47–8.
27 In Chapter 3, the genesis of an indigenous feminist ideology is located in the cunning of the Akan trickster figure, Anansi.
28 Moreton, *West India Customs and Manners*, pp. 14–15.
29 Ibid., pp. 153–4.
30 Pejorative term in Jamaica for unwed fathers. Connotes the juvenile character of irresponsible paternity. Louise Bennett's 'Registration' and 'Mass Wedding', discussed in Chapter 3, are satirical accounts of middle-class attempts to coerce working-class men and women into conformity to the conventions of marriage.
31 As both victim of Massa's indifference and active agent in the oppression of the black woman Misses cannot be simply dismissed as a footnote on the margins of my critique; nevertheless, she is not of central importance to the present study. Barbara Bush notes in *Slave Women in Caribbean Society* that '[a]lthough white women were also subject to patriarchal domination and contemporary records indicate that, in the early days of slavery, there was marked lack of respect for poorer white women, such class differences became less marked with the maturation of slave society, as all white women were elevated above black and coloured women' (p. 12). Indeed, the re-eroticisation of the white woman and her mulatto clone in late twentieth-century Jamaica, as evidenced in the preferred images of pin-up/calendar girls, advertising models for up-market products etc. inspires the following quip: 'The only thing worse than being a sex-object is not being a sex-object.'
32 D'Costa and Lalla, *Voices in Exile*, p. 144.
33 Defined in the *Dictionary of Jamaican English* as '[a]n exclamation of self-pity in Jamaica characteristically adding "boy", "gal", or one's name, in apposition to the "me" of the ordinary Engl phr "poor me".'
34 Moreton, *West India Customs and Manners*, p. 161.
35 Reproduced in *Voices in Exile*, pp. 31–2.
36 Ibid., p. 31.
37 Ibid., p. 134.
38 Edward Long, *The History of Jamaica*, Vol. II, p. 423.
39 Reproduced in *Voices in Exile*, pp. 12–13.

CHAPTER 2 'Culture an tradition an birthright': proverb as metaphor in the poetry of Louise Bennett

> Listen, no!
>
> My Aunty Roachy seh dat Jamaica people have a whole heap a Culture an Tradition an Birthright dat han dung to dem from generation to generation. All like de great philosophy of we Jamaica proverbs-dem. Mmmm.
>
> Well, sah! As she coulda seh de wud 'philosophy' so, one facety gal dem call Muches gi out an seh, 'A so-so foolishness Miss Roachy she dah chat! How yuh coulda put a deestant wud like philosophy wid de ole jamma bad talkin proverbs-dem?'
>
> See yah! Aunty Roachy never meck fun fi leggo tongue pon Muches. She seh, 'When goat laugh everybody fine out seh him no got no teet!' (Dat mean: some people shoulda keep silent to hide dem ignorance.)[1]

The metaphorical proverb recurs in the poetry and dramatised narratives of Louise Bennett to fulfil two vital functions as exemplified above. Thematically, the proverb provides conclusive evidence of the socially recognised truth of the argument that a particular Bennett *persona* articulates; structurally, the metaphorical proverb employs graphic imagery derived from everyday Jamaican life as the vehicle for social commentary. In both subject and structure the metaphorical proverb affirms Bennett's umbilical connection to that matrix of oral Jamaican folklore which she describes in 'Jamaica Philosophy' as 'Culture an Tradition an Birthright dat han dung . . . from generation to generation.'

Analysis of the use of metaphor in 'Jamaica Philosophy' is instructive. Muches, the unfortunate antagonist of the piece, is metaphorically described not only as the toothless goat but subsequently as a jackass: 'No strain yuh jaw bone pon de wud philosophy when yuh no know weh it mean.'[2] The strain on Muches' jaw bone is an obvious metaphor for the greater strain on her brain. In a clever twist of referent, Aunty Roachy introduces the metaphor of the jackass in a proverb that ostensibly describes herself, but which it is clear by implication is more appropriately applied to Muches: 'If yuh falla de philosophy a we Jamaica proverbs yuh woulda know seh dat "When yuh go a jackass yard yuh nuffi chat bout big aise!" (Don't offend people when you are in their domain. Mmmm.) So yuh shouldn come a me yard come call me foo-fool!'[3]

In addition to the use of these lucid metaphorical comparisons, Aunty Roachy employs a subtle technique to underscore Muches' stupidity: she paraphrases many of the proverbs she casts at poor Muches. The essence of a proverb is its immediacy of access to members of the community in which it has currency. The logic of Aunty Roachy's pointed paraphrases is that Muches is either an outsider or a fool. There is an Ashanti proverb, quoted epigraphically by Cundall and Anderson in their 1910 collection of Jamaican proverbs, that is particularly appropriate: 'When a fool is told a proverb, the meaning of it has to be explained to him.'[4]

Not all Jamaican proverbs are metaphorical in structure. The proverb may be a literal statement: 'If yuh no know bout no chat bout.' Or it may employ antithesis, alliteration, repetition and rhyme – mnemonic devices by means of which the proverb's potency is sustained. For example, antithesis: 'Farden pocket an poun a ches'; alliteration: 'Cratch an rub cyaan cure cocobeh'; repetition: 'Teck weh yuh can get so get weh yuh want.'[5] Mnemonic linguistic devices such as these are identified by Walter Ong in *Orality and Literacy* as the fundamental constituents of thought in primary oral cultures such as Jamaica largely is:

> In a primary oral culture, to solve effectively the problem of retaining and retrieving carefully articulated thought, you have to do your thinking in mnemonic patterns, shaped for ready oral recurrence. Your thought must come into being in heavily rhythmic, balanced patterns, in repetitions or antithesis, in alliterations and assonances, in epithetic and other expressions, in standard thematic settings . . . in proverbs which are constantly heard by everyone so that they come to mind readily and which themselves are patterned for retention and ready recall.[6]

In an important study of 'Figurative Language in Jamaican Creole' Velma Pollard analyses the use of proverb and riddle in the everyday speech of oral Jamaicans, and provides excellent examples of the way in which the proverb carries the weight of thought in ordinary discourse. I cite one of Pollard's examples and quote her discussion of it:

> **Informant**: mi neva get nof/bot mi breda/aa mi sista . . ./dem se *di hongriis kyaaf sok di muos milk*/
> (Me never get 'nuff' but my brother and my sister. . ./ Them say *the hungriest calf suck the most milk*)

> **Discussion**: In example 1 the subject is education. An old man explains that he is illiterate compared with his brother and sister. They represent the 'hungriest calf' since they were at a disadvantage in terms of family finance (he in fact worked in order to support them). There is an inverse relationship here between place in the family and eventual good fortune since the younger siblings, finally, are better off than he educationally. . . . Notice that after the first sentence the old man gives up and lays the burden of expression on the proverb.[7]

Pollard draws the following conclusion from her study:

> The suggestion is too often made that certain literary devices are beyond the understanding of individuals whose control of standard English is limited. Increasingly that view will have to be abandoned in the light of more and more evidence of the ease with which language is handled where standard English is not required. So that in the schools, for example, it is English that the children need to acquire, not the ability to understand or to handle the figurative use of the language.[8]

What Pollard thus illustrates is

> the ability of the folk to manipulate language not only effectively but with a certain distinctive style that is part of a tradition of verbal art forms available within or outside of a performance context. It is a style which surfaces again and again in the writing of the more sensitive and competent of the Caribbean artists.[9]

Louise Bennett is the quintessential Jamaican example of the sensitive and competent Caribbean artist consciously incorporating features of traditional oral art into the written literature. Mervyn Morris, in the introduction to his critical edition of Bennett's *Selected Poems* (designed for use in schools), draws deliberate attention to the poetry as both written text and oral performance:

> Louise Bennett's art is both oral and scribal; the forms are not mutually exclusive. The poem in print is, however, fully available only when readers are in touch with the oral and other cultural contexts the words imply.[10]

Similarly wishing to underscore the complexity of the art form, Rex Nettleford, in his 1966 introduction to Bennett's *Jamaica Labrish*, gently admonishes those who, responsive to the apparently artless vivacity of Bennett's performances, fail to recognise her careful craftsmanship – albeit in a 'bastard tongue':

> And those who indulge her rumbustious abandon and spontaneous inducement of laughter will sometimes forget that behind the exuberance and carefree stance, there are years of training – formal and informal – as well as this artist's own struggles to shape an idiom whose limitations as a bastard tongue are all too evident.[11]

The imagery of sexual licentiousness, used so naturally in this early post-Independence period by a Jamaican intellectual of such stature as Rex Nettleford, eloquently confirms the assumption of an almost instinctual correlation between linguistic 'slackness' and sexual (im)morality that is thoroughly bred into the Jamaican psyche.

Bastardy and corruption are negative attributes of the Jamaican language which is not generally perceived as undergoing the natural processes of morally neutral change – like all other living languages. Thus Bennett argues humorously, through the *persona* of Aunty Roachy, that just as the pedigree of respectable languages like English is never in question, Jamaican should be recognised as a legitimate language:

> Like my Aunty Roachy se, shi vex anytime shi hear people a come style fi wi Jamaican language as 'corruption' a di English language. Yu ever hear anyting go so? Aunty Roachy se shi no know we mek dem no call di English language 'corruption' a di Norman French an di Greek an di Latin we dem se English 'derived from'. Unu hear di wod? English 'derive' but Jamaica 'corrupt'. No massa, noting no go so. We not 'corrupt', an dem 'derive.' We derive to. Jamaica derive.[12]

Having creatively tested the limitations of the corrupt 'bastard tongue', Jamaican, Bennett has succeeded in helping to legitimise it.

Part of the legitimising process has been the writing down of the language. Oral discourse leaves the tongue open to slackness; writing trims the tongue, curtailing linguistic looseness. Bennett, herself, insists that she is a writer: 'From the beginning, nobody ever recognized me as a writer. "Well, she is 'doing' dialect"; it wasn't even writing you know. Up to now a lot of people don't even think I write.'[13] That assertion is no facile attempt to be retrospectively validated by the hierophants of the scribal tradition. Rather, it underscores the syncretic nature of her art. For Louise Bennett is herself literate. Her creation of oral *personae* such as Aunty Roachy is not simply a matter of spontaneous ejaculation; it is the product of a complex process of socio-linguistic accommodation. Ultimately, it is a political decision. Indeed, Bennett's choice of subject matter and language is an affirmation of what one might term *naygacentric*/nativist aesthetic values, rooted in the particular socio-political contradictions of Jamaica's history. As an aspiring poet in Jamaica in the 1930s, Bennett assumed that her exclusive models were the English Romantic poets; her ambition was to 'express [her] thought /And whims in dulcet poetry.'[14] But, responsive to the explosive sounds around her, Bennett abandoned dulcet poetry for dialect poetry. Like Claude McKay, Bennett was to discover an alter/native, dualistic oral/scribal aesthetic, grounded in both Jamaican popular culture and her formal (English) training in theatre.

Morris describes the genesis of her first dialect poem thus:

> One day she set out, a young teenager all dressed up, for a matinee film show in Cross Roads. On the electric tramcars which were then the basis of public transportation in Kingston, people travelling with baskets were required to sit at the back, and they were sometimes resentful of other people who, when the tram was full, tried to join them there. As Louise was boarding the tram she heard a country woman say: 'Pread out yuhself, one dress-oman a come' That vivid remark made a great impression on her, and on returning home she wrote her first dialect poem 'On a Tramcar' which began:
>
> Pread out yuhself de Liza,
> one Dress-oman dah look like seh
> She see di li space side-a we
> And wan foce harself een deh[15]

This literal spreading out of self is an evocative metaphor for the irrepressible survival instincts of Jamaica's dispossessed who refuse to be squeezed out of existence. The amplitude of the body becomes a figure for the verbal expansiveness that is often the only weapon of the politically powerless; tracings and other forms of verbal abuse are essential armaments in class warfare. The well-dressed young woman who is not to be allowed to sit with the market-women – at her convenience – must know her place; she cannot violate the social space that the ostracised market-women have come to claim as their own. Verbal confrontation on the public transportation system in Jamaica continues to be a popular safety-valve for ventilating social frustration.

In the poem 'Nayga Yard', published in 1948 in *Public Opinion,* Bennett celebrates the proverb-speaking rural and urban Jamaican *nayga* folk, for whom Jamaica is home, is yard. Bennett employs a vivid metaphorical proverb to introduce the poem's theme: 'Cock cyaan beat cock eena cock own yard'. The authority of the proverb is asserted: 'We all know dat is true', and then the problematic question is raised – 'Is who-for yard Jamaica is?/Is who dah beat up who?' (p. 102). The poem proceeds at the literal level to list a variety of professions and occupations and asks which race is dominant in Jamaica:

Tink omuch different race a people
Eena dis islan,
An tink who is de greates
Cricketer – a nayga man!

Who is de greates barrister?
A Jew? A Syrian?
Him white? Is Chiney? Coolie? No,
Him is a nayga man!

Call fi Jamaica fastes sprinters
Gal or bwoy, an den
De foremos artis, doctor, scholar –
Nayga reign again!

Go eena every school, ask fi
De brightes chile dem got –
An nineteen out a twenty time
A nayga deh pon spot!

Go eena prison, poor house, jail,
Asylum – wha yuh see?
Nayga dah reign predominant!
De place belongs to we! (p. 103)

The poem's irony is deliberate. Were it indeed self-evident that Jamaica *is* nayga yard, Bennett would not have needed to raise the question at all. The poem predates the happy fiction of our post-Independence national motto: 'Out of many, one people'; it exhorts nayga people to 'carry awn;/Leggo [dem] talents broad./Member de place a fi-[dem]/ Jamaica is nayga yard.' (p. 102)

'Nayga Yard' is a good example of the use of proverb to express metaphorically and euphemistically a socio-political statement that might appear inflammatory, were it baldly presented as merely the individual's personal opinion, and not a truism confirmed by popular wisdom. Mervyn Morris supports this view of the proverb as a framing technique in Bennett's poetry:

> proverbs often serve to widen the significance of a particular incident or situation: because they represent the distillation of generations of experience, reference to proverbs tends to suggest

> that the immediate difficulty or the immediate occasion for joy is not entirely new, and that the present moment is part of the flow of communal experience.[16]

A comic example of this widening function of the proverb appears in the poem 'Sweetie-Pie' which begins with two metaphorical proverbs: 'Donkey tink him cub a race-horse,/John crow tink him pickney white' (p. 48) and then furnishes a contemporary example of equivalent folly: 'Doah Teacher mark John sum-dem wrong/Him mumma seh dem right!' (p. 48) The laughter that the naiveté of John's mumma evokes is tempered by the audience's awareness that her weakness is not unique; her foibles are the common human condition. Further, the use of animal imagery in the proverbs to describe human characteristics suggests the ontological continuum of the human and animal worlds – a distinctive feature of the metaphysics of primary oral cultures. 'Sweetie-Pie', the poem's main subject, is variously described by his doting sister as 'de lickle heart-trob', 'de darlin chile' and 'de lickle dear'. The affectionate diminutives create a visual image that is not at all supported by Sweetie Pie's physical brawn. The Bennett *persona* is derisive:

> Beck whisper, 'Him a come!'
> Me tun fi greet de 'lickle heart',
> And den me tan up dumb!
>
> Me did expec one pretty
> Lickle bwoy bout six ear ole;
> Me see one big strong-muscle man
> Dah run fi fifty bole!
>
> De man mek up him face an grunt
> An stretch, an tare him yeye.
> Me seh, 'Massi, me lawd – a dis
> Becky call 'Sweetie-Pie'?[']
>
> But when me get over de shock
> Me laugh an seh: she right –
> 'Donkey tink him cub a race-horse,
> John crow tink him pickney white.' (pp. 48–9)

The best example of the sustained use of proverbs in *Selected Poems* and *Jamaica Labrish* is the poem appropriately titled 'Proverbs', first published in 1943 in the *Sunday Gleaner*. Bennett assumes the *persona* of a self-righteous 'dead-lef', an orphan who perceives herself as victimised by 'all kine a ole black nayga' (p. 53) now that her mother is dead. The use of judiciously-selected proverbs reinforces the speaker's view of herself as a hapless innocent abroad, facing a hostile world with only the traditional consolation of the proverb.

The poem's opening proverb immediately establishes through metaphor the young woman's perception of the grave social catastrophe that has befallen her:

> 'When ashes cowl dawg sleep in deh';
> For sence Ma dead, yuh see,
> All kine a ole black nayga start
> Teck liberty wid me. (p. 53)

The notion of the violation of social order is graphically expressed in the next verse by means of another metaphorical proverb:

> Me no wrap up wid dem, for me
> Pick an choose me company:
> Ma always tell me seh: 'Yuh sleep
> Wid dawg yuh ketch him flea'. (p. 54)

Temporarily abandoning the posture of social superiority, the woman describes her sense of vulnerability in the yard thus:

> Me know plenty a dem no like me,
> An doah de time so hard
> Me kip fur from dem, for 'Cockroach
> No bizniz a fowl yard'. (p. 54)

In these circumstances she recognises that one must observe the rituals of social decorum:

> Ah teck time gwan me ways an doan
> Fas eena dem affair;
> Me tell dem mawnin, for 'Howdy
> An tenky bruck no square'. (p. 54)

She confesses to an occasional gossipy chat with parson – her social equal – for '"Ef yuh no go a man fire-side, yuh no know/Ow much fire-stick a bwile him pot."' (p. 54) The consequence of which is:

> Sake-a dat, as lickle news get bout
> Dem call me po gal name;
> Me bear it, for doah 'all fish nyam man,
> Dah shark one get de blame'. (p. 54)

She absolves herself of all culpability:

> But when me go look fi parson
> Me ongle talk bout me soul,

For Ma use fi tell me: 'Sweet mout fly
Follow coffin go a hole'. (p. 54)

The final proverb with which she eulogises the dead mother is: '"Back no know weh ole shut do fi i/So tell ole shut tear of"'. (p. 54)

In the introduction to her 1925 collection of Jamaican proverbs, the expatriate anthropologist Martha Beckwith – somewhat in the tradition of Moreton's *West India Customs and Manners* – defines what she imagined to be the dominant mood of Jamaican proverbs: a fascination with deprivation and oppression. Beckwith's judgement appears to be based on a limited understanding of the Jamaican psyche, a failure to recognise the wry humour that permits us to 'teck bad tings mek joke'. Note the ubiquitous political graffiti, urban proverbs in the making. Beckwith, unlike Bennett's Muches, was an outsider, not a fool. Her description of the psychic consolation of the proverb, though limited in its general applicability, accurately defines one function of the proverb, as exemplified in the case of the Bennett *persona* analysed above:

> I was chiefly impressed with the dark sense of wrong and the nursing by the weaker folk of injuries real or fancied inflicted by those upon whom they were impotent to avenge themselves, which find voice in the apparently innocent or merely sententious retort. It is to be noticed how many of the proverbs apply to poverty, hunger, injury and want. Love is not celebrated, nor is heroism or beauty. Women are seldom mentioned, and then generally to belittle. It is the fate of the folk who are put upon by their betters and who smart under injury which is here expressed with an almost uncanny justness of observation; as if, by generalizing the experience of misery and poverty, each man became dignified in his own eyes. So he shares the common lot, and the hope of an eventual retribution appeases his particular sense of deprivation.[17]

A more inclusive view of the complex conceptual and emotional range of proverbs in African cultures – and in neo-African oral cultures like Jamaica – is that of Ruth Finnegan, who writes in *Oral Literature in Africa*:

> In many African cultures a feeling for language, for imagery, and for the expression of abstract ideas through compressed and allusive phraseology comes out particularly clearly in proverbs. The figurative quality of proverbs is especially striking; one of their most noticeable characteristics is their allusive wording, usually in metaphorical form.[18]

Louise Bennett has long recognised the evocative power of Jamaican proverbs as the locus of folk philosophy. In the words of Aunty Roachy:

> 'Dictionary seh dat philosophy mean "the general principles governing thoughts and conducts", "a study of human morals and character".... Dem-deh is we ole time Jamaica proverbs, an dem got principles governin thoughts an conducts an morals an character, like what dictionary seh. So doan cry dem dung, for what is fi-yuh cyaan be un-fi-yuh.'[19]

Though public acknowledgement of the cultural significance of Bennett's *oeuvre* has been grudging – there are yet the detractors who would ask 'A dat yuh modder sen yuh a school fa?'[20] – her ultimate consolation must be the certainty, expressed proverbially, that 'time longer dan rope'.

Notes

1 Louise Bennett, 'Jamaica Philosophy', in Mervyn Morris (ed.), *Focus* (Kingston: Caribbean Authors, 1983), p. 49.
2 Ibid.
3 Ibid.
4 I. Anderson, and F. Cundall (eds), *Jamaican Proverbs* (Kingston: Institute of Jamaica, 1910); rpt (Shannon: Irish University Press, 1972). Bennett's parenthetical glossing of the proverbs – in English – is clearly intended for the readership akin to Muches.
5 All proverbs cited above are from 'Jamaica Philosophy', p. 50.
6 Walter Ong, *Orality and Literacy* (New York: Methuen, 1982), p. 34.
7 Velma Pollard, 'Figurative Language in Jamaican Creole', *Carib* 3 (1983): p. 31.
8 Ibid., p. 32.
9 Ibid., p. 32.
10 Louise Bennett, *Selected Poems*, ed. Mervyn Morris (Kingston: Sangster's, 1982). Subsequent references cited parenthetically in text, indicated by *SP*.
11 Louise Bennett, *Jamaica Labrish*, ed. Rex Nettleford (Kingston: Sangster's, 1966); rpt 1975, p. 10. Subsequent references cited parenthetically in text, indicated by *JL*. The orthography of this collection differs from that of the later, more readable *SP*.
12 Louise Bennett, 'Jamaica Language', 'Yes M'Dear – Miss Lou Live', Island Records, ICT 9740, 1983.
13 'Bennett on Bennett', Louise Bennett interviewed by Dennis Scott, *Caribbean Quarterly* 14. 1–2 (1968): p. 98.
14 Louise Bennett, quoted in Mervyn Morris's 'Introduction' to *Selected Poems*, p. iv.
15 Ibid., pp. iv–v.
16 *Selected Poems*, p. xvi.
17 Martha Beckwith, *Jamaica Proverbs*, 1925; rpt (New York: Negro Universities Press, 1972), pp. 6–7.
18 Ruth Finnegan, *Oral Literature in Africa* (Oxford: Oxford University Press, 1970), p. 391. Cited by Pollard, op cit.
19 'Jamaica Philosophy', pp. 49, 50.
20 Quoted in Mervyn Morris's 'Introduction' to *Selected Poems*, pp. xii, xiii.

CHAPTER 3 That cunny Jamma oman: representations of female sensibility in the poetry of Louise Bennett

That cunning Jamaican woman, celebrated and satirised with equal gusto in Louise Bennett's ample corpus, is a composite character – an aggregation of the multiple *personae* employed by Bennett, the ventriloquist, to voice the lives of representative Jamaican women of all social classes. This multifarious heroine-victim of Bennett's comic/satirical sketches presents us with a diversity of social class values and behaviours that attests to the verisimilitude of Bennett's detailed portraiture. Indirection is the quintessential attribute, and/or dubious distinction of the crafty Jamaican woman, of whom Bennett is, herself, a prime example. For she creates with cunning irony, out of the raw materials of everyday Jamaican life, a dramatised world of paradoxical characters who simultaneously mask and figure forth the ambiguously shifting Bennett point of view.

Writing in 1978 on Louise Bennett's use of *persona* to present a wide range of female experience, Lloyd Brown observes in *West Indian Poetry* that

> Her poetic voice fascinates and challenges her audience precisely because her characters seem to be so irrefutably independent of a controlling artistic vision or authorial judgment. This partly explains the fact that the woman's experience which so clearly dominates her work remains, paradoxically, unobtrusive rather than explicitly reiterated. . . . Indeed, no other West Indian writer has dealt at greater length with the West Indian woman. And in no other writer has the world of the Jamaican (and the West Indies as a whole) been presented almost exclusively through the eyes of women, especially the rural women and the poorer women of the city. . . . Generally, Bennett eschews characters who make direct statements about the woman's situation, and instead allows her women to offer indirectly revealing, sometimes contradictory, levels of awareness of their sociosexual condition.[1]

The complacent ironies of the *personae's* self-disclosures account for much of the humour and subtlety of Bennett's work.

The proverbial cunning of the Jamaican woman is one manifestation of the morally ambiguous craftiness of Anansi, the Akan folk hero, transmuted in Jamaican folklore into Brer Nansi, the archetypal trickster. Folktales of the mighty outwitted by the clever proliferate throughout the African diaspora. The shared history of plantation slavery in the Americas consolidates within the psyche of African peoples in the hemisphere, cultural continuities, ancestral memories of sabotage and marronage, systemic resistance to servitude. It is within this broader tradition of neo-African folk consciousness – the Anansi syndrome – that Bennett's elaboration of Jamaican female sensibility can be best understood.

In the poem 'Jamaica Oman', the Louise Bennett *persona* employs an earthy metaphorical proverb to expose, with obvious relish, the *jinnalship* and fortitude of the Jamaican female:

> 'Oman luck deh a dungle',
> Some rooted more dan some
> But as long as fowl a scratch dungle heap
> Oman luck mus come![2]

In that body of Jamaican folk wisdom transmitted in proverb, Anansi story and riddle, is the genesis of an indigenous feminist ideology: the paradigm of a submerged and fated identity that must be rooted up, covertly and assiduously. The existential dungle, the repository of the accumulated waste of the society, becomes in the folk iconography the locus of transformation. It is the dungle, and the dehumanising social conditions that allow it, which are the enemy of woman, not the male.[3] Cunning, rather than overt male/female confrontation is the preferred strategy for maintaining domestic harmony.

This thematic/stylistic analysis of representations of female sensibility in Louise Bennett's poetry is organised under two broad subject headings: 'Eena Yard' and 'Outa Road', to quote a Bennett *persona*. I will examine domestic relations: male–female, and mother–child; and extra-domestic affairs: women and work, and women and politics.

In the witty 'Jamaica Oman' it is the positive, more so than the negative manifestations of the tricksterism of Anansi that Bennett affirms in her tribute to the resourcefulness of the Jamaican female in ordering her domestic affairs with the Jamaican male, amicably:

> Jamaica oman cunny, sah!
> Is how dem jinnal so?
> Look how long dem liberated
> An de man dem never know!
>
> Look how long Jamaica oman
> – Modder, sister, wife, sweetheart –
> Outa road an eena yard deh pon
> A dominate her part! (*SP*, p. 21)

The Bennett *persona* differentiates this tradition of indigenous feminism from 'foreign lan Oman lib', a more recent social movement:

> An long before Oman lib bruck out
> Over foreign lan
> Jamaica female wasa work
> Her liberated plan! (*SP*, p. 22)

The legendary Maroon Nanny, who 'teck her body/Bounce bullet back pon man', remains alive in Jamaican folklore because of her militancy against British soldiers, not Maroon men. The allusion to Nanny situates contemporary Jamaican 'oman lib' within a long-established heritage of consolidated male/female defence of cultural and political sovereignty.[4]

'Foreign lan Oman lib' is rejected by the Bennett *persona* because it is perceived as failing to acknowledge the strategic differences between men and women:

> Jamaica oman know she strong,
> She know she tallawah
> But she no want her pickney-dem
> Fi start call her 'Puppa'.
>
> So de cunny Jamma Oman
> Gwan like pants-suit is a style,
> An Jamaica man no know she wear
> De trousiz all de while! (*SP*, p. 22)

This 'tallawah' Jamaican woman knows when to be appropriately 'weak' as the complementary poem 'Tan-Up Seat' illustrates. The speaker there makes it clear that ritualised codes of decorum ought to govern male–female behaviour, particularly when a tired woman recognises an able-bodied male, seated, on a crowded tramcar:

> Me doan seh man kean tired to
> But wen dem want show-off,
> Dem sey ooman is 'weaka sex',
> An ooman frail and sof'.
>
> But wen man go pon tram and lef
> Dem mannas a dem yard,
> Dem gwan like ooman strong like man
> An cruff an rough an hard!
>
> An sometime when shame bun dem shirt
> Dem start gwan like dem shy,
> An sidung-man kean look straight eena
> Tan-up ooman y'eye![5]

It is the tenuous compromise that Jamaican women often make in order to live with their men which Bennett treats with such consummate craftsmanship in 'Jamaica Oman'. An excellent example of comic irony is the 'role reversal' by means of which women appear to have appropriated the male role as head of the household, but are simply functioning true to nature:

> Some backa man a push, some side-a
> Man a hole him han,
> Some a lick sense eena man head,
> Some a guide him pon him plan! (*SP*, p. 22)

Further, women will tolerate disparaging labels of powerlessness as long as they retain actual power:

> Neck an neck an foot an foot wid man
> She buckle hole her own;
> While man a call her 'so-so rib'
> Oman a tun backbone! (*SP*, p. 22)

The speaker's disdainful allusion to the biblical narrative of origins, conveys her contempt for a sanctimonious patriarchal prejudice that dehumanises women in the name of religion.

Bennett's portrayal of the cunny Jamma oman is not a solemn study of manipulative female politics, or simpering subservience. Good-natured humour, decidedly shading into satire, characterises her critique. For the poem ends on this ambiguous note:

> Lickle by lickle man start praise her,
> Day by day de praise a grow;
> So him praise her, so it sweet her,
> For she wonder if him know. (*SP*, p. 23)

Two mutually ironic interpretations of this verse suggest that (a) even when men concede the benefits of female power they may not be conscious of the *jinnalship* whereby women only appear to defer to conventional notions of appropriate behaviour, and (b) men may indeed suspect the ruses of women, and simply allow them free rein. In this second reading, jinnalship would not be the exclusive perquisite of the female, as the poem 'Racket' illustrates.

The speaker there berates the wiliness of the Jamaican male who resorts to subterfuge to escape emotional and material indebtedness during the season of goodwill to all persons:

As it come to Chrismus time
Dem drop de gal-frein 'biff!'
Becausen dem no waan fi gi
De gal no Chrismus gif! (*SP*, p. 21)

The biff/gif rhyme is particularly apposite. The onomatopoeic 'biff' – unlike a 'buff' – is lightweight; the rhyme thus carefully balances the weight of the negligent boyfriend's commitment against the worth of the missing gift. The deliberated drop is a temporary helping down of a burden to be assumed again, at a more convenient season:

Dem bwoy dah gwan too bad, yaw mah,
An smaddy haffi crack it!
Las ear, two weeks from Chrismus Day,
One po gal jus seh 'feh',
Her bwoy-frien start meck nize an row
An get bex an go weh!
Him meck de nice-nice gal spen Chrismus
Widout a bwoy-frien,
An de las week a January
Him crawl back een again! (*SP*, p. 21)

In a subversive reading of the poem one begins to suspect the speaker of a bit of unconscious malice. The intensity of her righteous indignation on behalf of the victim, as expressed in the opening four lines of the poem, seems somewhat excessive for the offence:

Tan! Oonoo know is what wrong wid
De Bwoy-dem nowadays?
Dem is a set a raskill, cho!
Dem got real dutty ways! (*SP*, p. 20)

By the final three lines, when the speaker is prepared to obliterate the duly punished male-turned-duppy, one is sure that the critique of gross male negligence has been inverted. The joke is on the mourner who is bawling louder than the primary victim: 'Ef dat gal was like me/Next ear him hooda haffi pick/Quarrel wid him duppy!' (*SP*, p. 21)

The ambiguous nature of Jamaican male/female relationships, satirised in several Bennett poems, appears antithetical to the singleminded zealousness of divisive 'foreign lan Oman lib' which has its Jamaican equivalent in the predominantly middle-class women's federation movement established in the 1940s under the patronage of the governor's wife, Lady Huggins.[6] This kind of organised movement is essentially different from the perennial struggles of predominantly working-class women to root out their dungle luck. Bennett's treatment of the movement is equivocal. In the poem 'Bans O' Ooman!', for example, one may detect satire, despite the speaker's laudatory intentions. In 'Mass Wedding' and 'Registration' tonal irony is even more readily apparent.

In 'Bans O' Ooman!' the female persona recreates the spontaneous excitement of the launching of the Jamaica Federation of Women designed to bring together women 'high an low, miggle, suspended,/Every different kine o' class.' (*JL*, p. 41). The comic use of the adjective 'suspended', which expresses the speaker's penchant for malapropism, also appropriately intimates the merely temporary suspension of ordinary class values which appear unimportant in the euphoria of the celebratory moment. Indeed, when the woman, who finds herself on the periphery of the gathering in St George's Hall, attempts to force her way to the centre of the event, she discovers that there is definite resistance to her upward social movement:

> Me was a-dead fe go inside
> But wen me start fe try,
> Ooman queeze me, ooman push me,
> Ooman frown an cut dem y'eye. (*JL*, p. 41)

Undaunted, she resorts to subterfuge, the rear-entry politics of potential sabotage:

> Me tek me time an crawl out back
> me noh meck no alarm,
> But me practice bans o' tactics
> Till me ketch up a platform. (*JL*, p. 41)

In the final two stanzas of the poem the satire becomes more pointed as one suspects a disjuncture of grandiose intention and actual accomplishment:

> Ef yuh ever hear dem program!
> Ef yuh ever hear dem plan!
> Ef yuh ever hear de sinting
> Ooman gwine go do to man!
>
> Federation boun to flourish,
> For dem got bans o' nice plan,
> An now dem got de heart an soul
> Of true Jamaican ooman. (*JL*, p. 41)

The optimistic certainty of the last two lines seems premature.

One of the many plans of the Federation of Women, to ensure that women enter into properly legal relationships with men, is the subject of 'Mass Wedding'. Rex Nettleford's gloss on the poem is succinct:

> The late Mary Morris Knibb of Kingston was a pioneer in the fight against bachelor fatherhood (taken up again in 1965 notably by the Soroptomist Club of Jamaica led by Edith Clarke, the anthropologist and social worker). One solution offered by Mrs. Knibb was the mass wedding, organized at little expense to the marrying parties, many of whom might have been living in common-law relationships for years. (*JL*, p. 30)

The speaker, who is hastily trying to secure one 'boonoonoonos man' (*JL*, p. 30), whom she has just met and is now stalking, seems on the surface to advocate the mass wedding. But when one notes the imagery of coercion she employs, one concludes that even she is aware that the frantic speed of the enterprise may be matched by the unwilling bridegroom's prowess at escape:

> Dat lady Mrs Married Knibbs,
> She is a real Godsen'
> For every man now mus tun husban,
> Dem kean be noh mo' bwoy frien'.
>
> Ah she meck nine-toe Berty
> Wed kaas eye Sue you know?
> An she force awn Mary Fowl-head
> Pon Miss Biddy cousin Joe.
>
> So fine a good man dat yuh hooda
> Like fe stan up beside,
> Den see Miss Knibbs an yuh will be
> Mongs de nex mass wedden brides. (*JL*, p. 31)

The speaker's vacillation between the redundant 'Mrs Married Knibbs' and the contextually deficient 'Miss Knibbs' seems unintentional and thus reinforces the poem's irony that ultimately the legal distinction is functionally unimportant. The class values of the Mary Morris Knibbses, as evidenced in 'Mass Wedding', go against the grain of a long-established Jamaican folk conviction that one ought not to marry, unless one can do it in style; they also violate the well-documented Jamaican superstition that the legal marriage ceremony can itself undermine the vulnerable balance of extra-legal male/female arrangements.

In the poem 'Registration', Bennett satirises yet another campaign of the well-intentioned Federation to coerce the working-class Jamaican male into conformity to the demands of middle-class propriety: the drive to register all fathers. The Bennett *persona* gleefully advocates the plan, citing three Jamaican proverbs to confirm the unequivocal authority of the proposed law:

> Every sore foot got him blue-stone
> Every tief got him las' deal,
> Noh care how smaddy dah-gwan bad
> Sinting deh fe spokes him wheel. (*JL,* p. 42)

Despite this apparent commonality of folk and middle-class values, what the speaker proceeds to do, apparently unwittingly, is to draw satirical attention to the social distance between the respectable middle-class ladies of the Federation, who have decent, responsible husbands, and the unfortunate, husbandless, working-class women whom the new legislation will seek to elevate. Upstanding middle-class women, with whom the speaker empathises, can afford to antagonise delinquent males because their own houses are in order:

> Guess how de man dem gwine bex wid
> De ooman Federation' (sic)
> Me glad mose o' de lady dem
> Married an got dem good husban.
>
> For like how somuch bwoy gwan weh
> And Jamaica short o' man,
> Dem ooman wat pass de law gwine have
> De dickans fe hook one! (*JL,* p. 42)

In a delightfully ambiguous line the speaker allows that unmarried middle-class women might themselves have a hard time hooking a man of their own in this period of social turbulence.

Long-chin James, who understandably objects to the legislation, is cursed by the woman: 'go weh, man a debil!' *(JL,* p. 42) But his quick reply is: 'dat is not no cuss,/For ooman a debil-mumma/So we kean tell which is wus.' (*JL,* p. 42) James is indeed perceptive, for what is evident from Bennett's wide-ranging portrayal of male–female relationships is that working-class men and women have much more in common than do middle-class and working-class women. In the Jamaican context, class rather than gender is the functional determinant of power.

But there is also evidence in Bennett's poetry of the internalisation of the values of middle-class domestic order by working-class women who believe that the state of wife, however transitory, is intrinsically superior to that of 'baby-mother' or girlfriend. In the words of one woman, who praises the war for its side benefits:

Soh me wi help de war, an ef
De war shoulda help me
Fe get married, me husban can
Gwan fight fe him country.

An ef my husban even dead,
Me don't seh me won't cry,
But de joy dat ah was married
Wi meck me satisfy. (*JL*, pp. 100–1)

Similarly, the speaker in the poem 'Praises' expresses great joy that with the establishment of the Sandy Gully American base, and the attendant employment opportunities it offers, her status changes:

Look how me an Joe did live bad.
But praise to Sandy Gully!
As him get de fus week pay him do
So baps – married to me.

An now him meck love sweeter mah
Him style me now as 'Honey'
Hear him – 'Ah dat way bout yuh Hons
Ah hopes yuh goes fo' me'. (*JL*, pp. 98–9)

There is the inevitable irony that the 'ten-poun baby pram' (*JL*, p. 99) bought in the first flush of prosperity, has to be converted into a fish-cart when Joe is laid-off and must revert to his usual occupation. Even though he is later recruited for the migrant labour scheme to the US, his wife's optimism – 'Wat a way we dah-go bruk sport/Wen we ketch a U.S.A.' (*JL*, p. 99) – must be tempered by the advice of yet another Bennett *persona*:

Betta yuh tan home fight yuh life
Than go a-sea go lose i.

De same sinting wey sweet man mout
Wi meck him lose him head,
Me read eena newspapa sey
Two farm-man meet dem dead! (*JL*, p. 94)

But the new wife's enthusiasm is unshakeable:

Me still love me Jamaica man,
But like a tenkful wife
Me haffa praise American
Fe put me eena life. (*JL*, p. 99)

It is this aspiration that their families be 'put eena life' which governs the child-rearing practices of Bennett's vocal women. The proverbial ring of James's uncomplimentary observation that 'ooman a debil-mumma' reinforces the fact that women – married or not – are largely responsible for the socialisation of children in Jamaica. Though there are very few Bennett poems that deal specifically with mother/child relations, there is a group, the theme of which is the aggressive ambition of mothers that their children, particularly their sons, acquire education, the entreé to middle-class culture. Fluency in the English language is an important rite of passage, which must be accomplished whether by formal schooling or as a consequence of living 'in foreign' or 'in town.'

The male *persona* in the poem 'Writing Home', expresses retrospective gratitude to his mother for her attention to his education: 'Ah did soh glad yuh did force me fe teck de zamination/Far now ah can demands a job fe suit me edication.' (*JL,* p. 117) There is pathos in the disparity between the young man's expectations and what he appears equipped to do. Indeed, the muted humour in the poem derives from the fact that though unemployed, he has joined a trade union and is 'on strike':

> I is not working now but ah
> Jine in a labour set
> An ah 'ope to keep awn strikin
> Tell some esteem jab ah get. (*JL,* p. 116)

A satirical portrait of an indulgent, self-congratulatory mother is given in the poem 'New Scholar'. The mother's misguided concern for her son's well-being is apparent in her words of advice to the boy's teacher, on his first day in school:

> No treat him rough, yah, Teacher;
> Him is a sickly chile:
> As yuh touch him hard him meck nize –
> Some people seh him pwile.
>
> Teck time wid him, yaw, Teacher –
> If him rude an start fi rave
> Dis beat annoder bwoy, an him
> Wi frighten an behave.
>
> For nuff time when him rude a yard
> An woan hear me at all
> Ah just beat de bed-poas hard, mah,
> An yuh wan fi hear Jack bawl! (*SP*, pp. 8-9)

A similarly satirical poem is 'Uriah Preach', which mocks the self-incriminatory pride of yet another misguided mother. Rhonda Cobham-Sander's gloss on the poem is accurate: 'Bennett recounts the vicarious pleasure taken by a Jamaican mother in the accomplishments of her children and especially in her son's ability to use his occasional ascent to the pulpit to lambast the family's enemies':[7]

> Fi-me famby is no peaw-peaw,
> Me daughter Sue dah teach;
> An when rain fall or parson sick
> Me son Uriah preach.
> . . .
> Him climb up pon de pulpit, him
> Lean over an look dung,
> Him look pon all we enemy
> An lash dem wid him tongue.
> . . .
> Him tell dem off, dem know is dem,
> Dem heart full to de brim;
> But as Uriah eena pulpit
> Dem cyaan back-answer him. (*SP*, pp. 60-1)

The general tenor of the mother/child relations described in Bennett's poetry is aphoristically expressed by the perceptive speaker in 'Bear Up': 'Noh mock mawga cow, him a bull muma.' (*JL*, p. 53)

The majority of Bennett's women are engaged in traditionally female, working-class occupations: domestic labour and higglering. Both are low-paid, higglering far less so in recent times, with the rise of the internationally-travelled female merchant class. The supply of prospective domestic labourers far exceeds demand, and employer/employee relations often reflect the market-value of the domestic servant. But a definite shift in the balance of power occurs when domestic servants come to recognise that their labour is essential to the smooth functioning of the middle-class household.

The female servant in 'Seeking a Job', for example, makes it clear that domestic labour is not her preferred vocation. God has not called her to this work; she is only doing it because s/he can't do better. She will condescend to certain quite specific tasks, stated in her job description:

> Ah cook an wash, but sake o' me nails
> Ah doan clean floor again
> But a (sic) can get a gal fe do
> Dat fe yuh now-an-den. (*JL*, p. 192)

Furthermore, if antagonised, she will simply withdraw her services:

. . . the las' ooman ah work wid
Didn' have no fault to fine.

Doah wen she start tek liberty wid me
Ah lif up and walk out,
For as ole-time people sey [']yuh play
Wid dawg dem lick yuh mout'.

Ah hooden stan her facetiness,
Far we wasn' company, *(JL,* p. 191)

Her citing of the proverb – 'as ole-time people sey' – is designed to give a measure of legitimacy to what is clearly unreasonable behaviour. Getting to work on time for a job she obviously detests, is definitely low down on the list of this woman's priorities; she is a dancehall regular:

Ef ah come een late a mawning time
Noh bada get eena fits
For every night me haffe go ketch
Me quatty dance a Ritz.

Pure high-class servant gal go dere,
For Ritz is all de craze,
An lots o' Busta Union bwoys
Go dance dere now-a-days. (*JL,* p. 192)

Her abusiveness to the prospective employer who, naturally, is not at all inclined to hire her, is matched only by her generosity in not bothering to pick a fight:

Is move off yuh dah-move off mah?
Yuh naw employ me? Gwan!
Yuh face tough like Spanish Tung han' cuff,
Mussa pon de ark yuh bawn.

Ah feelin' good dis mawning or
Ah hooda bruck a fight,
But ah don't feel eena a bad mood
Fe go sleep a jail tonight. (*JL,* p. 192)

Another humorous example of class antagonism between servant and householder occurs in the poem 'Me Bredda'. The speaker there is a vociferous domestic servant who cows a middle-class woman into submission in a dispute arising from the servant's tardiness in arriving for work – the very first day on the job. The housewife attempts to fire the woman on the spot, but is bombarded with a spate of abusive rhetoric:

Oono call me bredda fi me!
Beg yuh tell him come yah quick!
Tell him bring him pelt-yuh-kin cow-cod
An bus-yuh-open stick!

Me naw meck no joke wid yuh, mah!
Quick and brisk an pay me off,
Or ah call me bredda in yah
Meck him beat yuh till yuh sof! (*SP*, p. 18)

The aggrieved servant is offended because the householder has apparently broken her side of the agreement; she does not at all concede her own negligence:

Yuh answer me advertisement
Yuh come slap a me yard
Come tell me how de pay is big
An how de work no hard

Me never like yuh face, but when
Me bredda tell me seh
Dat yuh husban is a nice man
Mi decide fi come tedeh. (*SP*, p. 18)

The usual power-relationship between employer and employee is inverted; it is the housewife who answers the advertisement and is 'chosen' by the servant. The intended insult to the housewife is compounded in the servant's dismissiveness of the woman herself; it is only the husband's niceness that makes the wife a viable prospect. Class antagonism is complicated by latent same-sex gender hostility.

One is seduced into admiring the daring subterfuge of this outrageous servant who conjures up a fictitious brother to terrorise the housewife:

Yuh would like fi know me bredda?
Me cyaan help yuh eena dat.
Me hooda like know him meself,
For is me one me parents got! (*SP*, p. 19)

Yet one senses the impropriety of her victory; this trickster sabotages the very economic system she pretends to enter, employing Anansi tactics to accomplish pragmatic goals. There are several Jamaican proverbs that give clues to the origin of what appears to be an entrenched, counter-productive work ethic that seems to be the by-product of the slavery experience. The following pair of proverbs makes it clear that work simply will never be done willingly by tricksters like the woman above: 'You nebber see empty bag 'tan up'/'You nebber see full bag ben.' The hungry worker is too empty to stand, the well-fed worker is too full to bend. This proverb which has German, Italian, Haitian and Martinican variants, suggests that avoidance of work is not peculiar to any one 'race'. It seems to be a universal response to perceived exploitation.

In circumstances where workers feel that reward is not commensurate with effort, very little energy will be expended. Thus: 'Darg say before him plant yam fe look like mosquita foot, him satisfy fe tun beggar'; 'Darg say before him plant potato a pear-tree bottom mek it bear like mosquita shank, him we sit down look.' The most clearly evasive of the three: 'Darg say him won't work, him we si down and look, for him mus get a libin.' This optimism that one must get a living without needing to work seems to be founded in a sense of self-righteousness. Some divine benevolence must look after the poor since the benefits of work only accrue to the immoral, exploitative 'other' – the owner of labour. Thus: 'Backra work nebber done.' Since the white man's work is never done, there is no point in attempting to do it. The slave, the 'emancipated' indentured labourer and the modern, unemployable 'worker' alike, all recognise their alienation from the fruits of their own labour.

The uncharacteristically submissive domestic servant in 'My Dream' does not openly rebel against her truly exploitative counsin/employer, but instead displaces her aggression on the laundry:

> Ah swear dat ah mus fine a way
> Fi wounded cousin Rose,
> An ah tink it hooda hut her
> If ah start maltreat de clothes. (*SP*, p. 112)

She consoles herself, in proverb, with the knowledge that things are not always what they seem to be. There is the subversive possibility that beneath the posture of passive suffering lies a revolutionary rage that promises eventual justice: 'Dog a sweat but long hair hide i,/Mout a laugh, but heart a leap!/ Everthing wha shine no gole piece. (*SP*, p. 113) This sublimatory use of proverbs in a potentially explosive context of class antagonism is an excellent example of linguistic subterfuge, indirection as a strategy to preserve psychic equilibrium. These apparently divergent responses to domestic labour/economic exploitation – overt and covert sabotage – are essentially manifestations of the Anansi syndrome.

In 'Anansi – Jamaica's Trickster Hero', Laura Tanna identifies the universally problematic moral dilemma posed by the trickster figure:

> Trickster is actually an international phenomenon, a curious creature whose baffling nature can suggest an unmotivated, undifferentiated, amoral character, or a culture hero bringing ben-

> efits to mankind. . . . In every trickster tradition, his character traits are ambiguous, and in every culture, his attributes vary.[8]

In the specific case of Jamaica, Tanna suggests a clear class-determined ascription of negative and positive characteristics to Anansi:

> How Jamaicans react to Anansi depends upon who they are, what their position in society is, and how they view themselves, not that the specific application of Anansi need always be associated with colour and class. A wealthy businessman who outsmarts the tax collector or customs officer may liken himself to Anansi with pride. It is a question of who is doing the deceiving to get something for nothing. Since the middle and upper classes have more to lose, they tend to disparage Anansi the most, and use him as a symbol for much that is wrong with Jamaican society.[9]

The Anansi mentality is evident in the behaviour of the higglers who speak in 'South Parade Peddler' and 'Candy-Seller'. Their dramatic monologues counterpoint open cajoling of potential customers with *sotto voce* invective. Of 'Candy-Seller' Rex Nettleford notes: 'The professional salesman-charm of the local candy-seller can easily turn into abusive, if humorous, anger against the reluctant or unwilling customer. The "abusive asides" are a kind of stock-in-trade in the sorority of candy-sellers.' (*JL,* p. 28)

Even in circumstances where the labourer is engaged in work for herself, there is still a sense of victimisation, and thus the need to assert one's self in the way that these women know best – self-protective verbal abuse. Language is a kind of charm that wards off evil.

Come lady buy nice candy mam?
Dem all is wat I meck.
Which kine yuh want mam, pepper-mint?
Tank yuh mam. Kiss me neck!
One no mo' farden bump she buy!
Wat a red-kin ooman mean!
Koo har foot eena de wedge-heel boot,
Dem favah submarine.

Ah wey she dah-tun back fah? She
Musa like fe hear me mout
Gwan, all like yuh should'n walk a day,
Yuh clothes fava black-out.
Me kean pick up a big sinting
Like yuh so draw dat blank.
Afta me noh deh a war, me naw
Colleck no German tank.

Cho goh way – Come here nice white man
Don't pass me by soh sah!
See me beggin by de roadside
Come buy a nice wangla.
Wen w'ite people go fe ugly
Massa dem ugly sah.
Koo 'ow dat deh man face heng dung
Lacka wen jackass feel bad. (*JL*, p. 29)

Similarly employing the imagery of combat, the higgler in 'South Parade Peddler' declares open war on her customers. The references to 'bombin' plane', 'Graff Spe', 'Hair-raid' and torpedoed teeth indicate the tone and temper of her attack:

Hairnet, scissors, fine teeth comb!
Wey de nice lady dey?
Buy a scissors from me noh lady?
Hair pin? Toot' pase? Goh wey!
Me say go-weh aready, ef
Yuh doan like it see me.
Yuh dah-swell like bombin' plane fun'
Yuh soon bus up like Graff Spe.
. . .
Teck out yuh han' out o' me bax
Pu' dung me razor blade.
Yuh no gat no use fe it for yuh
Dah-suffa from Hair-raid!
. . .
Toot-brush? Ah beg yuh pardon sah
Me never see yuh mout',
Dem torpedo yuh teet' sah or
Yuh female lick dem out?
Noh bada pick me up yaw sah!
Yuh face look like a sey
Yuh draw it out o' lucky bax.
Noh bada me, go weh! (*JL*, p. 27)

This remarkable sales technique – aggressive verbal intimidation of prospective customers – is part of a repertoire of power-talking that is indeed likely to elicit submissive respect from its very victims. There is a deep-seated admiration in Jamaican society for the elegant control of language even in its most malicious forms. Tracing matches, for example, command a large audience of inflammatory onlookers.

Another higgler who eloquently affirms the importance of her trade for the well-being of her family is a single parent, whose market basket is apparently causing offence to a fellow passenger on a bus. She properly abuses the protesting lady whose stockings are at risk from the basket. The incongruous juxtapositioning of stockinged feet and market basket reinforces the social distance between the two women struggling to share the same public space:

> Weh yuh day kick me basket fa?
> Push i back eena place!
> Ah have a mine fi pick i up
> An lick yuh pon yuh face!
>
> Ah lick yuh yes! Yuh tink ah fraid?
> Yuh just galang, yaw, mah!
> Ef de basket tear yuh tockin
> Dat no gainst de law, mah! (*SP*, pp. 91-2)

The kick/pick/lick rhymes concentrate the woman's anger; her basket is an intimate friend and must be treated with due respect; indeed it has become a dependable substitute for the absent father who does not shoulder his responsibilities:

> Yuh can cuss me, yuh can beat me,
> Yuh can call me all de 'it':
> Do anyting yuh want wid me
> But lef de basket.
>
> For dis basket is me all-in-all,
> Me shillin, pence an poun;
> It is me husban an me frien,
> Me jewel an me crown.
>
> Me ha six pickney – an sence me
> Stop teck dem Pa to court
> Dis dutty, brucksy basket yah
> Is dem ongle support. (*SP*, p. 92)

If the higgler's sentimental attachment to her market basket seems humorously excessive in this ode, one must nevertheless recognise the seriousness of the woman's need to provide for her family under duress. She is prepared to go to jail to defend her right to make a living:

> So yuh can always pick me up,
> But pudung me basket –
> For me wi spen de res a me days
> Up a Rae Town fi it! (*SP*, p. 92)

The basket becomes a metonym for more general social privileges.

The efforts of women to support themselves in non-traditional occupations is the theme of 'Footworks'. The speaker there lauds the first female recruits into the Jamaica Constabulary Force:

> We haffe do we bes, tun eas,
> Tun wes, tun right about
> We kean afford fe meck de man
> Police dem beat we out. *(JL,* p. 70)

The choice of 'afford' appropriately emphasises the increased wages that women will earn in a traditionally male occupation, and which they dare not relinquish simply because they cannot manage the heavy police boots:

> Lif up yuh foot gal, practise up
> Fe tun ooman police.
> Oonoo mus bring two clothes-iron
> Fe tie pon oonoo foot.
> So we can practise how fe wear
> De heavy police boot. (*JL,* p. 70)

The clothes iron selected to assist women in their new field of work is a comic reminder of the domestic labour force from which they have now graduated. The final verse of the poem humorously suggests that there is no essential difference in the capacities of the male and female recruits:

> Go outa jail an watch good wha de
> Man-police dem do
> Yuh mighta fine nuff o' dem wid
> De same trouble as yuh. (*JL,* p. 71)

The engagement of women in the political process is similarly motivated by their desire to share with men the benefits of increased economic opportunities. Pragmatism characterises the attitudes of Bennett's women to politics. In a complementary pair of poems, 'New Govanah' and 'Mrs Govanah', it is evident that affairs of state are acknowledged as important only to the degree that they guarantee perceptible material benefits. Mervyn Morris's gloss on 'New Govanah' underscores the poem's ironies:

> The poem ridicules the fuss made over the arrival of a new governor (Sir John Higgins) in 1943. People, it says, are behaving as though the Governor were really valuable and worth worrying about, like steak, or white rice, or condensed milk – commodities scarce during the war. . . . Unlike those people who have dressed up, the speaker is not in awe of the Governor, and she wonders whether (in accordance with a common Jamaican decency) he has

> brought any message or parcel from her boy-friend Joe . . . There are courteous ironies within the final stanza. The Governor is implied to be irrelevant and out of key with ordinary needs and values: he has brought nothing for her, neither material things nor values. (*SP*, pp. 130-1)

Similarly, in 'Mrs Govanah', the speaker mistakes the commotion caused by the ritual passage of the Governor's wife through Nathan's department store as being precipitated by the distribution of 'free ile or green banana'. (*JL*, p. 126) Images of oral gratification are frequently used by these women in cynical reference to organised politics. In the poem 'Rightful Way', the speaker gives advice on the proper way to vote, noting that politicians, the main beneficiaries of adult suffrage, would be deprived of sustenance if the system were sabotaged:

> Yuh know how de genkleman dem
> Weh dah-gi speech all bout
> Hooda bex fe know yuh help fe teck
> De pap out o' dem mout. (*JL*, p. 135)

Female politicians are not exempt from ridicule. The speaker in the poem 'Which One?' questions the competence of all the candidates up for election, including the female representative:

> Pose we try a ooman an she
> Teck it put eena her lap
> An go get up absent-minded
> Meck we constitution drop! (*JL*, p. 136)

A more sympathetic, though equally problematic image of a female politician is given in 'Big Tings', which documents the in-fighting between two high-powered male politicians, the Hon. Sir Alexander Bustamante and the Rev. E. E. McLaughlin:

> Do po' ooman councillor nevah sey a ting,
> She stay quiet like lamb,
> She watch all de man dem antics
> An shet up her mout 'pam'.
>
> Me noh blame de po' ooman mah,
> Becausen is she one,
> An de po' ting mus feel frighten
> 'Mongs dem blood-t'irsty man. (*JL*, p. 151)

The female politician's silence is as eloquently damning as the verbosity of the American consultant in 'Distinguish 'Merican', imported to assist in launching the 'Be Jamaican, Buy Jamaican' campaign: '"Wuds, wuds, dem deh is wuds,/Is pure wuds dem a-chat."' (*JL*, p. 158) Grand words become a substitute for the meaning that ought to be released by the words. The popular image of the duplicitously loquacious politician is presented here; it is mirrored in the speaker's own inability to find the words to express her admiration of this American who has mastered the art of doublespeak: '"Gran wuds, me dear,/ Wuds can' express de wuds,/ Dat man mout full o' wuds yuh hear!"' (*JL*, p. 158)

The empowerment of the Jamaican woman, as portrayed in Louise Bennett's substantial poetry, is not accomplished by mere dependence on the flatulent rhetoric of politicians – though participation in the political process is essential for all:

> Everybody got a vote, an
> Every vote gwine swell de score;
> Missa Issa, Missa Hanna
> An de man wat sweep de store. (*JL*, p. 129)

What is of equal consequence is that meta-political conviction of intrinsic worth, validated by the proverbial wisdom of the folk, that 'Ooman day wi come at last.' (*JL*, p. 193) Out of the compost-heap of history the cunny Jamma oman, in her maternal role as mother hen, must root up for herself the prophetic certainty that 'oman luck mus come!' (*SP*, p. 23). This is the ultimate subterfuge: to evade domesticity in the very act of seeming to embrace it.

Notes

1 Lloyd Brown, *West Indian Poetry*, Twayne's World Authors Ser. 422 (Boston: Twayne, 1978), p. 116.
2 Louise Bennett, *Selected Poems* (ed.), Mervyn Morris (Kingston: Sangster's 1982) p. 23. Subsequent references cited parenthetically in text, indicated by *SP*.
3 See, for example, the poignant description of the dungle in Chapter 1 of Orlando Patterson's *The Children of Sisyphus* (London: New Authors, 1964).
4 For a feminist historian's account of Nanny's political significance, see Lucille Mathurin's monograph *The Rebel Woman in the British West Indies During Slavery* (Kingston: Institute of Jamaica Publications, 1975) pp. 34–7.
5 Louise Bennett, *Jamaica Labrish*, ed. Rex Nettleford (Kingston: Sangster's, 1966), p. 49. Subsequent references cited parenthetically in text, indicated by *JL*.
6 For an autobiographical account of her career in Jamaica, see Molly Huggins, *Too Much to Tell* (London: Heinemann, 1967).

7 Rhonda Cobham-Sander, 'The Creative Writer and West Indian Society: Jamaica 1900–50', dissertation, University of St Andrews, 1981 (Ann Arbor, UMI, 1984), p. 241.
8 Laura Tanna, 'Anansi – Jamaica's Trickster Hero', *Jamaica Journal* 16.2 (1983): p. 21.
9 Ibid., p. 25.

CHAPTER 4

Words unbroken by the beat: the performance poetry of Jean Binta Breeze and Mikey Smith

In a tersely sardonic meta-dub[1] poem, 'Dubbed Out', Jean Binta Breeze distinguishes her work from the rub-a-dub-a-dub monotony of facile performance poetry in which meaning is rubbed out in the dub:

> i
> search for words
>
> moving
> in their music
>
> not
>
> broken
>   by
> the
>
> beat[2]

The s/pacing of the lines jerking to a halt enacts the beating-down of sense and lyricism; the double-entendre, 'moving', extends the conventional conceit of poetry as music – emotive sound – to include the fluidity of the word released from the mechanical rigidity of the beat, and from the fix of the page. Poetry becomes verbal dance, transmitted word-of-muscle. This reading of 'Dubbed Out' not only evokes the embodied word in performance, but also requires a distinction between the poet as maker and as performer. For not only are the words in motion, unbroken by the beat, but the poet/performer, uncontained by the boundaries of the book, speaks face to face with an immediate audience. In an act of performative transference the speaker gets across the closure of the printed page.

The performance itself thus becomes a privileged reading of the text.[3] For example, the audio/visual/kinetic integrity of Breeze's repeatedly spectacular performance of her 'Riddym Ravings' classic cannot be fully anticipated from reading the relatively static (though richly allusive) words on the page. Somewhat like a musical score, the poem pressed to the page encodes performance. Breeze, fully possessing the rhythms of the body/text, achieves the music. She engenders the mad woman's despair with such absolute artistic control that the comfortable distance between madness and sanity, between actuality and the act is uneasily contracted. The audience becomes a collective *voyauditeur,* enjoying the aesthetic pleasure of exquisitely recreated suffering. The dissonant pain of the mad woman's debased condition is dignified, but not diminished, by her fleeting moments of total lucidity. The radio DJ in her head keeps her 'sane', comforting her in abject distress. In the passage below, the thin narrative thread of sanity stretches on the disturbing image of the living dead and snaps:

> Wen mi fus come a town
> mi use to tell everybady 'mawnin'
> but as de likkle rosiness gawn outta mi face
> nobady nah ansa mi
> silence tun rags roun mi bady
> in de mids a all de dead people dem
> a bawl bout de caast of livin
> an a ongle one ting tap mi fram go stark raving mad
> a wen mi siddung eena Parade
> a tear up newspaper fi talk to (p. 59)

The capacity to make metonymy and metaphor – rosiness and the rags of silence – is the privilege of the poet and the lunatic: 'The Lunatic, the Lover, and the Poet,/ Are of imagination all compact.'[4] In performance, Breeze's articulate dramatisation of 'the mad woman's poem', as 'Riddym Ravings' is ambiguously subtitled, confirms and obscures that cunning distinction.

Similarly, Mikey Smith's signature statement, his indelible voiceprint, 'Me Cyaan Believe It,' is a howl of incredulous anguish that dares to speak the unspeakable. That heart-rending 'Lawwwwwwwwd,'[5] the penultimate line of the poem, is the protracted pain of generations of sufferers whose affirmative voice the poet becomes in a single gesture of communal defiance. The poet/performer seems to assume the *persona* of Woman, for whom belly pain – 'me ban me belly /an me bawl' (p. 13) – is the specific anguish of child-bearing in a society that defies the poor to survive. Woman-pain is both an act of survival and evidence of defeat:

> Doris a modder of four
> get a wuk as a domestic
> Boss man move een
> an bap si kaisico she pregnant again
> bap si kaisico she pregnant again
> an me cyaan believe it
> me seh me cyaan believe it. (p. 14)

The refrain, 'bap si kaisico she pregnant again', in its adaptation of the nonsense words and rhythms of children's verbal play – 'bap si kaisico pinda shell'[6] – is a brilliant image of the generation of cycles of impoverishment. The woman's fertility is itself entrapping; her body bears its weight of nuts, and is then discarded, an empty shell. 'Boss man' sexual politics defines the rules of the adult game: no p/lay, no pay. The search for work thus exacerbates the repetitive pain of sexual exploitation that is often the poor woman's unwanted lot.

The power of the poem derives, in part, from the righteous anger of utterance. But the poet's performance, however privileged, is not authoritative. Indeed, the very 'text' of performance poetry, and its meanings, are dependent on complex variables beyond the absolute control of the poet as maker. Mervyn Morris, both poet and critic, defines the performance text/context thus: 'If the poem in print does, however minimally, alter with the specific context of its reception, the "performance poem" is even more difficult to fix, dependent for its meanings on the variable interaction between text, performer, audience and occasion.'[7] This fluidity of the text in performance is not inherently problematic except, perhaps, for the scribal critic wishing to keep the subject fixed in place and in proper perspective. In the two-way flow of the immediate moment of performance a discriminating audience, in contract with the poet/performer, functions as communal critic, endorsing (or not) the craft of the wordsmith and the authority of particular performances. The audience's familiarity with the words of the poem does not reduce the distinctive pleasure of each succeeding performance. For as the work becomes appropriated by the community – is known – an enjoyable tension between the new and the familiar is sustained, as in numerous other communal speech contexts: Anansi storytelling and political speech-making, for example.[8]

This interdependent relationship of performer, word, audience and occasion that invigorates the work of Jean Breeze and Mikey Smith is often compromised in the efforts of less accomplished practictioners who quickly become dubbed out. In the words of Gordon Rohlehr, '[d]ub poetry is at its worst a kind of tedious jabber to a monotonous rhythm.'[9] The search for the exact word and rhythm is abandoned as the dubber settles for the automatic reflex of cliché. The song-and-dance of 'performance' struggles to animate nonsense that cannot stand alone on the page or on the stage. In addition, an indiscriminate audience, relinquishing its responsibility to the artist and the medium, can simply opt out of the critical contract, applauding a noisy belch of vacuity as great oral art. Or the occasion for performance may not readily arise. Performance is often occasioned by commemorative events, for example, African Liberation Day, International Women's Day; or festivals – Reggae Sunsplash in Jamaica, the International Bookfair of Radical Black and Third World Books in London; or 'poetry readings' where performance itself is the celebrated occasion. The professional performance poet wishing to make a living must often seek out occasions for performance in which the essential interplay of word and audience may be subverted. Without patronage, whether state or private endowment, the performer, reduced to hand-to-mouth circumstances, often drivels.

In a punningly titled essay, 'Dub Poetry: Selling Out', Stewart Brown frankly assesses the contradictions of the commercially successful dub poet, cut off from a knowing community and in quest of a mass audience:

> As dub poetry becomes a commercial product, as its performers like Benjamin Zepphaniah (sic) or Mutabaruka or Ras Levi Tafari become media Stars and strive to entertain a mass, multicultural audience, there seems to me to be a real danger that the protest, the anger, the fire, becomes an act, while the image, the dub/rant/chant/dance becomes the real substance of the performance.[10]

Mutabaruka himself derides the notion of the incongruously entertaining 'revolutionary poet':

> revolutionary poets
> 'ave become entertainers
> babblin out angry words
> . . .
> yes
> revolutionary poets
> 'ave all gone to the
> creative art centre
> to watch
> the sufferin
> of the people being dram at ized by the
> oppressors
>   in their
>   revolutionary
>   poems[11]

The easy transformation of rage into entertainment disfigures the masquerading actor. For the 'act' is both performance, in literal theatre terms, and fraud, in the metaphorical, derogatory sense of that word. Mimicking performance, the commercial dub poet can put the audience on, assuming an anger that has not been earned. Particularly in a multi-cultural context like Britain, where negative stereotypes about Black culture seem to prevail, the act may become an un/conscious fraud perpetrated both by performers who exploit the low expectations and ignorance of their uncritical audience, and by the perversely 'liberal', patronising art establishment. For example, the sad case of Benjamin Zephaniah and the Professorship of Poetry at Oxford University.

The *Guardian* of Saturday, 20 May 1989 carried a witty front page article by Maev Kennedy headlined 'Dark horse in poetry contest bridles at sporting metaphor': the dark horse is and is not Zephaniah. It is, first of all, Duncan McCann, a renomination, who, according to the report 'was very indignant when he was described as "the bar room poet" five years ago, on being nominated by some friends from the King's Arms in Oxford.' McCann's objections to the sporting metaphor are sent up by Kennedy: 'The Professor of Poetry at Oxford University is still backing his own runner in the succession stakes despite the entry of a dark horse who bitterly disapproves of sporting metaphors cantering over sacred literary turf.' The newspaper article begs for deconstruction. The likely performance of the jockeying horses is forecast. The bar room poet is handicapped by his petulance; Seamus Heaney, the favourite, has the backing of the right credentials – '[i]t has been murmured that he is in line for a Nobel Prize for Literature.' According to Kennedy's pre-race analysis, Heaney's

> strongest competition comes from the Somerset-based poet, author and translator, Charles Sisson, and the Rastafarian dub-poet, Benjamin Zephaniah, whose work includes a New Year Rap for the Guardian with the prophetic lines:
> And when it comes to Nuclear Arms
> Where does Neil Kinnock stand?
> And where's that Marxist Theory
> Dat dey told us dey had planned?

Pure greeting-card doggerel, despite its clairvoyance. Intriguingly, in Kennedy's sporting review of the ratings, Zephaniah is the only entrant whose work is allowed to speak for itself. The black horse is unbridled and nothing further need be said about its chances. In the *Weekend Guardian* of that same date, the page 5 'Sound Bites' column reports a more viscerally outspoken appraisal of Zephaniah's work: 'Benjamin Zephaniah's chief claim to fame is finding the functions of the bowel a suitable topic for verse. Francis Bennion, barrister (letter to the *Daily Telegraph*).'

It is in this context of honest contempt, or worse, conspiratorial silence that Breeze, in a *Marxism Today* interview, makes a plea for accountability on the part of both the actor/poet and the critic/audience:

> I'd rather we had only two or three artists in our community that represent what is finest and truest about ourselves than a host of poseurs who have been allowed to take on the title of artist simply because they are black. . . . I'm tired of people preaching to the converted and saying it's art.[12]

For the poseur the image and the act are the degenerate substitute for genuine poetic ability. But for poet/performers like Breeze and Smith, both of whom are trained actors and talented poets, the act does indeed become quite literally 'the real substance of the performance'. It is the fulfilment of the promise of the words on the page.

Mervyn Morris, in his introduction to Mikey Smith's collection of performance poems which, as editor, he shaped for the medium of print, cites an oral account given by Honor Ford-Smith, one of Mikey's tutors at the Jamaica School of Drama, which stresses the poet's studious preparation for performance:[13]

> he would work hours and hours, sometimes the whole day, with his tape recorder which would have the backing tracks for the music, trying out different variations of rhythm. He was very very conscious of the variety that he could get in his voice. And you hear it in the voice, and you hear his consciousness of pace, when you listen to his recording, and when you hear him perform you would hear that he had worked hours on the pacing of his poetry, you know. So it wasn't just something that he improvised when he got on stage.

What is illuminating in this account is the suggestion that the process of making the poem is organically connected to the rhythms of its performance. In the programme notes to the 1988 Creation for Liberation national poetry tour of England done by Ntozake Shange and Jean Breeze, Mervyn Morris gives a similar sense of Breeze's theatrical control of the non-verbal elements of performance:

> Jean 'Binta' Breeze is, I think, the best of the performers. I think when Mikey Smith was alive he could have competed with her as a performer, but some of the things that I've seen her do in performance are really quite astonishing. I remember, for example, an occasion in London when the Mikey Smith book was being launched. Although I'd heard the poem, it was the first time I saw her perform the 'Mad Woman's Lament', 'Riddym Ravings'. A couple of gestures she made at that time were really astonishing; like a gesture, a sudden gesture for sort of putting the plug back in. It was really alarming you could feel everybody freeze at that moment. Obviously that kind of detail, I think, is very carefully calculated.[14]

This calculation and crafting are not to be expected when performance poetry is reduced to mere protest, anger and fire. The mode is declamatory and the emotional range of the poetry is accordingly contracted. 'Riddym Ravings' is a brilliant performance poem; a 'dub' parody could read like this:

oman a bawl
lice a crawl
een her head
waan fi dead
man wid gun
a come fi fun
belly big
like pig
a wallow
land fallow
pure gutter water
fi bathe di daughter
etc., etc.

The primary characteristics of this non-poem are its exteriorisation of consciousness; its facile word association dependent on rhyme; its short, lobotomised lines.

Mutabaruka's humorous, generic poem 'Dis Poem,' anticipates the parodic response of the jaded critic/audience fed up of poetrics passing itself off as poetry. It both illustrates and subverts the anxiety that the glib performance poem can generate. The wit of the poem depends on Mutabaruka's deliberate exploitation of the audience's uncomfortable suspicion of being put on. The hearer's dismay at the seeming nonsense of the many of the poem's lines thus becomes incorporated into the play of the text: 'dis poem is watchin yu tryin to make sense from dis poem.'[15] Not only is there this mockery of the audience's expectation of immediately intelligible lines – instant aural gratification – but the poet as non-entertainer insists that the audience actively participate in making the meaning of the poem. The poem therefore does not come to a fulfilling end; the listener is left hanging: 'dis poem is to be continued in your mind in your mind in your mind your mind.'[16] An ironic reverberation. This dub poem is thus self-satirical, consciously making fun of its own conventions. The genre has come of age: meta-dub.

Indeed, a broad thematic and tonal range characterises the work of the sophisticated performance poets. It is not all protest, anger and fire, an exclusively apocalyptic idiom. In Mikey Smith's 'Give Me Little Dub Music' the aggressive anger elicited by debilitating economic deprivation struggles for release in the sweet melancholy of the dub:

Give me little dub music
right ya so
tonight

A have dis haunted feelin
so meck we bat een
an ketch a reasonin

No bodder talk bout anyting too tough
Skip de usual stuff
dat yuh out a luck
a look fi wuk
an meck we seat up

We no mourners
We naw go watch weself
go down de road
like witherin flowers

An jus
give me little dub music
right ya so
tonight. (p. 32)

On the Island Records performance of this poem the elusive 'haunted feelin' of the plaintive voice is supported by the grounded instrumental accompaniment. Then there is the muted celebration of Breeze's 'Simple Tings' which on the 1989 LKJ Records release, *Tracks: Jean Binta Breeze*, quietly affirms, *a capella*, the solid peasant values of rural Jamaica, in particular the endurance of women: '(for Miss Adlyn and Aunt Vida)'. The counterpoint of English and Jamaican voices authenticates the poet's tribute. She is herself the product of both worlds:

de simple tings of life, mi dear
de simple tings of life

she rocked the rhythms in her chair
brushed a hand across her hair
miles of travel in her stare

de simple tings of life

ah hoe me corn
an de backache gone
plant me peas
arthritis ease

de simple tings of life
leaning back
she wiped an eye
read the rain signs

in the sky
evening's ashes
in a fireside

de simple tings of life. (p. 33)

This is not a sentimental pastoral. The seer divines the rain signs and the ashes of evening with equal calm; decline is simply accepted as part of the natural cycle of things.

In its sustained use of the imagery of radio transmission Breeze's 'Eena Mi Corner' is reminiscent of the harrowing 'Riddym Ravings'. But whereas the tone of the latter is dread melancholy, the former is drily humorous. The poem is a witty treatment of the theme of easy channel-changing men, whom the woman must learn to tune out in order to get rid of static:

flip a switch
tun mi receiva
to transmitta
checkin anadda one
wanderin troo
de sonic boom of a bassline
but wen mi see seh
dis one a forward pon de same riddym station
breed een
breed out
mi memba
how it easy
cho
mi haffi
mi haffi
mi haffi jus
check out (p. 27)

'Holly', a bitterly ironic warning to beware the power of sexuality and the corresponding shortness of the male attention span, is developed in naturalistic imagery that suggests the organic nature of the perennial problem:

so hole strang gal
fi wen man look pon yuh
like im is sun

talk
like breeze
run im han oba yuh
wid cool coconut cream
waiting to flow troo yuh
like im is ribba
nex ting yuh know
flood yuh wid crop
draw back
an lef yuh liddung
fallow
a tiad
hardened soil
weh ongle macka grow (p. 67)

In Jamaican folk etymology, the biblical injunction to dig up one's fallow ground often becomes the digging-up of folly ground. The sexual imagery of the poem, for example the crop/crap/clap overtones, grounds multiple levels of meaning.

'Lovin Wasn Easy', transposed into a blues/jazz idiom in the LKJ *Tracks* recording, is an equivocal celebration of mutual affection that survives, for a while, the harshness of material poverty threatening to erode it:

wasn easy at all

cep wen
warm
eena de tear up tent
a we blanket
jine wid we glue
we use to watch mawnin star
rise
troo de hole
eena de bamboo shack (p. 69)

In 'Ordinary Mawning' despair prevails. In its very ordinariness, the sameness of the struggle to eke out an existence is overwhelming:

was jus anadda
same way mawning
anadda clean up de mess
after dem lef mawning
a perfectly ordinary
mawning of a perfectly

ordinary day
trying to see a way
out

so it did hard fi understand
why de ordinary sight of
mi own frock
heng up pon line
wid some clothespin
should a stop mi from do nutten
but jus
bawl (p. 49)

In Smith's 'Sunday a Come' the pathos of the speaker's impotence is imaged in the dark disjunction of skin and world:

Sometime a siddung
wid me heart full up an me face wet up
for is a shame when yuh mumma breast wither up
an yuh waan cry an yuh cyaan bawl
for darkness between yuh world and yuh skin (p. 25)

In the prophetic 'Sunday' this pain is transmuted, quite unsentimentally, into a visionary acceptance of both the necessity of earthly sacrifice and the possibility of martyrdom:

I sit
Sunday

not meditating on
people clapping
shouting

meek
shall inherit earth

but meditating
freedom

I
shall not die
a natural death
but fighting (p. 37)

Then there is the grim humour of 'I an I Alone' that records the verbal battles between the buyers and sellers in the marketplace, as both sides struggle to keep flesh on the bone. Hustling becomes a way of life. The folk thrift encoded in the proverb 'every mickle meck a muckle' – it all adds up – is devalued into a raw competitiveness for scarce goods that commodifies human relations:

> De people-dem a teck everyting meck a muckle
> Dem a try fi hustle down de price
> fi meck two ends meet,
> de odder one a try fi push up de price
> fi meck de picni backbone get sinting fi eat.
> But two teet meet an dem a bark
> dem cyaan stan de pressure,
> dem tired fi compete wid hog an dawg,
> but dem mus aspire fi someting better
> although dem dungle-heap ketch a fire. (p. 28)

The insults fly in a dissonant mix of market noises: the warnings of the preacher and the sales-pitch cries of other unperturbed sellers:

> 'Shoppin bag! Shoppin bag! Five cent fi one!'
> 'Green pepper! Thyme! Skellion an pimento!'
> 'Remember de Sabbath day, to keep it holy!
> Six days shalt thou labour,
> but on the seventh day shalt thou rest.'
> 'Hi, mam, how much fi dah piece a yam deh?
> 'No, no dat; dat! Yes; dat!'
> 'Three dollars a poun, nice gentleman.'
> 'Clear out! Oonoo country people too damn tief!'
> 'Like yuh mumma!'
> 'Fi-me mumma? Wha yuh know bout me mumma?
> Look ya, a might push dis inna yuh!'
> 'Yuh lie! A woulda collar yuh!'
> 'Bruck it up! But, dread, cool down!'
> 'Alright, cool down. Rastafari!' (p. 27)

Even a less accomplished poem like 'I Sight Up Tacky' which is rather prosaic in its loose rhythms, facile rhymes and glib, up-beat exhortations,

> If yuh waan two ends fi meet
> only yuh can do it,
> by awakenin yuh soul to yuh reality
> an determine not to devalue yuh dignity.
> Stan up like Tacky!
> Regardless of de term
> Yuh haffi stan firm
> fi we chart we destiny. (p. 48)

is redeemed from absolute banality by the sudden switch to an altogether different register: 'Yuh feel de heat?/Who will suck anodder kisko-pop?' (p. 48) The intrusive practicality of the seller's question takes the heat of the poem's rhetoric down several degrees. This kind of incongruity is funny, intentionally or not.

It is the range of poems such as these that makes one sympathetic to Mervyn Morris's privileging of the term 'performance poetry', a more inclusive designation than 'dub':

> if we say that 'dub poetry' incorporates, or is performed to the accompaniment of reggae rhythms, we are forced to acknowledge that 'dub poetry' constitutes only a fraction of the output of the writers/performers we call 'dub poets'. 'Performance poetry' encompasses more of the work they do, and the term may have the further advantage . . . of encouraging the recognition that there are performance poems among the works of many poets we more often associate with print.[17]

An excellent example of the latter is the poet Lorna Goodison whose performances resonate with the oracular authority of 'chant' and in whose work metaphors of 'calling', 'mission' and 'channel' recur. Goodison often assumes the public *persona* of 'sojourner poet carolling for peace/calling lost souls to the Way of Heartease.'[18] In performance, seemingly translucent lines such as these – that can indeed look like doggerel on the page – acquire opacity and weight in the phrasing. A pensive pause on 'poet' and between 'souls' and 'to', for instance, slowing down the brisk pace of the dactylic feet, subtly alters the rhythm and meaning of the seemingly glib lines. An understated, counter-rhythmic reading allows the subversive possibility of self-mocking irony. The poet's mask does not always fit smugly in performance.

But the 'further advantage' of the broader term 'performance poetry' includes its own limitations. What is lost is the allusive power of the emotive label 'dub', with its onomatopoeic drum resonances and its recognition, in the naming, of the roots of this artistic movement in the reggae culture of urban revolt: working a rhythm that is the dub-side of both middle-class respectablility and the somewhat constricting conventions of the iambic pentameter, to use Kamau Brathwaite's metaphorical turn of phrase in *The History of the Voice*: 'What English has given us as a model for poetry, and to a lesser extent prose (but poetry is the basic tool here), is the pentameter. . . . There have, of course, been attempts to break it.'[19] He continues: 'It is nation language in the Caribbean that, in fact, largely ignores the pentameter.'[20] Oku Onuora's definition of dub poetry similarly focuses on its distance from the conventions of English metrics: 'It's dubbing out the little penta-metre and the little highfalutin business and dubbing in the rootsical, yard, basic rhythm that I-an-I know. Using the language, using the body. It also mean to dub out the isms and schisms and to dub consciousness into the people-dem head. That's dub poetry.'[21] When 'dub' poetry is dubbed 'performance' poetry it goes genteelly up-market, somewhat like the Third World Band.

Nevertheless, the all-encompassing term does have the decided advantage of confirming the breadth and complexity of the performance/print, oral/scribal literary continuum along which both 'performance' and 'non-performance' poets operate. For before performance comes composition, the conceiving, writing and rewriting of the script. With bad 'performance' poets it is all an organic process of decomposition. Though Breeze, herself, images the creative urge as a natural bodily function – composition versus constipation[22] – the evidence of her words on the page and in performance is not flatulence. By her own admission she engages in a search for the moving word. Similarly, Mikey Smith acknowledges both the flash of inspiration and the slow, evolutionary process of making the poem:

> A man seh, 'Boy, me can't believe it, that the thing gone up, yu know.' Me seh, 'Rahtid, a it that, you know! We can't believe it. And when you can't believe it and you look and you see the things that you can't believe!' And then me go home now and me seh, 'Yeh. Poem now. I waan get a poem. "Cyaan believe it". That's the poem I want.' And then it slowly evolve. It might work out. You might jot it down – line, piece a line – and you go weh and you leave it, and then you come back an you build on it. Or it might come 'roops', right out. The whole intensity just come right out and you just really – release it. Or sometimes a rhythm come to me first. You know, is a rhythm, and me seh, 'Dah rhythm-ya feel nice, you know, feel nice.' And then me try remember the rhythm . . . and then I build up under that and catch me breaks and the bridges. Just like how a musician a work out.[23]

It is evident from an account such as this that the disjuncture of sense and sound, of word and beat that often characterises simple-minded performance poetry is likely to be less a function of the orality of the medium and more a measure of the skill (or lack of it) of the composer. For like literacy, oracy requires the mastery of hierarchies of knowlege: the concrete and the abstract, the literal and the metaphorical. Indeed, oracy is not merely the absence of literacy; it is a way of seeing, a knowledge system. Practitioners like Breeze and Smith who are both literate and orate employ the conceptual conventions of both discourses. Thus in the process of creating and in the later analysis of the product it may be difficult, if not impossible, to discriminate between orate and literate constructs. Mikey Smith's statement above illustrates the difficulty. It used to be possible to employ purely linguistic criteria: English was the language of literacy; Jamaican the voice of orality. But the gradual spread of literacy in Jamaican, largely through the efforts of our creative writers, raises the politicised issue of the degree to which the authority implicit in English, as the official language of literacy, may now be assumed by/for Jamaican. Experiments in Caribbean Creoles as literate languages of analysis suggest their extended range of possibilities.[24] Determining a functional, generally agreed-upon Creole orthography is essential for the full development of Creole literacy.

In his 'Introduction' to *Voiceprint: an Anthology of Oral and Related Poetry,* Gordon Rohlehr provides a brisk summary of the historical problem, especially as it relates to Caribbean poetry:

> Nowhere has the 'dialect' versus 'standard' polemic been more bitter than in the question of whether serious poetry can grow out of a dialect base. Since it was widely believed that dialect was a restricted code, incapable of expressing abstract ideas, sublimity or complexities of thought and feeling, the functions permitted dialect were those of drama and energetic folksy humour.[25]

Acknowledgement of the 'oraliteracy' of Jamaican might come to mean not only a recognition of the capacity for abstraction and subtlety of feeling and expression on the part of speakers/writers in Jamaican, but it may also require a de-privileging of abstraction; or at the very least, a revaluation of the making of metaphor as a kind of literal-minded process of abstracting. The metaphorical is to oracy what abstraction is to literacy – a way of generalising. I am not proposing a simplistic opposition of the form:

literacy:abstraction: : orality:metaphor

as though literacy is not itself rooted in metaphor. Rather, I wish to suggest that Caribbean literary criticism (and linguistics) needs to more fully investigate *how* Creole orality uses metaphor to generalise. Devonish's work, cited above, represents an important development. Like Louise Bennett, he recognises, for example, the weight of the metaphorical proverb in translating the abstractions of English into a readily accessible form for Creole speakers.

But poetry, whether performance or not, is not a language of generalities. It is a celebration, in the making, of particulars. It is a return to the roots of language in oracy. Unlike the transmitter of traditional Jamaican oral texts – for example, Anansi stories, riddles, duppy stories, Big Boy jokes, proverbs – who inherited a body of knowledge that was memorised and re-presented with or without modification by the performer, the contemporary performance poet makes his/her own text. Elements of traditional lore are inevitably incorporated into these texts. Mikey Smith's use of tags from ring games and folk sayings is particularly effective. In the following verses he fuses a children's ring game ('Room fa rent, apply widin, when I run out you run in'); a proverb ('Waan good/nose haffi run'); allusions to two English nursery rhymes – with ironic wit. In a metaphorical slide the horn-blower seems to become an unwelcome, self-aggrandising suitor – perhaps politician, or lover bearing the seeds of more children:

> Room dem a rent
> me apply widin
> but as me go een
> cockroach rat an scorpion
> also come een
>
> Waan good
> nose haffi run
> but me naw go siddung pon high wall
> like Humpty Dumpty
> me a face me reality
>
> One little bwoy come blow im horn
> an me look pon im wid scorn
> an me realize how me five bwoy-picni
> was a victim of de trick
> dem call partisan politricks
>
> an me ban me belly an me bawl (p. 13)

Similarly, in Breeze's 'Warner', ironic biblical imagery – Herod's sword – merges with the apocalyptic sing-song rhetoric of the Afro-Christian, Kumina Warner Woman, Mother to the flock, who breeds fear in the presumably promiscuous baby-mother:

> an de baby madda
> clamp dung pon er stomach muscle
> lack er foot tight
> fah Herod sword nah come een tonight
> an river nah rush no more
>
> Madda tek pickney by de han
> an de cymbal start sing
> she sayin I
> I come to bring a warnin
> fah de Lawd Gad say to tell you

dat de day of your sins is upon you
dat de day of tribulation is nigh (p. 22)

It is this interweaving of disparate elements from oral and scribal literary sources that characterises the neo-oral performance poetry of both Breeze and Smith. Poems such as these will inevitably become part of the communal repertoire just as Louise Bennett's poems have been appropriated and performed by other actors. This process of communal appropriation raises the paradoxical issue of originality: that which already existed or that which is newly made. Old-fashioned Western, scribal definitions of the poet as maker – a lonely individual talent – collapse into broader oral notions of the poet as transmitter of 'pre-packaged' cultural forms and values which are realisable only in specific contexts of production and reception. Karin Barber, of the Birmingham School of African Studies, argues in a brilliantly eclectic essay on 'Yoruba Oriki and Deconstructive Criticism', that

> Deconstructive criticism, despite its rhetoric of writing, of inscription and textuality, appears to have moved silently and, as it were, surreptitiously into a position from which oral literature takes on a paradigmatic quality; oral texts are what the deconstructive critics say all literature is – only more so.[26]

In traditional oracy, performance is, quite literally, the making of the text, which has no 'existence' or authoricity independent of its voicing. Performance itself is thus a privileged skill. Indeed, would-be performance poets with limited abilities in composing might well be advised to forfeit the attractions of short-term originality and concentrate their efforts instead on performing well the classic works of our accomplished poets. To subversively paraphrase Derek Walcott's homage to Gregorias, such lesser talents ought to abandon apprenticeship to the errors of the communal soul, and thus repossess aboriginal force.[27]

As composed text, the performance poetry of Jean Binta Breeze and Mikey Smith illustrates the sensitive deployment of a range of rhetorical styles of both Jamaican and English provenance. The pure orality of Jamaican folk poetics (both rural and urban, folk song and reggae) engages in constructive dialogue with the scribal conventions of English metrics – in which both poets have been schooled, Breeze somewhat more so than Smith. As performance text, the meta-dub script of these skilled actors allows them to fully demonstrate their command of a broad repertoire of theatre idioms. In performance, the word – unbroken by the beat – speaks volumes.

Notes

1 I use 'meta-dub' to suggest the transformation of the somewhat more limiting term 'dub' into 'performance' poetry. See the discussion of the pros and cons of the terms, below.
2 Jean Binta Breeze, *Riddym Ravings and Other Poems*, ed. Mervyn Morris (London: Race Today Publications, 1988) p. 29. Subsequent references cited in text. For my somewhat limited analysis of individual poems as *performance* (I am aware that my critical vocabulary is largely print-oriented), I depend on my memory of events in which I have participated, and on recordings.
3 I am indebted to Stewart Brown, in conversation, for this formulation/wording of the process.
4 Theseus in *A Midsummer Night's Dream,* V, i: 6–7.
5 Michael Smith, *It A Come,* ed. Mervyn Morris (London: Race Today Publications, 1986), p. 14. Subsequent references cited in text. The Island Records LP album ILPS 9717, *Me Cyaan Believe It*, and again, my composite reconstruction of performances, is the 'performance text.'
6 'peanut' – '<Kongo (Angola) *mpinda,* ground-nut, peanut,' *Dictionary of Jamaican English*. '[ad. Pg. *pinda,* ad. Congo *mpinda,* Mpongwe *mbenda*; carried by negroes to America.] W. Indian and Southern U.S. for the ground-nut or pea-nut,' *OED.*
7 Mervyn Morris, 'Gender in Some Performance Poems,' unpublished conference paper, Seminar on 'Gender in Caribbean Culture,' Women and Development Studies Project, U.W.I., Mona, June 1987, p. 2.
8 See also Erna Brodber's subtle fictional account of the paradoxical pleasures of familiar story-telling ritual, which is introduced thus: 'At New Year's eve our clan gathers never tired of tears and never weary of the warmth of sadness.' *Jane and Louisa Will Soon Come Home* (London: New Beacon Books, 1980) pp. 13–14.
9 Gordon Rohlehr, 'Introduction' to Stewart Brown, Mervyn Morris and Gordon Rohlehr, eds. *Voiceprint* (London: Longman, 1989) p. 18.
10 Stewart Brown, 'Dub Poetry: Selling Out.' *Poetry Wales* 22.2 (1987) : pp. 53–4.
11 Paula Burnett, (ed.), *The Penguin Book of Caribbean Verse in English* (Harmondsworth: Penguin, 1986) pp. 80–1.
12 Jean Breeze, interview by Andrea Stewart, *Marxism Today,* November 1988, p. 45.
13 *It A Come,* p. 10.
14 Leila Hassan, (ed.) *Women of the Word* (London: Creation for Liberation, 1988), p. 13.
15 Mutabaruka, 'Dis Poem', poster, Kingston, Jamaica, lithographed by Stephenson's, n.d.
16 Ibid.
17 'Gender in Some Performance Poems,' p. 1. See also Morris's review of Paula Burnett, ed. *The Penguin Book of Caribbean Verse in English*, in *Journal of West Indian Literature* 1.2 (1987) : pp. 73–5, in which he questions the editor's segregation of the poets (and texts) into 'oral' and 'literary' camps.
18 Lorna Goodison, *Heartease* (London: New Beacon Books, 1988) p. 41. In an unsympathetic review of *Heartease,* 'Exiles and heartlands: new Caribbean poetry', *Third World Quarterly* 11.4, (1989): p. 273, Stewart Brown somewhat

sceptically allows that 'performance' might redeem what looks like clearly bad poetry on the page: 'Lorna Goodison is renowned for her public readings, and one can see how the admirable sentiments that underpin many of these poems would be well received in such circumstances. Some of them, however, read as rather limp and self-indulgent on the page.' This critical dissatisfaction with limpness may very well be an exclusively male, performance-related anxiety; admittedly, the female recipient of a limp performance (poem) may also feel, self-indulgently, that it simply is not enough.

19 Kamau Brathwaite, *The History of the Voice* (London: New Beacon Books, 1984), p. 9.
20 Ibid., p. 13.
21 Statement made at a seminar on 'Dub Poetry', Jamaica School of Drama, 17 January 1986. Transcript of excerpts done by Mervyn Morris.
22 *Marxism Today,* 44.
23 Mikey Smith, interview by Mervyn Morris, 27 May 1981, in *Jamaica Journal* 18.2 (1985): p. 41. Quoted by Morris in the 'Editor's Notes' to *It A Come,* pp. 9–10.
24 See, for example, Hubert Devonish, *Language and Liberation* (London:Karia Press, 1986), particularly Chapter 7, pp. 122–34, which eloquently answers the question, 'How does one go about expanding the linguistic resources of Creolese in order for it to adequately perform its new functions?' p. 129. See also my own experiment with Jamaican as a language of literary analysis in the critique of *Lionheart Gal* in Chapter 5.
25 *Voiceprint,* 1.
26 Karin Barber, 'Yoruba Oriki and Deconstructive Criticism,' *Research in African Literatures* 15 (1984): p. 498.
27 Derek Walcott, *Another Life* (London: Jonathan Cape, 1972, 1973), p. 59: 'Gregorias abandoned apprenticeship/to the errors of his own soul/ . . ./he possessed/aboriginal force'.

CHAPTER 5 Writing oral history: Sistren Theatre Collective's *Lionheart Gal*

Lionheart Gal: Lifestories of Jamaican Women is an experiment in narrative form that exemplifies the dialogic nature of oral/scribal and Creole/English discourse in Jamaican literature. For *Lionheart Gal* is dialogic in the old-fashioned, literal sense of that word: the text, with three notable exceptions, is the product of a dialogue in Jamaican and English between each woman of Sistren and Honor Ford Smith, the sister confessor, who herself confesses all in solitary script, immaculate in English.

In the fashionably modern, Bakhtinian sense of the word dialogic, *Lionheart Gal* is impeccably subversive. For it engenders an oral, Jamaican subversion of the authority of the English literary canon. Further, its autobiographical form – the lucid verbal flash – articulates a feminist subversion of the authority of the literary text as fiction, as transformative rewriting of the self in the *persona* of distanced, divine omniscience. *Lionheart Gal,* like much contemporary feminist discourse, does not pretend to be authoritative. Indeed, the preferred narrative mode of many feminist writers is the guise of intimate, understated domestic writing by women: letters, diaries or what Sistren, in an oral/Creole context, simply calls testimony. The simultaneously secular and religious resonances of 'testimony' intimate the potential for ideological development from the purely personal to the political that is the usual consequence of this process of communal disclosure.

It is important to distinguish between actual letters and diaries written by women, and the literary use of this sub-genre as fictional frame. For the artifice of these feminist narrative forms is that they are artless, the author having receded in Joycean detachment to pare, and perhaps paint her fingernails, leaving the tape-recorder or word-processor on automatic. For example, Alice Walker in *The Color Purple* describes herself as 'A. W., author and medium', and courteously 'thank[s] everybody in this book for coming'.[1] She presumably ghost-writes the text.

With *Lionheart Gal* this feminist illusion of narrative artlessness is complicated by the mediating consciousness of Honor Ford Smith, the editorial *persona* who performs a dual function in the making of the text. As testifier, Honor records her own story in 'Grandma's Estate'. As amanuensis, she transcribes the testimonies of the other Sistren (except for 'Ava's Diary' and 'Red Ibo'), shaping the women's responses to her three leading questions:

'How did you first become aware of the fact that you were oppressed as a woman? How did that experience affect your life? How have you tried to change it?'[2]

The full weight of the unprepossessing editorial 'with' on the title page – 'SISTREN with Honor Ford Smith, editor' – is revealed in the polemical 'Introduction', particularly in the section 'How This Book Was Made'. The editorial explanation of the collaborative process is an illuminating sub-text, as interesting as the stories themselves. For the 'Introduction' offers an ideological frame for the stories that attempts to define the boundaries of their meaning: the stories assume a sociological authority that the improvisational authorial process cannot readily support. The sociologist Herman McKenzie, in his review of the text, issues an instructive *caveat*:

> There are methodological doubts, however, which make me feel that perhaps it is wiser to view these stories as illustrative of generalisations previously arrived at by other means, rather than as providing an independent basis for such generalisations about women in Jamaica.[3]

Editorial intervention in the making of the text is clearly an important issue in *Lionheart Gal*. In an early review Evelyn O'Callaghan argues that 'the life stories related in *Lionheart Gal* stand somewhere *between* fiction and research data. These stories have been so shaped by selection, editing, rewriting and publication that they have become to a large extent "fictionalised".'[4] As editor, Honor seems to doctor the text – less in the pejorative sense of that word and more in the sense of obstetrician. This metaphor signifies both the active creativity of the labouring woman telling her own story, and the somewhat more passive efficiency of the enabling mid-wife dilating the passage of the text. This distinction between text and story, between ideological necessity and narrative autonomy is central to the problem of authorship and authority in *Lionheart Gal*.

In her 'Introduction' Honor acknowledges a methodological uncertainty in the making of *Lionheart Gal*: a tension between illustration and testimony – what I call text and story:

> This book started life as a documentation of the work of the theatre collective. The first section was to put the work in the context of Jamaican society and focus on the conditions of life of Jamaican women. It was to include testimonies from Sistren as illustrations of pre-determined themes and then discuss how we work on our plays. Soon it was clear that the testimonies would not sit neatly into an introductory section. They refused to become supporting evidence of predetermined factors. They threatened to

> take over the entire project and they would not behave. So, in the end we gave up trying to trim them and silence them and we decided to change the nature of the entire project. (pp. xxvi–ii)

Lionheart Gal does not entirely transcend its ambiguous origins in social history; but perhaps it ought not to. For as Herman McKenzie concedes in his lively critique, the hybrid nature of the text is a major source of its appeal:

> The collection, therefore, while its mode of presentation (and appeal) places it firmly within the arts, suggests conclusions that challenge social scientists to consider both the problems as well as potential contributions, not to say advantages, of this approach.[5]

Indeed, the ideological frame does not totally circumscribe the range of meanings of the stories. For *Lionheart Gal* is literary less by intent than intuition. Somewhat like *Jane and Louisa Will Soon Come Home* (whose author, Erna Brodber, once artlessly described herself as 'innocent of literature',[6]) *Lionheart Gal* subverts the conventional generic boundaries between literature and social document, between autobiography and fiction, between the oral and the scribal traditions.

As story, *Lionheart Gal* is, for the most part, clearly oral. The language of narration is Jamaican, employing proverb, earthy metaphors and folk-tale structures, particularly repetition and apparent digression. In addition, the rural setting of many of the stories reinforces the sense of a 'folk' perspective. The life-stories illustrate what Derek Walcott calls the 'symmetry' of the folk-tale: 'The true folk tale concealed a structure as universal as the skeleton, the one armature from Br'er Anancy to King Lear. It kept the same digital rhythm of three movements, three acts, three moral revelations.'[7] In the case of *Lionheart Gal,* narrative structure is shaped by Honor's three informing questions which compress female experience into riddle. Decoding the riddle is the key to identity and the moral of the fable.

As text, *Lionheart Gal* somewhat ironically affirms the authority of the written word. Documenting the ideological development of the Sistren Theatre Collective cannot, apparently, be fully accomplished in the medium of theatre. The plays do not adequately speak for themselves: thus the scribal intention of the original project. Further, the search for what Honor calls a 'throughline for each story' (p. xxviii) superimposes on these misbehaving, idiosyncratic oral accounts a decidedly scribal narrative necessity. The looping, circular line of oral narration becomes diametrically opposed to the unidirectional, ideological throughline. The autonomous oral stories revolt against the constricting, scribal narrative intention of the predetermined thematic project.

This oral/scribal contradiction is quintessentially linguistic – Jamaican/

English – with clear resonances of social class. For, as Honor observes somewhat evangelically in her 'Introduction':

> Those who speak standard English easily are usually middle-class. They usually write in English, but a few also write in Patwah (usually poetry or drama only). Those who are working-class and speak Patwah, write English too – or at least very few write Patwah (usually poetry or drama). This means that Patwah is written for performance, which is excellent, but what is not excellent is that it is not written for silent reflection or for purposes other than entertainment. Yet we all know that Jamaican people reflect all the time in their heads or in conversations in Patwah, and we also know that reflection is part of the process of gaining control over one's own life. So why are certain kinds of written language still dominated totally by English? (pp. xxviii–ix)

This is the seminal/ovular question. But Honor's own written performance, both in the autobiographical 'Grandma's Estate'[8] and the explicatory 'Introduction', serves to confirm not the appropriateness of the Jamaican mother-tongue, but the imperial authority of the English father-tongue – more often phallic pen – as the instrument of serious, written reflection. But perhaps it is indelicate to notice: the subversive subverted.

In an unpublished 1986 conference paper, entitled 'Creole and the Jamaican Novelist: Redcam, DeLisser and V.S. Reid', Victor Chang, more sceptical than Honor, poses a series of challenging questions to our writers, which *Lionheart Gal* as story, if not as text, eloquently answers:

> We have been increasingly told that the resources for expression in Creole are no more limited than in Standard English. If this is so, why then is it not used for internal musing and reflection? Could it be that there is still a persistent belief that Creole just will not serve in certain situations, that certain registers require standard English, or that our writers still have yet to learn to manipulate the Creole with total freedom? Perhaps it could be argued that the very spoken nature of the Creole, its very physicality, militates against its use for inner reflection and introspection.[9]

Perhaps it could be argued; but the compelling counter-argument – of sophisticated performance poets like Louise Bennett, Jean Breeze and Mikey Smith, whose reflective, multi-tonal words are energised, not broken, by the beat; of Sistren's own commanding theatrical productions that move across a wide emotional range, in Jamaican; of Michael Thelwell's linguistic *tour de force* in the novel *The Harder They Come*; of Bob Marley's musing, introspective lyrics; of the DJs' penetrating noises – seems to decisively lay that backward, dead-end line of argument to final rest.

Recognising the dialogic nature of oral/scribal and Jamaican/English discourse in the story/text *Lionheart Gal;* and seeking to narrow the social distance between the language of the stories and the language of textual analysis, I wish to engage in an experimental Jamaican subversion of the authority of English as our exclusive voice of scholarship. My analysis of the testimonies of the women of Sistren – their verbal acts of introspective self-disclosure – will now proceed in Jamaican. I use the Cassidy orthography which differs markedly from the English-oriented orthography of the *Lionheart Gal* text.[10]

'We come together and talk our life story and put it in a lickle scene.' (p. 72) A so Ava se Sistrin staat aaf: a tel wananada stuori. So yu tel, mi tel, so tel di huol a wi fain out se a di wan stuori wi a tel: Uman stuori. Di siem ting uova an uova. Bot it no iizi fi get op tel piipl yu bizniz ma! It tek plenti haat. So Foxy se iina fi har stuori. Shi se:

> Plenty women used to talk bout di children dat we have and di baby-faada problem. At first me was shy to talk about myself. Di impression women always give me is dat dem is a set of people who always lap dem tail, tek yuh name spread table cloth. Me did feel sort a funny at di time, having children fi two different man, especially since me never like Archie. Me never discuss it wid nobody. When me come meet Didi and hear she talk bout her baby faada and how she hate him after she get pregnant, me say, 'Well if yuh can say your own me can say mine', for we actually deh pon di same ting. Me and she start talk bout it. (p. 253)

An a di siem Foxy shii kom fi fain out se dat di tingz dem dat hapn tu wi jos bikaazn wi a uman, dem de tingz supuozn fi kaal 'palitiks', jos laik eni a di ada big tingz de, we a gwaan iina 'palitriks' az di wan Tosh im se. Den wat a wie dem kil im aaf iin! Mi no nuo if a big Palitiks dat, ar a likl palitiks, bot sinting mos iina sinting. Bot dat iz anada stuori. An di ail dat frai sprat kyaan frai jak, so sumaal frai aal laik mii no supuoz fi bizniz iina dem de tingz.

So hier hou Foxy se shi staat fi fain out bout dis uman palitiks:

> Tings develop so-till we start meet more people and talk bout woman and work and woman and politics. We discuss what is politics and how it affect woman. After we done talk ah get to feel dat di little day-to-day tings dat happen to we as women, is politics too. For instance, if yuh tek yuh pickney to hospital and it die in yuh hand – dat is politics. If yuh do someting to yuh own child dat damage him or her fi di future, dat is politics. If yuh man

> box yuh down, dat is politics. But plenty politicians don't tink dose things have anything to do wid politics. (p. 253)

A truu. Far yu kyaan andastan 'di little day-to-day tings dat happen to we as women' if yu no andastan se dat di huol ting set op gens plenti uman fram di die dem baan. Tek far iinstans hou so moch a di uman dem we a tel dem stuori iina *Lionheart Gal* jos fain out se dem prignant. Yes! It kom iin laik wan big sopraiz. Grab bag. A no notn dem plan fa. A no laik hou yu hier dem piipl pan di riedyo an t.v. a tel yu se 'Two is better than two many' – laik se pikni iz somz: ad an moltiplai an divaid an subtrak! Wier yu down tu notn. Naat. Dat a we prignant du plenti uman. Nat iivn uman gud. Yong gyal. Fuors raip an blaitid.

Bot iivn duo laif haad, di uman dem stil a trai. Hier hou Barbara put it: 'Di pregnancy a never someting me plan or choose. It just happen. Nadine born '71. After she born, me did just love her. Me always feel a tenderness inside me dat me no waan do notten fi hurt her. At di same time me no pet her till she spoil.' (p. 138) Bot uman an pikni kyaan liv pan suo-so lov. An a wen di uman dem staat fi trai fi fain likl wok dat stuori kom tu bomp. Far a den di palitiks biit dem down. Uongl sertn kain a piipl fi du sertn kain a wok. An daag nyam yu sopa if *yu* no wan a dem. Aal yu fi du a fi luk afta ada piipl bizniz. Yu no hav no bizniz fi luk afta. Dat a we hapn tu Doreen. Neva iivn get a chaans fi go a die skuul. Pyor iivnin skuul, an naa laan notn:

> Me did waan learn, for me did waan be nurse, or a teacher, but me couldn't grasp notten. Me know definitely seh if me no pass di exam, me nah go get di job me did want. As di months pass by and me see seh me couldn't manage di work in di evening school, me know dere and den seh me nah go noweh in life. After school, ah used to walk past di residential areas and wish it was in deh me live. Sometime me used to pretend seh me live deh and dat me get fi go a school like dem pickney. (p. 92)

So nou wen pikni prablem jain aan pan no-get-fi-go-a-no-gud-skuul, kyaan get no wok, hafi a sidown wiet pan man fi set yu op, dat a wen di palitiks get hat. Dat a Didi stuori. Hier har:

> Sometime when yuh no have notten and yuh have di pickney dem and dem a look to yuh fi food and fi shelter, yuh haffi do sometings weh yuh no really waan fi do, just fi survive. Sometimes a better yuh cyaan do, mek yuh tek certain man. Sometime yuh really in need. A man might use dat fi ketch yuh. Yuh might know a so it go, but yuh in need. Yuh want it, so yuh haffi tek it. (p. 201)

Bot a no aal di taim yu kyan tek it. Fa 'mait az wel' ton iina livin hel. Far nou man aal waan biit yu if yu no mek op yu main fi du we *him* se. An if yu marid to him, dat no mek no difrans. It kuda aal wos, far nou im dairekli fiil se im uon yu. Dat a di preke Yvonne get harself iin. Shi se:

> Ah say ah have me three pickney now and ah married. Dem time deh when yuh married, dem say yuh married fi life. Ah never expect fi me and him separate. Me depress and unhappy. Everyting just get confuse inna me brain. Me feel seh me life mash up tru me never understand bout sex and man. Me never know what me could a do bout di problem. Me say is everyday problem. It cyaan change. Me grow in it. A so life hard. Me no chat to nobody more dan so. Me no know no odder woman fi talk to. Me never have no consideration. Me, like me unconscious. (p. 151)

Dem de bluo gud fi kil yu. Lik yu down flat. Di uongl ting fi bring yu bak fram griev-said a fi fain out se a no yu wan. Ada uman iina di ring wid yu a go help yu pen op di bul. So yu taak, ak out yu likl siin, an neks ting – yu iina buk.

So hou dem mek di buk? Askaadin tu di ring-liida, Honor, di huol ting staat aaf wid shi a aks di Sistrin dem kwestyan bout hou dem gro op, an di difran-difran tingz dat hapn tu dem fi mek dem fain out se laif haad. An dem go roun an roun, an taak an taak, laik se dem a plie 'Shuo mi yu muoshan'. Aal dis taim dem a tiep evriting we dem se. Den Honor shii lisn bak tu di tiep, an fiks-op fiks-op wat shi tink si Sistrin dem a se, an dem gwaan taak an takk so tel dem en op wid laas vershan. An den dem rait it down.

Plenti a di stuori dem soun laik a so di uman dem taak. Bot some a dem mek mi wanda. Dem no soun so kyasier. Tek, far instans 'Ava's Diary'. It kaina miks-op miks-op. It kom iin laik se hou shi taak a har yaad iina war wid hou dem did waant har fi taak an rait a skuul; an di skuul naa win! Siit ya nou:

> Since me and the children are alone, if a man come to me other than him, I would have to leave them and go out with him. Therefore I have decided not to have any relationship with another man for the time being.
>
> Bertie know seh me no have no man friend, so him come if him want to come, till me and him start to talk good and him start come intensively. (p. 271)

Den nou, 'Grandma's Estate' an 'Red Ibo'. Mii neva laik hou di tuu a dem jos primz op demself iina suo-so Inglish. An dem no ina no taakin bizniz, mi dier; a pyor rait dem a rait. Skuul definetli win out yaso. An it luk lai se Honor shi did nuo se piipl a go aks har bout it, far shi trai fi klier op harself. Shi se:

> With the two middle-strata members of the group, the oral interviews did not work well. Accustomed to standard English and the conventions of academic expression, their stories sounded stilted when spoken, full of jargon, and hollow. Both 'Red Ibo' and 'Grandma's Estate' were written responses to the interview questions. (p. xxviii)

An yu nuo, mi tink mi andastan: Paasn krisn dem pikni fos. Bot mi stil se, supuozn dem did gi wi di chaans fi hier wat dem did *se*? Miebi notn neva rang wid it. Den neks ting: It no soun laik se dem a se se dem kyaan *taak* gud, dem kyan uongl *rait* gud? Mi no nuo; mi jos a wanda. Den agen, yu no si se fi dem stuori no persanali diil tu dat wid no man an uman bizniz; no likl ruudnis. Bot mii naa se dem fient-a-haat bikaazn dem naa tel piipl di huol a fi dem persnal an praivit bizniz – laik di ada laiyanhaat gyal dem! Iz jos dat fi dem stuori kom iin laik se yu a trai fi eksplien yuself, yu nuo se piipl a lisn, so yu hafi fiks it op. Red Ibo stuori it aal soun laik se shi a priich. Bot no testimoni miitn! Evribadi a testifai iina dem uona wie. Bot mi dier, mek mi lef it. Far pus an daag no hav di siem lok, an mi no waan nobadi se a bad main mi bad main mek mi a aks dem ya likl kwestyan.

An stil far aal, yu hafi gi it tu dem. A truu se Ella an Red Ibo stuori soun laik buk. Bot wat iz fi-yu kyaan bi on-fi-yu! An muor taim dem stil kech wan nais likl ruuts vaib ina di Inglish. Hier hou Red Ibo shii staat aaf fi har stuori kolcharal: 'When I think of childhood, I think of a village squatting on hillslopes with a river running through it and a bridge and a fording midway along the road which ran by the river.' (p. 221) An a Ella grani nierli spwail op di puor likl pikni. No waant har fi aks no kwestyan bout har piipl dem. Shi fi go riid buk. Nat iivn plie di likl pikni kyaan plie. Puor ting. Shi se:

> I packed leaves of croton and pimento into a basket I found in the kitchen. I twisted a piece of cloth into a cotta and put it on my head. I placed the basket on top of it and practised walking while balancing it on my head. Then I stepped off down the pathway arriving with my produce under Grandma's window. 'Lady, Lady, yuh want anyting to buy, maam?' I readjusted the basket which proved difficult to control.
>
> At first there was no answer, so I repeated, 'Lady, Lady, yuh want anyting to buy, maam?'
>
> My grandmother pushed her head through the window.
>
> 'Ella! Come inside at once and put down that basket!'
>
> I obeyed.
>
> What do you think you are doing, Miss?'

Playing market woman, Grandma,' I said, not sure what I had done wrong.

'Never let me see you doing that again.'

'Why Grandma?' I asked. 'What is wrong with market ladies?'

'Ladies? They are not ladies. They are women. Go and take a seat in your room.' (pp. 180–1)

A so it go. *Lionheart Gal* iz a siiryos buk. An unu beta riid it. It maita likl haad fi kech di spelin fi di fers, bot afta yu gwaan gwaan, it no so bad. Den wan ting swiit mi: Yu nuo hou som a fi wi piipl simpl; fram dem si sinting set down iina buk dem tink it impuortant. So nou plenti a dem uu neva go a non a Sistrin plie, dem siem wan a go riid Sistrin buk, bikaazn buk hai. Dem a go get kech. Far a siks a wan, haaf dozn a di ada: uman prablem, man prablem, pikni prablem. Plenti palitiks. An huol hiip a juok! Far yuu nuo, hou wii nuo hou fi tek bad tingz mek juok. Stap yu fram mad, go aaf yu hed. Doreen nuo hou it go. Hier har no: 'All my life, me did haffi act in order to survive. Di fantasies and ginnalship were ways of coping wid di frustration. Now me can put dat pain on stage and mek fun a di people who cause it.' Go de, Sistrin. Laas lik swiit.

Notes

1 Alice Walker, *The Color Purple* (New York: Washington Square Press, 1983), p. 253; first published 1982.
2 SISTREN with Honor Ford Smith (ed.), *Lionheart Gal: Life Stories of Jamaican Women* (London: The Women's Press, 1986), p. xxvii. Subsequent references cited parenthetically in text.
3 Herman McKenzie, Review of *Lionheart Gal*, *Jamaica Journal* 20.4 (1988): p. 64.
4 Evelyn O'Callaghan, Review of *Lionheart Gal*, *Journal of West Indian Literature* 2.1 (1987): p. 93.
5 Herman McKenzie, op cit., p. 63.
6 In an unpublished talk to students in the West Indian Literature class, Department of English, UWI, Mona, 1984.
7 Derek Walcott, 'What the Twilight Says: An Overture', in *Dream on Monkey Mountain and Other Plays* (New York: Farrar, Straus and Giroux, 1970), p. 24.
8 Ella does use Jamaican when she role-plays as the market lady: '"Lady, lady, yuh want anyting to buy, maam?" I readjusted the basket, which proved difficult to control.' (p. 180) A Freudian slip?
9 Victor Chang, 'Creole and the Jamaican Novelist: Redcam, DeLisser and V. S. Reid', unpublished paper, Sixth Annual Conference on West Indian Literature, UWI, St Augustine, 1986, p. 5.
10 I am indebted to Celia Blake for transcribing my text into the Cassidy orthography. For my English-based original, see S. Slemon and H. Tiffin (eds) *After Europe* (Mundelstrup, Denmark: Dangeroo Press, 1989) pp. 52–6.

CHAPTER 6 Country come to town: Michael Thelwell's *The Harder They Come*

Michael Thelwell's novelisation of the Perry Henzell/Trevor Rhone film, *The Harder They Come,* is an experimental transaction somewhat like *Lionheart Gal.* Both texts explore the intertextuality of oral and written performance. Though Thelwell's acknowledged debt to the film is 'considerable',[1] the writer, apparently constrained by that very debt, attempts to distance his novel from the 'inherent limitations of the [film] medium' (p. 7). This is a splendid irony and not a little hubris. For film (and its TV/video spinoffs) is *the* post-literate, twentieth-century popular art form *par excellence.* Further, as anyone who has attended the cinema in predominantly oral societies like Jamaica will attest, film is an art-form in which an open-ended dialogue with the narrative/visual text is transacted. Loud comments on the action, not simply non-verbal laughter or tears, articulate the viewer's responses to this intimate medium. Characters are addressed directly and are often warned of impending danger; the viewer, after all, is more knowing than they and can 'read' the meaning of events that the character merely experiences. Responses to the action are also kinetic, ranging from simple 'shadowing' of dramatic movements to the kind of total theatre that is immortalised in the story of a cinema in Kingston that had to have a concrete screen built because of enthusiastic gunmen in the audience firing back at hostile characters: the ricochet effect. This kind of 'naive' response to the artifice of film can be simply dismissed as the habitual unsophistication of the illiterate mind. But it does signal the viability of film as a powerful non-scribal medium that can circumvent the usual alienation of the orally-educated from immediate access to the pleasures of extended narrative.

In the Caribbean where the Ivans and Fisheyes of literature are themselves often not literate, it is the reading of film that provides an oral equivalent of the interpreting of written literary texts. At a screening of the film adaptation of Alice Walker's *The Color Purple* at Kingston's Carib Cinema, one of the largest in the region, the audience responded to the film text in much the same way that they might have read the novel: for example, at a primarily thematic level of analysis, the outraged audience collectively denounced the suggestions of lesbianism in the text in raucous censorial comments such as 'nastiness', 'slackness', 'cut it out' – to the accompaniment of loud booing. The audience clearly does not read uncritically. In a witty account of the Carib theatre audience response to the 1990 propagandist American film, *Marked for Death*, which features dreadlocksed, Jamaican drug-dealing villains (who achieve heroic stature in subversive rereadings of this scandalously racist movie),[2] Paulette Williams notes:

> I don't know what it is but these guys rarely wait until the credits go up . . . as soon as the sound track signalling the beginning of the end starts, or as soon as the anti-hero falls, my 'co-patrons' start filing out of the cinema in a steady stream. Then outside in the thickness of bodies, as everyone scrambles to catch his bus or taxi, the saga continues. The movie is postmortemised, not in terms of the acting, the technical flaws, weaknesses of script and casting and all that hifalutin stuff. It is all cut up in terms of whether for example 'Screwface' "bad nuh $&*#$??##&"' or 'Bad him blouse nawt . . . and di w'ite bwoy race 'in up suh!' or in another instance: 'Dem star bway dey a eediat, mek ooman trick 'im dem way deh . . .' That's if it's espionage and as usual the smarter women get the better of the men after they've settled scores in bed![3]

Admittedly, the usual fare in many Caribbean cinemas is the western/kung-fu/espionage action film in which the universe is reduced to a simple schematic conflict between good guys and bad guys and woman (as accessory) is stereotyped as whore or virgin; the text becomes an archetypal drama of predictably recurring plots: back to Eden. Earl Lovelace's treatment of the role of film, particularly the western, and its carnivalesque constructions of masculinity (and femininity) is powerfully accomplished in the novel *The Dragon Can't Dance*. Fisheye, the diminished hero of Lovelace's folk epic, embodies frustrated energy imaged in terms of both dispiriting sexuality and demonic possession; excitement and bedevilling impotence:

> He began to go to the cinema. Every night almost, he went to Royal or Empire, whichever was showing a western double; and after the show, walking home up the Hill, the picture fresh in his mind, walking kinda slow, he would feel for a few moments his strength, his youth, his promise fill him, and he would walk, the fastest gun alive, his long hands stiff at his sides, his fingers ready to go for the guns he imagined holstered low on his hips. But no one wanted to draw against him; and he would pick his way between the garbage and the dog shit with his secret power and invisible guns, his eyes searching the shadows for a hidden gunman – in which movie was it that someone had said: 'Every

> shadow is a gunman?' – but all he saw was maybe a few fellars gambling under the street light, or a man and his woman quarrelling. Back in his room, he felt crushed by his own strength, spun by the quickness in him. Now and again he would punch the boards of the partition, and he would overhear his neighbour's resigned comment: 'The devil in there with that boy.' The devil remained with him.[4]

The imperial resonances of the names of the cinemas underscore the delusions of grandeur of the alienated Fisheye, lost in his lonely fantasies of vicarious power. Fisheye's total identification with film heroes, like Ivan's, is clearly pathological and must be distinguished from the discriminating responses of habitual moviegoers in the Caribbean, as described, for example, by Paulette Williams, who are ultimately able to maintain a sane critical distance from the text. However much they might immerse themselves in the action for the fictive moment in the cinema, outside, they return to relative normalcy in the reintegrative process of communal analysis.

The socio-cultural significance of the screening of a Jamaican movie in Jamaica can thus be fully understood in the somewhat contradictory terms of the viewer's usual ability imaginatively to enter the escapist 'foreign' action film most intimately and knowingly, and the reader's unique capacity to be both subject and critic of this particular fiction with its 'realistic' Jamaican setting. Using the example of the pleasures of 'bad words', in this case *bombo claat* (roughly translated as 'menstrual pad' but with far from sanitised resonances), Paulette Williams generalises about the distinctive appeal of the familiar once it is transformed into film:

> it never fails to amaze me how turned on we become at the sound of two good Jamaican BBcs which we all are shouted around us daily (sic). But coming off the screen, they take on new significance and we love it to death. Unlike regular lines, utterance of a B.C. ig (sic) is reason enough to stop the show for a full three or so minutes . . . and this while the word is echoed and reechoed around the cinema. In the middle of the furore, some smart ass shouts out 'Sound! Sound! A whey di #$&**c??$$ them tek dis ting fa! Tun up di soun!' – Of course you and I know why no sound is coming forward – until some other smaties (sic) starts shouting SH-SH-SH and the hint is taken and the noise subsides.[5]

In the specific case of 'bad words', there is not only the simple aesthetic pleasure of recognising the familiar as art, but also the thrill of collectively breaking taboos. At the 1990 Carib theatre world premiere of the Island Records movie, *The Lunatic*, a screen adaptation of Anthony Winkler's novel of the same name, it was noteworthy how indulgent the predominantly 'up-town' audience was in their liberal refusal to receive as 'slackness' the generous use of bad words. Just like the masses. Much to their amusement, '*bombo!*' becomes the battle cry of the satirised expatriate feminist, Inga, who represents the despotic terror of the rule of foreign *pum-pum*. The latter word, meaning 'female genitalia' in Jamaican, would not ordinarily be used in polite society or in respectable art forms. Indeed, these same 'bad words', used in 'Roots Plays' or in popular song, are subject to censure. Even a critic as well-intentioned as Willams seems caught in the class double-standard, establishing a conspiratorial complicity with her newspaper readers ('Of course you and I know why'), in mockery of the naive, undisciplined behaviour of her presumably lower-class 'co-patrons' at the Carib cinema.

But the practitioners of 'down-town' art forms and their audience, contesting the social distance between the licensed and the licentious, simply assume freedoms that Establishment critics would deny them. Thus, Peter Tosh in a 1984 *Pulse Magazine* interview passionately argues for honesty against the class double-standard:

> when me say 'bombo-claat', a guy wan tell me say me mouth is dirty and I'm using 'indecent language'. And under no sector of laws or constitution can a guy show me or clarify to me why is it this word is indecent. A guy say 'damn you', 'fuck you' and a guy don't say nothing! But as a man say 'bombo-claat' him vex. It has too much spirituality. Is the effectiveness that the word has. Me have a song name 'O Bombo-Claat' which me sing, and me sing it with dignity. Seen? If you listen to the song, from the first verse to the last, me wrote so many verses to clarify my song, because me know our middle-class nice, decent, clean people out there don't like that. But they do the most devious and evilous bombo-claat things in the society that even the Devil himself is ashamed of, but them don't wan hear me say bombo-claat. A can't tek dat.[6]

Conventional definitions of spirituality, dignity and decency are clearly undermined in Tosh's revisionist, *bombo-claat* philosophy.

Similarly, Edward Brathwaite, in a typically metaphorical reading of the film version of *The Harder They Come*, foregrounds its subversion of colonial rhetorical strategies in the repositioning of subject/object–viewer/viewed relations:

> The premier (sic) of the Jimmy Cliff roots/reggae film, *The Harder They Come* (Kingston 1972) marked a dislocation in the socio-colonial pentameter, in the same way that its music and its stars

> and their style marked a revolution in the hierarchical structure in the arts of the Caribbean. At the premier, the traditional 'order of service' was reversed. Instead of the elite, moving (complimentary) into the Carib Cinema watched by the poor and admiring multitude, the multitude took over – the car park, the steps, the barred gates, the magical lantern itself – and demanded that they see what they had wrought. 'For the first time at last' it was the people (the raw material) not the 'critics', who decided the criteria of praise, the measure and ground of qualification; 'for the first time at last', a local face, a native ikon, a nation language voice was hero. In this small corner of our world, a revolution as significant as Emancipation.[7]

Somewhat paradoxically, Brathwaite's enthusiastic recognition of the power of *The Harder They Come* as revolutionary aesthetic practice seems to reinforce notions of the absolute authority of the scribal 'elite' critic, in its silence on the loudly oral critical activity in which his unindividuated 'multitude' always engage whatever the provenance of the film. Continuous feedback throughout the screening, and the critical post-mortem, though focusing largely on content analysis, must be taken into account as legitimate acts of 'self-conscious' criticism. A reversal of 'raw material'/processor-critic positions is only the first step (although an admittedly big step) in the direction of the much more complicated process of dislocating underlying assumptions about the nature and function of the critical act itself. Is 'criticism' an extension of the pleasure of reading the text ('outside in the thickness of bodies') or a discrete activity turned in on itself?

From the perspective of Black Britain, Paul Gilroy, much less reverential than Brathwaite, views the movie and its successors as part of an elaborate marketing campaign devised by Island Records to sell reggae music internationally (outside its market of origin). This exploitation of 'raw materials' – part of the development process – is deconstructed by Gilroy as a reinscribing of colonialist discourse:

> The gradual involvement of large corporations with a broad base in the leisure industries in the selling of reggae stimulated important changes reflecting a conscious attempt to separate the product from its roots in black life. Whatever the effect of the reggae film *The Harder They Come* in the Caribbean (Brathwaite, 1984), in Britain it marked the beginning of a new strategy for white consumption. The film was presented as little more than visual support for the sound-track recording made available by Island Records, an Anglo-Jamaican company. Cinemas showing the film became artificially insulated spaces in which images of black life,

> in this case as backward, violent, sexist and fratricidal could be consumed without having to face the difficulties associated with sharing leisure space with real live black people. Island Records, the company who pioneered this ploy, elaborated it further in subsequent films of reggae artists in live performance and in the 'adventure fantasy', *Countryman* in 1982. This last film, a tale of Obeah and adventure, was based on a simple inversion of the Robinson Crusoe myth. 'Friday,' recast in the form of a Rasta hermit-fisherman endowed with magical powers that originated in his total harmony with the natural world, saves and protects two young white Americans who fall into his Eden as the result of a plane crash. They are unwittingly involved in the drug business but with his help are reunited with their families and sent back to the US once the villains, the military wing of Michael Manley's socialist government, have been put in their place. This plot is less significant than the fact that the film was billed as 'A Tribute to Bob Marley'. This time, the soundtrack featured his songs.[8]

Thelwell's version of *The Harder They Come* is clearly closer in spirit to Brathwaite's revolutionary consciousness than to Gilroy's hard-nosed anti-capitalist polemics. But implicit in the writer's claims for the superiority of the novel form *vis-à-vis* film is a covert privileging of 'originality' and a somewhat reactionary view of the novelist as the (admittedly alienated) 'genius working out of his own ego' from whom Thelwell distances himself, at least in theory. There seems to be a fundamental contradiction at the heart of Thelwell's project. The conservative, writerly instinct to valorise the mimetic scribal act seems to require the devaluation of the original 'oral' film text, itself the product of collaborative writing. In this revisionist project, Thelwell's own collectivist aspirations are called into question:

> You know there is an unexamined, largely, notion about modernism in art, which is that it is private, subjective, that the artist is some kind of alienated genius working out of his own ego. And there is a countervailing African–Caribbean tradition that the artist is a man anchored in his society, anchored among his people, working out of the collective experiences. . . . the collective sensibilities, the collective values of the people, and as a consequence only a medium through which the people's reality is expressed. So that when black writers embrace European modernism they are really turning their back against their tradition and making themselves absurd and historically irrelevant. And I intend this novel to be a kind of political statement about the role literature can play.[9]

Because of book prejudice, film is dismissed as an inferior, limited form not having the same aesthetic potential as politically correct literature. It is this same book prejudice that motivates Sistren's written documentation of life stories. The oral accounts of the self in the medium of theatre or film are not adequate. You have to have a book; you have to sell yourself in as many forms as possible. In the case of Thelwell one is forced to recall in Gilroy's pragmatic terms that whatever the author's passions as a collectivist writer-medium, the book, like the film, seems to have had its genesis in the capitalist instincts of a far-seeing producer/publisher who recognised its market potential in the reggae music industry.

The novelisation project did not originate with Thelwell. In his own words:

> The film, *The Harder They Come*, has become a cult in America and so a New York editor, Kent Carroll of Grove Press, asked me to turn it into a novel. I rejected the idea of a straight novelisation, but agreed to do a much more ambitious narrative based on the film.[10]

To give Thelwell his due, the 'originality' of his ambitious response to that backward request to write 'the novel from which the film might have been derived were the process reversed, as is more usually the case' (p. 8), is that the writer as *griot* (in the tradition of Vic Reid) gives back to Ivan his origins, filling in the void of his past and thus civilising the silences and spaces in the film text. Ivan becomes more than *leggo beast* in the jungle of Kingston: *im come from somewhere.* The major advance of the novel beyond the film has little to do with the author's assumptions about the 'inherent limitations' of the film medium; the novel's authority is ideological. In its establishment of a context for urban drift the novel, much more than the film, humanises Ivan and detoxifies his society. It provides a psycho-sociological account of the making of a Rhygin, defining the trajectory of the meteoric rise and fall of Ivanhoe Martin from naive country bwai to city slick star bwai, and finally, hunted rude bwai/gun man. Gilroy's critique of the British voyeur's passive consumption of the movie's 'backward, violent, sexist and fratricidal' images of Jamaican life must itself be recontextualised.

The epigraph to Chapter 1, 'Village Bwai,'

> 'so me get it, so me give it, . . .
> Jack Mandora, me no choose none . . .' (p. 13)

is both a ritual affirmation of the non-originality of the folk-tale and a conventional disclaimer whereby the teller distances self from the moral improprieties of the tale. In 'Me And Annancy', Louise Bennett explains:

> At the end of each story, we had to say, 'Jack Mandora, me no chose (sic) none,' because Annancy sometimes did very wicked things in his stories, and we had to let Jack Mandora, the doorman at heaven's door, know that we were not in favor of Annancy's wicked ways. 'Me no chose none' means 'I don't choose to behave in any of these ways.'[11]

'So me get it, so me give it' thus signifies the entangling chain of production that binds the writer in a well-known plot. In Thelwell's view Ivan's wholeness could only be restor(i)ed in the expansiveness of the novel, not in the conventional two-hour film. He rationalises the need for the novel thus: 'I mean, there are certain kinds of social and political contexts, social history which you simply couldn't put in a movie unless it were eight or nine hours long, which is quite impossible. You can do that in a novel.'[12] This either/or extemporising seems deliberately to suppress the discrete pleasures of film as visual/oral art-form with its unique capacity to depict social history. The ironic disclaimer, 'Jack Mandora me no choose none', coming at the beginning of the tale, seems to be an acknowledgement of Thelwell's own emplotment, Anansi-like, in a somewhat unusual cultural transaction apparently beyond his will.

The epigraph can thus be interpreted as an indigenous sign of how to read the relationship of the novel to the film. The writing of the novel is a retelling of communally-generated narrative, the setting down of yet another version of legend: experiencing the pleasure of reformulating the familiar. Here is Thelwell's model African–Caribbean novelist 'working out of the collective values of the people'. The country setting of the first quarter of the novel becomes much more than 'background'. It encodes narrative strategies that structure a counter-discourse to the fiction of the Hollywood western to which *The Harder They Come* as film pays reluctant tribute. Stuck with writing the novel of the film of the legend, Thelwell nevertheless attempts to struggle out of the straitjacket of the plot in which he is implicated. The novelist's evocation of the multivalent 'problem tale' retextures the flat planes of the familiar film story. *The Harder They Come* is transformed into a subversively open-ended 'problem tale' that interrogates justice in an historically unjust society.

The problem tale narrated by Joe Beck at the shelling match, one of the high points of the first quarter of the novel, is one for which 'the audience would have to decide what the wise and just ending should be'. (p. 50) The story of the king, his daughter (who unreasonably refuses all suitors) and the two brothers who compete to claim her, combines elements of two types of tales as classified by Alice Werner in her 1907 'Introduction' to Walter

Jekyll's *Jamaican Song and Story*: (a) the tale in which 'the hero is robbed of the fruit of his achievement by an imposter stepping in at the last minute' and (b) the tale of the 'robber-bridegroom'. In 'Yellow Snake', the most delightful of the five examples of group (b) in Jekyll's collection, the gullible bride is almost completely swallowed by the duplicitous snake husband; marriage ruthlessly devours the fickle woman who 'never can find her fancy. Everybody come she say: "Lard, this one hugly, me no like him at all!"'[13] The tale is a clear warning of the deceptiveness of beauty as surface signifier. It ends with a proto-feminist moral and a *caveat*:

> From that day she never marry again for she feel the hand of marry.
>
> So everybody that pick too much will come off the same way.[14]

In Thelwell's version of the problem tale, the king, impatient with his daughter's choosiness, threatens her thus:

> 'So . . . no man no please you nuh? We gwine see. Any man who can ketch me a wild bull without use rope or gun or anyt'ing but 'im hands dem, gwine get you fe married. An' Ah don' care if 'im ugly, Ah don't care if 'im fool. Any man who can tame wild bull can tame you.' (p. 50)

Ivan is enraged by the solution proposed to the problem of who should marry/subdue the stubborn girl – not the determined, older brother who actually kills the bull, but the younger, more temperate brother who claims victory after he sees his brother and the bull go over a precipice and assumes that they are both dead:

> Where was the justice in that story? How would Joe Beck – wicked ol' red-ibo brute – like it if it was him did ketch the bull an' the people cheat him so? It woulda did serve dem right if the older brother did come back by night an' burn the town down like Samson an' the Philistine corn. Anyway, he reflected angrily, he didn't really like shelling matches: too much woman and pickney and petty talk. Bet you if it was a digging match nobody would agree with such a decision. But those were men's events, when new land had to be cleared and plowed by hand. No woman, pickney or old man, but only strong young man dem who could work hard, hard. (p. 54)

Joe Beck's advice, with its emphasis on the feminised wisdom of age, is no consolation to headstrong Ivan:

> 'Ah, mi son,' Joe Beck said. 'You young but you wi' see. If you was a king or a faddah you would see different. Justice is not a straight t'ing you know, is a crooked and curvy t'ing. It have to twis' an turn and ben' up – here he made a sinuous, twisting motion with his pipe – 'to get to where it mus' get to.' (p. 53)

Book One, 'The Hills Were Joyful', with its biblical resonances and its echo of the Roger Mais novel, carefully fleshes out the rural world that shapes Ivan's sensibility, invoking the interconnected forces that both define his sense of place and community, and precipitate his revolt. Chief among the powerful early influences on the child are the spiritual values which he inherits from his grandmother – the pious Christianity of Miss 'Mando's Sankey hymns fused with the possessive authority of Kumina. There is also the religious fervour of his Uncle Nattie's Garveyism and the intimate knowledge of storytelling ritual. The wisdom of the folk-tale that affirms the sinuous twists of justice offers complicated alternatives to the seductive half-truths of *The Harder They Come* as Hollywood film script. The accumulation of proverbs and cautionary tales in Book One constitutes a meta-text, a rewriting of the story that Thelwell is forced to tell. For example, Miss 'Mando's optimism that Ivan "wi learn"' is expressed proverbially:

> No, him spirit really strong, she thought, sitting there in the glow of the fire, it really strong. But him is not a bad pickney at all, y'know. Him is just one of dem people who tink say dem can box-box up the world an' spit in life face. But him wi' learn. She felt like the mother pig who, when asked by her pickney why her mouth was so long, merely grunted and said, 'Aai mi pickney, you young but you wi' learn. (p. 19)

But the idealistic faith of the old that the young will accept the values that have sustained the community is challenged in graphic metaphor. Ivan's view of the hill country in which he is reared is that it is a pen that threatens to transform him into a trapped animal: 'Dem think say man a go pen up yah 'pon mountainside like goat-kid all 'im life? Cho them wrong dereso. Definite!' (p. 68) The image recurs. With proverbial cunning, Jose, Ivan's prime antagonist in town, attempting to exonerate himself after betraying Ivan to the police, defines the young man's overweening ambition in vivid excremental detail: 'If nanny goat diden know how 'im batty hole stay 'im shouden did swallow pear seed.' (p. 339) These competing constructions of rural life as stability/entrapment, conservatism/backwardness, safety/boredom determine the reader's wavering sympathies in attempting to decode the problem story of Ivan's rise and fall.

When Ivan comes to town after the death of his grandmother and the disintegration of his familiar way of life he finds in the fiction of film a substitute for the clearcut justice that is undermined in Joe Beck's problem tale. The narrator gives a vivid account of Ivan's first encounter with the fantasy world of film with its fundamental moral certainties that seem to reconnect the wide-eyed innocent to his rural past:

> But great as the action was, it was something else that intoxicated him. The world of the movie was harsh and brutal, yes. But it was also one where justice, once aroused, was more elemental and deadly than all the hordes of evil. He thought Mass' Nattie would approve of such a world. (p. 149)

The brutality of the action is thus redeemed by its superimposed ideological meanings. The description of the audience's animal identification with the triumph of star-bwai Django in the face of apparent defeat contains the divergent motivations of the drama: cathartic satisfaction of a lust for violence as well as vicarious fulfilment of an optimistic belief in the heroism of the underdog – an Old Testament morality. The swift, simple justice of 'an eye for an eye and a tooth for a tooth' triumphs over the twisting wisdom of the problem tale:

> A low, approving, anticipatory visceral growl rose from the audience, becoming a joyous hysterical, full-throated howl of release, of vindication and righteous satisfaction as Django, grim-faced and alone, the very embodiment of retribution and just revenge, raked the masked killers, hot bloody destruction spitting from the Gatling gun on his hip. Men were torn apart, picked up and flung to earth in grotesque spinning contortions. The giant bearded face, tight jawed, crazy eyed, each line and furrow magnified 100 times, glared out at the audience, a powerful and primal force, an avenging angel in a sombrero. (p. 149)

For these impressionable young men adrift in the city, local events acquire the resonance of spectacle and are interpreted in terms of film metaphors. When Prince Emmanuel David and his 'strange army' (p. 209) of Rastafarians attempt to capture the city of Kingston and exorcise the spirit of colonialism, Widmark (an appropriated name) moved by the ritual grandeur of the occasion, whispers 'it only want Charlton Heston fe come down wid de commandments now' (p. 207) thus bringing together in a single image both the Rastafarians' identification with the avenging power of the Old Testament Jehovah/Jah, and the young men's vicarious political/moral victories in the idealised world of the cinema. But the waiting crowd of onlookers, like so many film extras, fully enjoying the pure drama of the moment, become annoyed that the Rastafarian takeover seems purely symbolic; they want action: '"Cho rass – is dis me walk so far to see?" a man complained. Wait? Dem t'ink a so man capture city nuh? Is mus' joke dem man yah, a joke.' (p. 211) The Rastafarians soon attempt to capture two 'Babylon' as sacrificial victims, and the crowd is placated: '"Whaiiee, watch de Babylon dem a run. Haw, haw. Me say run Babylon!" The sight of the police in headlong flight pleased them mightily and their good spirits were immediately restored at the prospect of seeing something really unusual like a sacrifice.' (pp. 211–12) It is Cowboys and Indians, with the cowboys as the villains: the ethos of the film, *The Harder They Come.* In this passage three voices and perspectives converge – Jamaican, biblical English and the language of the tourist/voyeur: the native and the foreign, mediated by the ritual language of film.

When the police assemble their counter-army it is Widmark, again, who remarks 'Spartacus to blood claat.' (p. 212) The omniscient narrator/*griot* concurs: 'And indeed, with the Biblical robes of the Rastas and the lines of shields and spiked helmets, the scene resembled nothing so much as the Roman legions against the slaves.' (p. 212) After the defeat of the Rastafarians, it is Bogart, 'the cool, the unchallenged leader, the man of respect . . . by day Ezekiel Smith, a mechanic's apprentice' (p. 201) who sums up the profundity of their failure: 'even Victor Mature couldn't did help them'. (p. 213) And even Bogart's 'real' name, Ezekiel Smith, the visionary worker in metals, returns us via the Old Testament prophet to the film fantasy of *The Ten Commandments* and the apparent failure of Jah to protect the righteous.

Film thus remains a powerful icon in Thelwell's rewriting of *The Harder They Come.* Notions that 'star-bwai can' dead', compounded with the sense of the inevitable triumph of goodness that is embedded in the western, shape the narrative, accounting for Ivan's increasingly daring, self-aggrandising acts that fly in the face of commonsense reason. Ivan's ambition of success in the city as star-bwai singer gradually becomes subsumed in his cowboy fantasy:

> It wasn't long before his judgment matured and his taste became more selective. Gangster movies didn't appeal to him much, they seemed to lack the clean-cut heroism of the westerns. Of course there were certain names: Humphrey Bogart, Edward G. Robinson, . . . which evoked a certain style, a cynical tight-lipped toughness which he liked. But in his innermost heart Rhygin was a cowboy. To miss a western, almost any western, brought sadness and deprivation to his spirit. (p. 195)

Ivan's fight with Longah, which marks his formal initiation into a disassociated life of crime, is visualised in film terms: 'It was just like watching the scene in *From Here to Eternity* where Lancaster and Borgnine are in the bar. He heard himself say, "If it's a killing you want Fatso, it's a killing you get." From a distance he saw himself. . .'. (p. 257) Later, when he greedily tests the feel of the guns with which Cowboy tempts him, Ivan is completely seduced by his star-bwai/gunslinger role: 'He twirled them backward western style by the trigger guards, pleased at the easy graceful way they settled back against the heel of his hand. "Rahtid," Cowboy breathed. "Gunslingah to rass. Is a star-bwai dis!"' (p. 310)

It is significant that Ivan actually buys the guns only after he comes to realise that he has no 'country' to go back to. When he returns to his village to find it intact only in memory, he yearns for that sureness of personal history and connectedness with the communal past that he has lost in his drift into the anonymous city. The guns are acquired to redefine his sense of identity and protect him from his newly-discovered vulnerability:

> He sat under the tree numbly. The smell of rotting fruit filled his nose and his head was full of the humming of the flies that buzzed around the sweetness. It was not easy to come to grips with the shock and desolation he felt. Ah shoulda did stay. Ah shoulda did stay an' tek care of de place, he thought. The worst insult that people had was the sneering 'Cho, you no come from nowhe'.' For the first time he was feeling what that really meant. Now he realized how important this sense of place was to his most fundamental sense of himself. He had the same urge he had the day his grandmother died to put his hands on his head and bawl and holler. He wanted to get a machete, to cut a path to the graves and clear the bush away. But . . . what de rass is de use. . . . What's de fucken use? He felt empty, and frightened, futile, miserable, and very alone. He would never, he swore, come back ever. (p. 321)

Ivan has become the parrot about to be destroyed by the hawk, of which his grandmother had moralised tendentiously, to little effect: 'We see ol' hawk ketch 'im. But is 'fraid kill 'im. If 'im did stay ina the guava trees wid the rest of 'im generation dem, the hawk never coulda catch 'im. But is fraid, 'im fraid cause 'im to fly out. You see?' (p. 42)

As a child, Ivan empathises with the parrot's daring, lonely flight; his adult life is a constant flying past his nest, a refusal to be mere carrier pigeon victimised by the predatory hawks in the ganja trade. It is Ivan's painful acceptance of his absolute loss of 'im generation dem' that thus precipitates his metamorphosis into rude bwai/gunman, that elusive folk-hero Rhygin who embodies the collective revolt of the deracinated tribe. As reggae/rebel singer in the concrete jungle of Kingston Ivan becomes an inciting voice crying out in the desolate wilderness of Babylon, wailing the dread of a generation of youthful sufferers. As rude bwai/gunman he becomes the star-bwai in his own movie firing down judgement on the villains in the wilds of western Kingston and their up-town accomplices. After Ivan shoots his first policeman he fully enters the fantasy of the western: 'He saw himself as a calm, cold-eyed and very cunning desperado outsmarting posses and search parties.' (p. 342) In his rewind of the incident Ivan becomes both viewer and viewed: 'The image of the cop flashed before him, rammed backward as if he had ridden into a steel cable. This time it was sanitized, distanced, purged of fear or guilt or any sickening sense of destruction. It was pure, abstract motion and power, like something on the screen.' (p. 346)

These film references culminate in the staging of the final ritual shoot-out. The confrontation is imaged in the familiar terms of Hollywood stereotype: Rhygin Ivan impatiently awaits the arrival of the police for the showdown at his hideout. Fully believing that 'star-bwai can' dead,' Ivan fears that he will be cheated of his triumph by the anti-climactic caution of the enemy. So he breaks cover:

> 'So what dem a wait for – is *Sands of Iwo Jima* dis to rass? Is mus' Iwo Jima dem t'ink dem deh.'
>
> He had to fight the laughter that rose up in him. Were they real – or another scene from a movie? They certainly seemed in no hurry to move. If he just lay in the thick grass they would never find him. Not cowering on their bellies like that. He realized with a great astonishment that Babylon, with all their long guns, were afraid of him. Eight, or more like twelve, with long-range guns crawling like so many turtles in the sand.
>
> 'Me one, an' dem 'fraid me . . . Show doan over a rass! Star-bwai can' dead after all. . . .' He rose to his feet shouting and staggering in the loose sand. 'Cho – done de army business!' he challenged, laughing. 'Who is de bad-man unu have? Sen' 'im out, nuh – one man who can draw. Sen' 'im out!' (pp. 389–90)

Inverting the myth of the underdog as hero, the novel, like the film, is an apparent betrayal of the romance of the western. Ivan's show *is* over. Indeed, the realistic ending of Ivan's movie is prefigured in one of his dreams during that span of delirious time he spends hiding out in the cave:

> Then, there were scenes from movies he had seen – familiar westerns but a mysterious, black cowboy astride a Honda kept riding into the scenes, changing the ending. Every time he appeared, guns spitting and engines roaring, the crowd in the theatre would erupt into cheering. A new scene came on, D'Jango was

> about to make his move. The crowd was watching for the black cowboy but a cold arrogant voice cut into their excitement: '*Show cut. Unu believe now say show cut?*' The black cowboy did not appear. (p. 374)

Ivan, the black cowboy – a contradiction in terms – is cut out of the action and reduced to 'a pile of bloody rags'. (p. 391) But just as the pleasures of gratuitous violence become moral victories in the world of the western, Ivan's 'destruction' is immortalised in legend. For example, Louise Bennett's wicked tribute to Rhygin, 'Dead Man', balances acceptance of the moral propriety of his necessary demise against the vicarious thrill of identification with his apparently indomitable badness:

> When smaddy dead dem dead fi true!
> Koo yah, koo police man
> Tan up over Rhygin an dah
> Finger-print up him dead han!
>
> Member dem days when big fraid
> Hole we everywhe we tun?
> Ef dem hear a car back-fire
> People seh a Rhygin gun!
>
> Night time every tree was Rhygin
> Or one a Rhygin spy:
> Ef peeny-wally blink him light
> Dem seh a Rhygin yeye!
>
> Police dress wid gun an bayonet
> Dissa stamp bram-bram all bout:
> Dem big boot a warn Rhygin fi
> Careful when him walkin out!
>
> Koo omuch time him slip police!
> Koo omuch blood him shed!
> But no care how man seh dem bad,
> Man cyaan badder dan Dead!
>
> Wid all a Missa Rhygin
> Carrin-awns-dem, me did know
> Seh Dead was backa him dah teck
> Him meck big poppy-show!
>
> From de beginnin a Rhygin
> Narvasness an terror spread:
> An look pon de en a Rhygin –
> Bullet-hole up, harmless, dead!

Koo de fus picture him pose fa,
Gun dem ready, blazin lead!
Koo de las picture him pose fa,
Eena dead house, lidung dead!

But ah wonder what would happen
To de picture-man, Miss Sue,
Ef when him dah teck de picture
Rhygin duppy did seh 'boo'![15]

The final verse of the poem, undercutting the proverbial certainty of the first, humorously suggests that Rhygin as duppy/legend may be even more deadly than Rhygin as living gunman.

In terms of the twisting justice of the problem tale, a positive reading of Ivan's life is required by the several references in the novel that image him as a subversive Christ figure, despite his criminality. That long void of time he endures when he first comes to Kingston and is broken by the anonymous harshness of urban life is a kind of wilderness experience that prepares him, in part, for his trials in the yard of Preacher Ramsay. It is a call to suffering as ritual purification. Having survived the dehumanising beating that is his punishment for cutting up Longah, Ivan remains buried in his room for three days as Elsa nurses him back to life. When he returns to Kingston from his disillusioning visit to his lost home in the country he again suffers ritual death and remains locked in his room for three days. He becomes an outcast prophet without kin or place; his sole commitment is to his mission. It is Ivan who becomes the scapegoat for the ganja traders' collective revolt against the inequities of the trade; he is the sacrificial lamb that must be slain for the resumption of trade – the life-blood of the community of sufferers. With proverbial authority, Sidney, recognising Ivan's symbolic power, recklessly urges the traders to refuse to betray him for blood money:

> 'Me is not so criminal dat me no know who abuse me, who scorn me, who down-press me all me life. . . . Ol' time people say, 'every fish nyam man, but is shark alone get blame.' José say Rhygin is stranger – not one a we – well, dem say 'when tiger wan' nyam him pickney, him say dem favor puss.'. . . All a we is little dutty criminal to dem – alla we. Mek Ah tell you. . . . If dem high-up man a go pay all dis money fe de life a one dutty little criminal, den dem really a buy somet'ing much biggah. You evah see dem give way money yet? Somet'ing much more dem want, man, an' dat is what Sidney who sell everyt'ing a'ready, *will not sell*. Unu can do what unu want, but dis little dutty criminal nah go sell. Sidney nah sell Rhygin so. . . . Nah sell 'im so. . . . Nah sell 'im so.' (pp. 379–80)

Even when Ivan *is* sold by Elsa, this betrayal is a carefully contemplated act of sacrifice for the life of Man-I, the next generation. But Elsa's motives are complicated; she has never believed in Ivan's dreams. Ivan becomes a victim of the possessive, domesticating love of women who would keep him from his divine mission as agent of social justice. With the exception of Miss Ida, that voluptuous literary precursor of those sporting ladies in the dancehall who celebrate their sexuality so brazenly, the women in Ivan's world represent forces of resistance to the urbanisation of peasant culture. Miss Ida, whose cafe introduces Ivan to the pulsating sensuality of urban reggae music, gives him a vision of an exciting alternative to the country pen in which he is trapped: 'This was city music, cafe music, the music of pleasure and fleshly delight, and Miss Ida was its incarnation. She was a dancer moving effortlessly with the melody, anticipating the brassy variations of the trombone, but always coming back to the heavy rolling drumbeat that seemed to drive and control the bumping, grinding motions of those massive, insistent hips.' (p. 29) Miss Ida is carefully contrasted with the respectable women of the district: '"Some a the Christian people in Blue Bay, the postmistress and teacher wife and so, them no like Miss Ida . . . Dem say she is a *sportin' lady*."' (p. 24) In the eyes of the enthralled Ivan, Miss Ida is desire embodied:

> She was a woman, as were his grandmother and her friends, but there the similarity ended. He couldn't take his eyes off her. Her lips were red, and when she smiled, as she seemed to do a lot, there was a flash of gold. A thick wave of black hair swung down to her shoulders, which were bare. And what shoulders they were – wide, smooth, black – and below them, outlined clearly under a tight red blouse, depended two round outthrust globes fighting against the fabric and coming to perfect points some distance in advance of the rest of her. When she walked her hips, which flared dramatically from a tightly belted waist, rolled with a majestic rhythm as though to call attention to themselves. And indeed, the checker game was temporarily suspended when she emerged from behind the bar.
>
> 'Lawd,' one of the men breathed reverentially, but loud enough for the tribute to carry, 'what a woman walk nice, sah?' He shook his head slowly in rapt devotion. (p. 27)

Though Miss Ida's transfiguration in dance is compared with that of the women at Miss 'Mando's pocomania meetings, it is the humorous incongruity of the analogy that is underscored by the narrator: 'but the dreamy expression on her face, the smile on her painted lips were not very spiritual'. (p. 29) Indeed the separation between the two worlds is comically represented in Miss 'Mando's refusal to listen to church music on Ivan's newly-acquired transistor radio: 'she regarded it as sacrilege to play God's music on the same devil's instrument that brought the sinful music of Babylon.' (p. 69) Miriam, Ivan's country girlfriend, feels a similar sense of violation when the blaring transistor radio intrudes into the post-coital peace of their love-making. But for Ivan, sex with Miriam, like reggae music, is one of a range of sensual experiences that mark his passage from innocent country bwai to worldly-wise, city slick rude bwai. For Miriam, sex means the promise of family and a commitment to reproducing the way of life which she knows intimately. So she tries to get Ivan to give up his dream of going to Kingston. In Elsa are combined both Miss 'Mando's piety and Miriam's sensuality. Attracted to the bad man in Ivan, Elsa nevertheless struggles to redeem him.

Ivan consistently rejects all of Elsa's attempts to mould him into a nice and decent, Christian young gentleman. Indeed, the sacrificial pie-in-the-sky morality of deferred gratification that she upholds is analogous to the long-term justice of Joe Beck's problem-tale that Ivan contemptuously dismisses as a woman thing. In this matter of submission to the demands of a feminised respectability Ivan single-mindedly follows the advice of his substitute father, Mass Nattie: '"One mo' t'ing – bwai, you *can'* done pussy. Yu gwine ha' fe tek some an' leave some. You *can' done pussy* so don't mek it rule you. You can' done it *a rass*."' (p. 112) Refusing to be undone by pussy, Ivan disregards Elsa's aspirations to piety, opting for the quick rush of immediate success in the here-and-now. His dream career as star bwai reggae singer offers the promise of material success. But it is a slow business. There are so many potential stars for the producer to exploit in what is decidedly a buyer's market. It is entirely logical that Thelwell's portrayal of Hilton, the gun-toting, macho record-producer manages to suggest both his superior social distance from the likes of Ivan as well as their shared, culture-specific, masculinist identity that transcends social barriers. The Jamaican male, whatever his class, enjoys a common instinct for handling pussy. Of the ever-ready white American female tourists and their apparently deficient male counterparts at home Hilton contemptuously muses in the spirit of Mass Nattie that: 'the man dem up there confuse, not sure what them supposed to do. Then the women dem run down here and want to kill off the male population wid pussy. But we up to the task man, more than up to it.' (p. 245)

The age-old story of men collaborating in the control of pussy is replicated in the difficult case of Thalia, Rufus/Longah and Coolie Roy. In an urban update of the tale of the woman who never can find her fancy, combined with a version of the Robber Bridegroom tale, Thelwell presents us with another problem narrative of shifting sympathy. Ambitious Thalia, 'an extremely pretty black girl' (p. 226) who works as nursemaid in the same household as Rufus, the garden boy, has nothing but contempt for the young black men who aspire to her bed:

> 'Since when me and you is frein'?' she demanded. 'Me is you *love*? What I would want wid all like you? What you have dat I want? You have money? You have looks? You have color? You have education? No! You doan have nothing in you favor. You ugly, you poor, you ignorant and you black. When you see me a street don't talk to me, y'hear?' She sucked her teeth, tossed her head, and started off, her proud batti rolling with indignation.
>
> 'After you is nothing but a damn *garden bwai*,' she called over her shoulder. 'You think garden bwai money can get me?' (p. 227)

The collectively humiliated garden-boys temporarily console themselves with the knowledge that Thalia as woman is congenitally vulnerable: 'As one young man said philosophically,"Well, if me can't get her, mi brother bound to." "What you mean? Who is you breddah?" "Everyman."' (p. 227)

Impatient Rufus, the immediate object of Thalia's disdain, engineers a brilliant scheme to hasten Everyman's revenge. He conscripts Coolie Roy, 'an inordinately handsome coolie-royal boy with a very sweet mouth and impeccable maners', (p. 227) to court Thalia. In a last-minute switch Rufus takes his place in Thalia's bed and thus acquires his nickname when she exclaims '*"WAIEE, Lawd Jesus – it longah dan first time*."' (p. 229) Thalia is swallowed hook, line and sinker by the snake suitor:

> Next afternoon Thalia, prim and prissy in her uniform, walked her charges down the avenue past the hedges hiding the smooth lawns, but her walk turned out to be a gauntlet. At that time of the afternoon the garden boys she had scorned were busy watering their lawns, and from behind every hedge she was greeted with cries of, '"Lawd Jesus, me no have nowhere fe put all that! Waiee Roy, *it longah dan first time!*"'
>
> She endured it for a week, then left her job with very little explanation. Rufus became known as Longah-dan-first-time, And then simply Longah. But he didn't escape unscathed either, because boys who didn't like him, of which there were a few, lost no opportunity to pant imploringly, 'Lawd Miss Thalia, beg you mek Ah finish, nuh' whenever he came in sight. (pp. 229–30)

The sinuous justice of the problem-tale makes it difficult to determine who is victor and who victim in the long run. Generic 'Everyman' is a composite victor; individual men will still have to negotiate with the Thalias of this world to finish what they start.

In the short term the victory of the garden-boys over Thalia with her middle-class aspirations is a celebration of native wit, that duplicitous cunning of Anansi who learns how to cut crooked to go straight. Conversely, Ivan's brash, headlong confrontation with his adversaries in class war precipitates his death. But Rhygin's apotheosis, like Jimmy Cliff's rise to superstardom as his reincarnation, is the victory of the growling underdog that dares to bite back: 'I'd raddah be a free man in mah grave/ dan living as a puppet or a slave.' (p. 281) It is also the triumph of reggae music:

> It seemed to [Ivan] a sign and a promise, a development he had been waiting for without knowing it. This reggae business – it was the first thing he'd seen that belonged to the youth and to the sufferahs. It was roots music, dread music, their own. It talked about no work, no money, no food, about war an' strife in Babylon, about depression, and lootin' an' shootin', things that were real to him. (p. 221)

The image of the suffering underdog reconnects Ivan's fate with that of the despised Christ. When Ivan's banned hit song 'De harder dey come' is finally played on the radio as a perverse requiem, it is Ras Peter who affirms the parallel with the crucified Christ in words that echo 'It is finished': '"Tu'rn (sic) it off! Ah say to tu'n it off!' But of course they didn't. 'It done,' he said. 'It really done now."' (p. 391) The crucifixion motif is continued: 'Over the gulley, in the shacks and hovels of Trench Town, for the space of half an hour, silence reigned.' (p. 392)

Rhygin will be resurrected in the collective imagination of succeeding generations of youth for whom he will become an eternal role-model as boys continue to play out the stereotypical film roles of badman and sheriff, cowboy and indian, ghetto youth and Babylon:

> 'Bram, Bram, Bram!' He leapt from cover, guns blazing.
>
> The posse returned fire. 'You dead!' the sheriff shouted. 'Cho man, you dead!'
>
> 'Me ah Rhygin!' the boy shouted back. 'Me can' dead!'
>
> He again swept the posse with withering fire before dancing back under cover. His clear piping voice sang out tauntingly, 'Rhygin was here but 'im jus' disappear. . .'. (pp. 391–92)

This is the triumph of the black cowboy, astride a Honda, who keeps on riding into the scenes, changing the ending. It is also an affirmation of the subversive, revolutionary energy of Rastafari.

The deferral of closure in the problem tale which requires that the audice determine the appropriate ending encodes the endless interrogations of the postmodernist sensibility. Ivan's conservative, backward folk culture is surprisingly modern, providing models of interpretation that defy the simple logic of clear-cut closure: Riddle me this, riddle me that, guess me this riddle and perhaps not.

Notes

1 Michael Thelwell, 'Author's Preface', *The Harder They Come* (London: Pluto, 1980), p. 7. Subsequent references cited in text.
2 See, for example, G. Fitz Bartley, 'Jamaican stars in "Marked for Death"', *Jamaica Record*, Sunday, 28 October 1990, p. 1C.
3 Paulette Williams, 'I Just Love The Carib', *Flair Magazine (The Daily Gleaner)*, 5 November 1990, p. 17.
4 Earl Lovelace, *The Dragon Can't Dance* 1979; rpt (London: Longman, 1985), pp. 64–5.
5 Paulette Williams, op. cit., p. 17.
6 Peter Tosh, interview by Carolyn Cooper, *Pulse*, June 1984, p. 12.
7 Edward Brathwaite, *History of the Voice* (London: New Beacon Books, 1984), p. 41.
8 Paul Gilroy, *There Ain't No Black in the Union Jack* (London: Hutchinson, 1987), p. 169.
9 Quoted by S. M. in a review of *The Harder They Come*, 'Rhygin . . . and now the book', *Sunrays, Sunday Sun Magazine*, 29 June 1980, p. 18.
10 Quoted by W. J. Weatherby, 'When Literary Worlds Collide', *Guardian* (London), 28 May 1980.
11 Louise Bennett, 'Me and Annancy', in Walter Jekyll, ed. 1907; rpt *Jamaican Song and Story* (New York: Dover, 1966), p. ix.
12 S. M., p. 18.
13 Walter Jekyll, p. 102.
14 Ibid., p. 103.
15 Louise Bennett, *Selected Poems*, ed. Mervyn Morris (Kingston: Sangster's, 1982), pp. 56–7.

CHAPTER 7 Chanting down Babylon: Bob Marley's song as literary text

Critical evaluation of Bob Marley's song as literary text raises recurring questions about the tricky, Anansi-like mutability of the oral/scribal literary continuum in Jamaica. Verbal creativity clearly does not spontaneously divide into discrete categories, orature and literature. The performance poetry of Louise Bennett, Mikey Smith and Jean Breeze illustrates the interpenetraton of oral and scribal forms; there are fundamental ideological contradictions at the heart of Sistren Theatre Collective's *Lionheart Gal* project that exemplify the practical difficulties that arise in attempting to separate the voice and the pen; Thelwell's fictive practice embodies orality despite the author's privileging of the scribal mode. Bob Marley's songs similarly illustrate the fusion of scribal and oral literary influences – the former, largely derived from the Bible (as interpreted by Rastafari), which is, admittedly, often transmitted orally; and the latter, originating in what Louise Bennett simply calls 'Jamaica philosophy': 'a whole heap a Culture and Tradition an Birthright dat han dung . . . from generation to generation.'

The reggae songwriter's art is a dynamic process in which words, music and dance are organically integrated within an afrocentric aesthetic. The composition and performance of lyrics is multi-modal; by contrast, artificial transmission of the reggae songwriter's lyrics as transcript is monologic and thus somewhat counterproductive.[1] The lineal act of writing down lyrics distorts the performance process. In the attempt to 'catch the words' and pin them down for close inspection one can develop a somewhat antagonistic relationship to the music. The energising reggae beat and the pulsating melodic line that normally extend the meaning of the performer's words – especially in the case of an accomplished artist like Bob Marley – become disquieting diversions. Occasionally, in order to 'fix' the text for rereading, one is forced to make an educated guess and simply grab a meaning. This ordering academic enterprise, with its subjects controlled by the analytic imperative, can become another bastion of establishment Babylon that must be chanted down.

Nevertheless, one does feel the shape of the music, like a phantom limb, in the very process of attempting to concentrate solely on the disarticulated, transposed words. And there are compensations. Reflective evaluation of the words fixed on the page does allow distinctive pleasures: overtones of meaning reverberate. Potential readings, that may be muted in the total theatre of performance, are isolated and released. The strength of Bob Marley's lyrics is that his words, detached from the emotive musical context in which the songs are most fully realised, retain a compelling, allusive authority.

Indeed, the lyrics become open to a wide range of interpretations. Asked about the possible meanings of the *Kaya* album, Marley himself advises in good 'reader response' criticism: 'You have to play it and get your own inspiration. For every song have a different meaning to a man. Sometimes I sing a song and when people explain it to me I am astonished by their interpretation.'[2] This permissive astonishment seems to derive from the creative artist's recognition that the power of the word cannot be contained within the boundaries of the individual author's 'intention'. It also seems to point to the dynamics of 'interpretation' in oral, communal contexts of performance. The roots of interpretation – 'to spread abroad among' (OED) – seem to be grounded in oral discourse. The audience, as much as the performer, engages in the making/spreading of the text and its meanings. Inspired interpretation – both oral and scribal – thus becomes another 'performance' of the text, another opportunity to disclose its multiple meanings.

The act of criticism as 'interpretation' is thus essentially a process of signification, not obfuscation; when the criticism itself needs to be interpreted it becomes pointless cross-talk. In my own reading of Marley's lyrics and even more so the lyrics of the DJs, which are not usually viewed as susceptible to serious critical analysis, I am guided by a missionary instinct for interpretation that attempts to reclaim the often derided 'gibberish'/ verbal creativity of 'illiterate' Jamaicans. Not only can signifyin' itself be dismissed as monkey talk, but also the critical act of 'interpreting' the meaning and significance of that talk.[3] Given my liberalising political prejudice, I clearly do not claim any authority for my own readings, except for that given by Bob Marley, above, which may, naturally, provoke resistance.

Marley's skilful verbal play – his use of biblical allusion, Rastafarian symbolism, proverb, riddle, aphorism and metaphor – is evidence of a highly charged literary sensibility. His words require the careful critical attention ordinarily accorded verbal performances in the written medium. This evaluation of Marley's lyrics is based on eight albums produced over the ten-year period 1973–83. These are *Burnin'* (1973), *Natty Dread* (1974), *Rastaman Vibration* (1976), *Exodus* (1977), *Kaya* (1978), *Survival* (1979), *Uprising* (1980) and the posthumous *Confrontation* (1983).

Marley began writing and recording songs long before the 1972 release of *Catch a Fire*, the Wailers' first album, as distinct from a collection of individual hits. His first recording 'Judge Not', was released a decade earlier. But, it was with the rise and fall of the original Wailers triumvirate that Bob Marley's distinctive talents unquestionably emerged.[4] Further, the very nature of that early Wailers cooperative makes it difficult to ascribe authorship to several of the songs released by the group before 1972. Stephen Davis, one of Marley's biographers, describes the collaborative improvisation of early Wailers' lyrics thus, underscoring the role of Lee Perry – alias Little, Scratch, Upsetter – the Wailers' producer and co-writer:

> While Bob strummed and brooded, Perry would croak out catch-phrases and doggerel, trying to find the right lyrics to match the spluttering, bumpity Afro-style percussion tracks that the Barrets were experimenting with. Perry . . . was . . . a witty and imaginative lyricist who contributed immeasurably to the great records the Wailers made with him. As to who actually wrote the songs (Bob or Scratch – Peter's and Bunny's songs are unmistakably their own), confusion still reigns. . . . Most likely, they were written by both men and the band, improvising in the studio.[5]

An excellent example of the verbal spontaneity of group improvisation is evident in the shaping of the lyrics of the Wailers' classic, 'Small Axe', attributed to Marley. Recounting a tale that may very well be apocryphal, Stephen Davis notes:

> When the Wailers originally merged with Lee Perry, Upsetter Records was facing competition from the 'big three' studios in Kingston – Federal, Studio One and Dynamic. One day Bob and Peter and Scratch were playing with lyrics at the Upsetter shop and Scratch was complaining about the 'big t'ree'. Brash and boasty as usual, Tosh spoke up: 'If dem is the big t'ree, we am (sic) the small axe!' And one of the canniest double-entendres in reggae music was born.[6]

Tosh's spontaneous verbal wit illustrates how artistry in oral composition functions – as in the written tradition. The literariness of an utterance is dependent on the particular skill of an individual talent, shaping communally-shared verbal techniques. Double entendre, metaphor, proverb and riddle, characteristic elements of everyday oral discourse in Jamaica, constitute the heightened language of orature. In another account of the genesis of the song 'Small Axe', Sebastian Clarke notes in *Jah Music* that:

> Psalm 52 was used by Bob Marley to create 'Small Axe'. The Psalm opened with: 'Why boastest thyself, O mighty man? The goodness of God endureth continually.' Marley changed or scram-

> bled the words around to say, 'Why boastest thy self, O evil man? The goodness of Jah endureth for Iver.' The song was also strengthened by the inclusion of bits of Ecclesiastes 10: 'He that diggeth a pit shall fall into it.' Marley's slightly changed lyrics say, 'And whosoever diggeth a pit shall fall in it.'[7]

The interrelated issues of individual authorship, originality and influence, raised in these complementary accounts of the evolution of 'Small Axe', are central to an understanding of oral formulaic thought and expression as employed by Bob Marley. Walter Ong observes in *Orality and Literacy* that:

> Poets, as idealized by chirographic cultures and even more by typographic cultures, were not expected to use prefabricated materials. If a poet did echo bits of earlier poems, he was expected to modulate these into his own 'kind of thing.'[8]

By contrast, the art of the oral poet is essentially formulaic. According to Ong:

> formulaic style marks not poetry alone, but more or less, all thought and expression in primary oral culture. Early written poetry everywhere, it seems, is at first necessarily a mimicking in script of oral performance. The mind has initially no properly chirographic resources. You scratch out on a surface words you imagine yourself saying aloud in some realisable oral setting. Only very gradually does writing become composition in writing, a kind of discourse – poetic or otherwise – that is put together without a feeling that the one writing is actually speaking aloud.[9]

Ong's formulation, 'a mimicking in script of oral performance', is a useful way to conceptualise the transformation of the performed song into transcript. The metaphor of mimicry also approximates the symbiotic process of oral/scribal composition, whereby literate artists create and perform within an oral mode. The emphatic voice of Louise Bennett's Jamaican-speaking *personae*; the reggae-rhythmic chant of the 'dub' poet; the ubiquitous song of the reggae musician; the apparently inscrutable art of the DJ together constitute an oral performance continuum in which the voice, in dialogue with an audience, is of primary aesthetic importance.

The message of these contemporary oral poets is often a 'drumbeat . . . playing a rhythm/resisting against the system', to quote Bob Marley.[10] Erna Brodber and J. E. Greene in their 1979 study, 'Reggae and Cultural Identity in Jamaica', conclude that

> The transmitters of reggae . . . are by and large committed to a

> belief structure, Rastafarianism, whose roots are in Africa, in Jah, Haile Selassie, the Emperor of Ethiopia. The themes of their messages are rooted in their despair of dispossession, their hope is in an African or diasporan solution. As a result, their messages emerge as an ideology of social change.[11]

The central ideological concern of Bob Marley's songs is indeed radical social change. The existing social order, metaphorically expressed in Rastafarian/New Testament apocalyptic iconography as Babylon, the whore, the fallen woman of St John's Revelation, must be chanted down.

Bob Marley's chant against Babylon is both medium and message. For Babylon, the oppressive State, the formal social and political institutions of Anglo/American imperialism, is bolstered by the authority of the written word, articulate in English. 'Head-decay-shun', the cunning inversion of the English word 'education', is antithetical to the cultural practices of Rastafarians, whose chant against Babylon has biblical resonances of the fall of Jericho. The power of the spoken word is emotively affirmed in the distinctive language of the Rastafarian. Malika Lee Whitney notes in *Bob Marley: Reggae King of the World* that:

> The Rastafari way of speaking or 'reasoning' is not illiteracy as some would have you believe, but the tailoring of the European language for more identifiable self-expression and modification of it to highlight the positive. Changes in vocabulary and syntax are also a conscious act of protest against the established mores of 'Babylon'.[12]

References to Babylon recur throughout the Marley collection. In the traditional 'Rastaman Chant', from the *Burnin'* album, for example: 'I hear the words of the Rastaman say/ Babylon you throne gone down, gone down/ Babylon you throne gone down.' In 'Revolution', from the *Natty Dread* album, though there is no explicit reference to Babylon, the apocalyptic imagery of imminent collapse graphically suggests the fall of Babylon and the implosion of the political system:

> Revelation, reveals the truth
> Revelation
> It takes a revolution to make a solution.
> . . .
> Never make a politician grant you a favour,
> They will always want to control you forever.
> So if a fire make it bu'n
> And if a blood make it run.
> Rasta there on top, can't you see.

We got lightning, thunder, brimstone
Fire.

In 'Crazy Baldhead', from the *Rastaman Vibration* album, the theme of revolution is amplified. The social institutions of Babylon – the inter-related religious, educational and penal systems, are perceived as dysfunctional. 'Brain-wash education' must be subverted and the con-man/crazy baldhead put to rout:

Build your penitentiary
We build your schools
Brain-wash education to make us the fools.
Hateraged (sic) you reward for our love
Telling us of your God above.
We gonna chase those crazy
Chase those crazy bunkheads
Chase those crazy baldheads
Out of town.
Here comes the con-man
Coming with his con-plan
We won't take no bribe
We got to stay alive.

In the title-track from the *Exodus* album, the driving message is the metaphysical flight of 'Jah people' from Babylon/Egypt to Ethiopia, the Rastaman's Eden. The unproblematised identification of oppressed Africans in the diaspora with biblical Jews, as evidenced here in the motif of the exodus from Egyptian slavery, underscores the incongruities of cross-cultural mythologising:

Open your eyes and look within.
Are you satisfied with the life you're living?
We know where we're going
We know where we're from.
We're leaving Babylon
We're going to our father's land.
Exodus!
Movement of Jah people.

In 'Time Will Tell', from the *Kaya* album, in which Marley appears to move away from the militant social and political preoccupations of the earlier songs, there is an anxious affirmation of the moral righteousness of dread: 'Jah would never give the power to a baldhead,/Run come crucify the Dread./ Time alone oh! Time will tell.' The urgency of flight in *Exodus* is transposed into the reflective philosophising of the more sombre *Kaya*.

'Babylon System', from the *Survival* album roundly denounces the systematic brutalisation of the downtrodden and asserts the authority of the autonomous will to rebel:

> We refuse to be
> What you wanted us to be.
> We are what we are
> That's the way it's going to be.
> You can't educate I
> For no equal opportunity
> Talking about my freedom
> People freedom and liberty.
> Yeah!
> We've been trodding on the winepress
> Much too long
> Rebel, rebel.

The imagery of parasitism is appropriate:

> Babylon system is the vampire
> Sucking the children day by day.
> Babylon system is the vampire
> Sucking the blood of the sufferers.
> Building church and university
> Deceiving the people continually.
> Me say them graduating
> Thieves and murderers,
> Look out now
> Sucking the blood of the sufferers.
> Tell the children the truth.

The motif of the internalisation of liberation, 'we are what we are', is elaborated in the lyrical 'Redemption Song', from the *Uprising* album. The opening lines telescope time, compressing a whole history of exploitation and suffering. The heroes of Empire are demythologised, reduced to common criminals; Africans engaged in the mercenary enterprise that was slavery are also implicated by that neutral 'they':

> Old pirates, yes
> They rob I
> Sold I to the merchant ships
> Minutes after they took I
> From the bottomless pit

But my hand was made strong
By the hand of the Almighty
We forward in this generation
Triumphantly.
Won't you help to sing
These songs of freedom?
Cause all I ever have
Redemption songs.

The religious and commercial resonances of 'redemption' suggest both divine grace and the practical justice of freeing a slave by the payment of ransom money. Liberation becomes much more than the freeing from physical chains, for true freedom cannot be given; it has to be appropriated. Authenticity comes with the slave's reassertion of the right to self-determination. Emancipation from 'mental slavery' thus means liberation from passivity – the instinctive posture of automatic subservience that continues to cripple the neo-colonised:

Emancipate yourselves from mental slavery
None but ourselves can free our minds.
Have no fear for atomic energy
Cause none a them can stop the time.
How long shall they kill our prophets
While we stand aside and look?
Some say, 'it's just a part of it,
We've got to fulfil the book.'
Won't you help to sing
These songs of freedom?
Cause all I ever had
Redemption songs.

'Chant Down Babylon', from the posthumous *Confrontation* album is incendiary, a celebration of the potency of reggae music as an inciting force, a manifestation of collective revolutionary energy:

Come we go burn down Babylon
One more time.
Come we go chant down Babylon
One more time.
For them soft, yes them soft,
Them soft, yes them soft.
So come we go burn Babylon
One more time.
Music, you're, music you're the key

Talk to who, please talk to me
Bring the voice of the Rastaman
Communicating to everyone
. . .
A reggae music, chant down,
Chant down Babylon . . .

The 'burn down'/'chant down' ambivalence denotes a fundamental paradox in Marley's apocalyptic vision. Like the biblical prophets, whose message of impending doom also conveyed the promise of divine forgiveness, with repentance, Bob Marley sings of both destruction and regeneration. Implicit in his message of damnation is latent hope for the redemption of Babylon and the establishment of Jah's kingdom of righteousness. Like the divine horsemen of Revelation, Natty Dread rides 'thru the mystics of tomorrow', chanting retributive justice:

All and all you see a gwan
Is to fight against the Rastaman
So they build their world
In great confusion
To force on us the devil's illusion.
But the stone that the builder refuse
Shall be the head cornerstone
And no matter what games they play
There is something they could
Never take away
Something they could never take away.
And it's the fire, it's the fire, the fire
Only the birds have wings.
No time to be deceived
You should know and not believe
Jah says this judgement
Could never be with water
So no water could put out this fire
This this fire, this this fire
This this fire, ride Natty ride
Go deh Dready, go deh,
Dready, go deh.[13]

In practical political terms, the 'burn down'/'chant down' variant also perhaps denotes Bob Marley's awareness of the actual power of Babylon in the real world. The polemical language of overt political confrontation – 'burn down Babylon' – and the covert language of ideological optimism –

'chant down Babylon' – cleverly converge. Marley, who on 3 December 1976, survived a brutal ambush in the night at his Tuff Gong residence, concedes in a 1978 *Melody Maker* interview that:

> Pure politics can hurt certain people so you 'ave to get hard, get soft, 'cos guns don't argue, an' you talk too much an' get too strong, they'll kill ya because Babylon set up (their) own system an' it no want nobody to change it. . . . So is not everything you can talk 'bout 'cos them kill ya'.[14]

Bob Marley's consistent use of metaphorical language – the quality of his style that Petrine Archer Straw aptly defines as 'the hidden depth of reasoning'[15] in his work – is evidence of the Jamaican folk wisdom compressed in proverb that warns 'you haffi play fool fe ketch wise'. Thus, for example, in the menacing 'I Shot the Sheriff', with its aggressive, derisive flaunting of Babylonian authority, the primary mood is one of defiance – Rhygin style:

> I shot the sheriff
> But I didn't shoot no deputy, oh no
> I shot the sheriff
> But I didn't shoot no deputy, ooh, ooh, ooh
> All around in my home town
> They're trying to track me down
> They say they want to bring me in
> Guilty
> For the killing of a deputy
> . . .
> Freedom came my way one day
> And I started out of town, yeah
> All of a sudden I saw the sheriff John Brown
> Aiming to shoot me down
> So I shot – I shot him down
> And I say
> If I'm guilty I will pay.

Yet, despite the bravado and the willingness to accept responsibility for a conscious act of 'self-defence', there is also a sense of an impersonal fate working itself out. The final verse of the song employs two proverbs, in a structural device of completion, which confirm the inevitability of reflexive ghetto justice:

> Reflexes got the better of me
> And what is to be must be
> Every day the bucket go a well

One day the bottom a go drop out
One day the bottom a go drop out.

Similarly, 'Who the Cap Fit', from the *Rastaman Vibration* album employs riddling proverb to restate allusively the theme of the song, hypocrisy, which is presented initially in a series of straightforward truisms:

Man to man is so unjust
You don't know who to trust
Your worse enemy could be
Your best friend
And your best friend, your worse enemy
Some will eat and drink with you
Then behind them susu pon you
Only your friend know your secret
So only he could reveal it
Who the cap fit
Let them wear it

The deceptively innocent neutrality of the proverb – 'Me say me throw me corn/Me no call no fowl' – is deliberately and ironically undercut by the onomatopoeic fowl call – 'I saying cok, cok, cok, yeah/cluk, cluk, cluk.' Subterfuge, riddling language – signifyin' – is thus used by Marley to voice his vision of the healing of the breach between man and man.

This vision of redemptive love also encompasses the need to transform potentially exploitative male/female relationships. Babylon, as woman/whore, must be redeemed. Three categories of Marley songs denote distinctive responses to this dualistic Babylon symbol – woman and social system. First, there is a cluster of songs, particularly from the *Exodus* and *Kaya* albums in which intimate issues of domestic power and powerlessness, love and suspicion are of central importance. For example, 'Waiting in Vain', 'Is This Love?' and 'She's Gone'. Secondly, there is a smaller group of songs in which the correlation between socio-political and domestic issues is explicity drawn, for example 'Johnny Was' from the *Rastaman Vibration* album. Finally, there is a group of songs in which the very conceptualisation of Babylon as fallen woman poses ideological problems: woman, in both her literal and symbolic manifestations, is intrinsically evil, a seductive, malevolent force enticing the morally innocent Rastaman from the path of righteousness into slackness.

The songs in the first grouping illustrate one of the remarkable accomplishments of Marley's lyrics – the seriousness with which he treats sexual love, a subject that is often trivialised in Jamaican popular music. 'Is This Love?' opens with the man's positive statement of intent:

I wanna love you, and treat you right
I wanna love you, every day and every night
We'll be together, with a roof right over our heads
We'll share the shelter of my single bed
We'll share the same room, Jah provide the bread
Is this love, is this love, is this love
Is this love that I am feeling?

The poignant image of the shared shelter is reinforced by the ambiguous 'single' bed, which both denotes the intimate warmth of material poverty, and connotes a commitment to monogamy. (One should not permit details of Marley's colourful biography to delimit the range of meanings of the songs themselves.) The allusion to gambling, 'So I throw my cards on your table', is primarily an admission of honesty; there is nothing up the man's sleeve. But the very metaphor of the game suggests the dicey nature of male/female relationships. The complex thematic movement of the song is from the intention, 'I wanna love you', to the question, 'Is this love?' and finally the declaration, 'Oh yes, I know.' The lover calls no trumps.

In 'Waiting in Vain', from the *Exodus* album, the lover's ardent supplication modulates into mild reproof. There is a definite suggestion that the dilatory woman is functioning somewhat like a whore, with a long line of lovers in attendance. The all-too-willing Rastaman is forced patiently to wait to negotiate a space for himself, however much he may not want to wait in vain. The tension betweeen the wanting and the waiting defines the pathos of this song:

I doan wanna wait in vain for your love
From the very first time
I blessed my eyes on you girl
My heart says follow through.
But I know now that I'm way down on your line
But the waiting feel is fine.
So don't treat me like a puppet on a string
Cause I know how to do my thing.
Don't talk to me as if you think I'm dumb
I wanna know when you gonna come.
See, I doan wanna wait in vain for your love.
. . .
Cause it's summer is here
And I'm still waiting there
Winter is here

And I'm still waiting there
Like I said
It's been three years
Since I'm knocking on your door
And I still can knock some more
Oooh girl, oooh girl
Is it feasible
I wanna know
For I to knock some more?
Ya see
In life I know there's lots of grief
But your love is my relief
Tears in my eyes, girl
Tears in my eyes, girl
While I'm waiting
While I'm waiting for my turn

The superhuman endurance of the tearful lover is reinforced in the reference to the magical number three; after a three-year period of protracted suffering, marked by the cycle of the seasons, the knight errant may, perhaps, find the not-too-holy grail.

In 'Turn Your Lights Down Life', also from the *Exodus* album, the lover *lyrics*[16] the woman in true Jamaican style:

Turn your lights down low
And pull your window curtains
Oh let Jah moon come shining in
Into our life again
Saying, oooh, it's been a long, long time
A get this message for you girl
But it seem I was never on time
Still I wanna get through to you, girl
On time, on time.
I want to give you some good, good loving
Oh I, Oh I, Oh I
Say, I want to give you some good, good loving
Turn your lights down low
Never try to resist, oh no
O let my love come tumbling in
Into our life again
Saying, oooh, I love you
And I want you to know right now
Cause I, that I

I want to give you some love
I want to give you some good, good loving

This is classic sweet-mouth talk: the man admits his shortcomings – 'it seem I was never on time' – and hopes for the best, or at least another chance.

The elegiac 'Johnny Was', from the second grouping of songs, evokes the dread power of the Babylonian state in the intimate terms of a mother weeping for her son who has been destroyed by the arbitrary violence of ghetto life:

Woman hold her head and cry
Cause her son
Had been shot down in the street
And died
From a stray bullet.

The song ends with a rhetorical question that eloquently renders the pathos of the woman's despair: '"Can a woman tender care"/She cried . . ./"Cease towards the child she bear?"' The biblical quotation generalises the woman's suffering beyond the immediate context of guerrilla warfare in urban Kingston. Like all mothers who have lost their sons to war, this woman wails the anguish of senseless suffering. Similarly, in 'No Woman No Cry,' from the Bob Marley and the Wailers *Live* album, the woman's tears are not only an expression of her personal grief but a more general lamentation for an irretrievable past:

No woman no cry
Cause I remember when we used to sit
In a government yard in Trench town
Observing the hypocrites
Mingle with the good people we meet
Good friends we have
Oh, good friends we have lost
Along the way.
In this great future
You can't forget your past
So dry your tears, I say

The vacillation between the good friends we have/have lost underscores the sense of separation and loss that is the song's primary theme.

In the third grouping of Marley songs a central tenet of Rastafarianism is expressed: the Adamic Rastaman, susceptible to the wiles of Babylonian Eve, becomes the passive victim of female cunning. The biblical image of Babylon as whore, the fallen woman of *Revelation,* defines contemporary gender relations, founded on the essential frailty of (fe)male flesh. The female is ambivalently perceived as both deceiving and vulnerable to deception. Maureen Rowe notes in her pioneering 1980 essay, 'The Woman in Rastafari' that:

> For the Rastafari male, it was significant that the first female mentioned in the Bible was unfavourably mentioned. This was interpreted as a clear warning against the potential evil in the female. While the interpretation is widely held by Rastafari males their response to it differs. Some brethren are sympathetic in their response arguing that the evil was in the devil and that Eve was the victim. . . . The other attitude is more judgemental. It argues that the female is impure and must be kept from corrupting the male. It is also implied wherever this attitude is manifested that females should not get together because of the potential for sinful thinking and practices. The female then must be guided, instructed and restricted by the male.[17]

This ambivalent response to woman that is characteristic of Rastafarian fundamentalism is evident in Marley's songs and in his statements about his work. In a 1975 *Caribbean Times* interview Marley is alleged to have said: 'me never believe in marriage that much . . . marriage is a trap to control men; woman is a coward. Man strong.'[18] Although one must reasonably distinguish between Marley's attitude to woman and to marriage, one must note that the image of woman as entrapper rears its ugly head. The man, fearful of 'control', turns the woman into a double-headed monster that is both manipulatively emasculating and emotionally vulnerable. But in that same interview Marley expresses admiration for the vocal asssertiveness of an Angela Davis: 'dat woman in America . . . Angela Davis, a woman like that who defends something: Me can appreciate that.'

'Pimper's Paradise' from the *Uprising* album is a good example of Marley's ambivalent response to 'fallen' woman. The song opens with the man's indictment of the fashion-conscious, pleasure-seeking, drug-addicted woman:

> She loves to party
> Have a good time
> She looks so hearty
> Feeling fine
> She loves to screw,
> Sometime shifting coke
> She'll be laughing
> When there ain't no joke

A pimper's paradise
That's all she was now.
. . .
She loves to model
Up in the latest fashion
She's in the scramble
And she moves with passion
She's getting high
Trying to fly the sky, eh!
Now she is bluesing
When there ain't no blues.

But the enigmatic line, 'Every need got an ego to feed', suggests empathy for the woman who has perverted natural desire into self-destructive obsession. The reference to paradise subtly connotes Eve's fall from innocence, seduced by Satan, the first world pimp. The song moves towards a clear statement of sympathy: 'I'm sorry for the victim now.' The singer then addresses the woman directly, abandoning the initial, dismissive 'throw-word' stance:

Pimper's paradise
Don't lose track
Don't lose track of yourself, oh no!
Pimper's paradise
Don't be just a stock,
A stock on the shelf
Stock on the shelf

The woman becomes more than exploited commodity; she is challenged to reclaim her humanity.

The compassionate ambiguity of Bob Marley's response to Babylon/woman extends as well to Babylon/system, but with greater reservations. The sexual appeal of woman at the interpersonal level covers a multitude of sins; it cannot mediate hostilities at the systemic, socio-political level. For example, in 'We and Them' from the *Uprising* album, the polarisation of good and evil is clearly articulated:

We no know how we and them
A go work this out, oi!
We no know how we and them
A go work it out
But someone will have to pay
For the innocent blood
That they shed every day
Oh children mark my word

It's what the bible say
Yeah! Yeah.
. . .
Dem a flesh and bone
We no know how we an dem a go work it out
But we no have no friends
In na high society
We no have no friends
Oh mark my identity

Yet, in the very recognition of a fundamental antagonism between 'we and them', between spirit and flesh, there is an implied acknowledgement of the possibility that a way could be found to 'work this out'. In the chant against Babylon is the religious faith in a transformed earth where Jah's creation will be restored to original perfection. Ecological and moral issues become one:

But in the beginning Jah created everything
He gave man dominion over all things
But now it's too late
You see men has lost their faith
Eating up all the flesh from off the earth.

In the *upful* 'Forever Loving Jah' from the *Uprising* album, Marley affirms a steadfast faith in divine guidance. Employing several biblical allusions as well as the *susu/sese* rhetoric of Jamaican street talk, this song asserts the righteousness of the Rastaman's cause, despite the ill-will of *badminded* detractors:

We'll be forever loving Jah
Some, they say, 'see them walking up the street'
They say we are going wrong
To all the people we meet
But we won't worry
We won't shed no tears
We've found a way
To cast away the fears
Forever, yeah!
. . .
So, Old Man River
Don't cry for me
I've got a rolling stream of love you see
So no matter what stages, stages
Stages they put us through

In everything
No matter what rages, oh rages, changes
Rages they put us through
We'll never be blue
We'll be forever loving Jah
Cause there's no end.
Cause only a fool
Lean upon, lean upon his own misunderstanding
And then what has been hidden from the wise and the prudent
Been revealed to the babe and the suckling
In everything
Cause just like a tree
planted, planted, by the rivers of water
That bringeth forth fruits
bringeth forth fruits in due season
Everything in life got its purpose
Find its reason
In every season
Forever, yeah
We'll be forever loving Jah

Marley's vision, like that of John the Revelator, is for a new heaven and a new earth from which the former evil has passed away:

> And he cried mightily with a strong voice, saying, Babylon the great is fallen, and is become the habitation of devils, and the hold of every foul spirit, and a cage of every unclean and hateful bird. For all nations have drunk of the wine of the wrath of her fornication, and the kings of the earth have committed fornication with her, and the merchants of the earth are waxed rich through the abundance of her delicacies.[19]

Bob Marley's song, like all great local literature which we come to call 'universal', speaks first to the particular circumstances of his own time and place; its meaning expands in ever-widening circles of compassion, levelling barriers of race, class, gender and geography. Bob Marley lives in the rich legacy of song he has bequeathed us. Give thanks!

Notes

1 I am indebted to Garth White, Research Assistant at the African–Caribbean Institute of Jamaica for his transcription of five of the Marley albums, an ACIJ project. I quote from his transcriptions to which I occasionally make slight

modifications of lineation and punctuation. I transcribed the songs quoted from the *Natty Dread*, *Exodus* and *Confrontation* albums. I am also indebted to Garth White for his invaluable *The Development of Jamaican Popular Music with Special Reference to Bob Marley: A Bibliography* (Kingston: Jamaica: African–Caribbean Institute of Jamaica, 1982).

2 Basil Wilson and Herman Hall, 'Marley in His Own Words: A Memorable Interview', *Everybody's Magazine* 5.4 (1981): p. 24.

3 See, for example, Claudia Mitchell-Kernan's definition of 'signifying' quoted in Henry Louis Gates Jr, *Figures in Black: Words, Signs, and the 'Racial' Self* 1987; rpt (Oxford University Press, 1989), p. 240: 'The Black concept of signifying incorporates essentially a folk notion that dictionary entries for words are not always sufficient for interpreting meanings or messages, or that meaning goes beyond such interpretations.'

4 For a vivid account of the complex professional relationship between Peter Tosh, Bunny Wailer and Bob Marley, see Peter Tosh, interview by Carolyn Cooper, *Pulse*, June 1984, pp. 14–15.

5 Stephen Davis, *Bob Marley* (London: Panther/Granada, 1984; rpt of Arthur Barker Ltd), pp. 118–19.

6 Ibid., pp. 120–1. The story is also narrated by Timothy White in *Catch a Fire* (New York: Holt, Rinehart and Winston, 1983), p. 23. The bravura with which White narrates – verbatim – conversations that he could not possibly have overheard, raises suspicions about the credibility of the entire biography.

7 Sebastian Clarke, *Jah Music* (London: Heinemann, 1980), p. 55.

8 Walter Ong, *Orality and Literacy* (London: Methuen, 1982), p. 21.

9 Ibid., p. 26.

10 'One Drop', *Survival*, 1979.

11 Erna Brodber and J. E. Green, 'Reggae and Cultural Identity in Jamaica', Working Papers on Caribbean Society, Sociology Department, UWI, St Augustine, Trinidad, Series C, No. 7, 1981, p. 26.

12 Dermott Hussey and Malika Lee Whitney, *Bob Marley: Reggae King of the World* (Kingston, Jamaica: Kingston Publishers, 1984), p. 115. See also Velma Pollard, 'Dread Talk – The Speech of the Rastafarian in Jamaica', *Caribbean Quarterly*, 26.4 (1980): pp. 32–41.

13 'Ride, Natty, Ride', *Survival*, 1979.

14 Quoted in Sebastian Clarke, 1980, pp. 109–10.

15 Petrine Archer Straw, 'Christopher Gonzalez's "Bob Marley Monument": Masterpieces from the National Gallery', Lecture No. 8, *Sunday Gleaner*, 18 May 1986.

16 In Jamaican slang 'to lyrics' means, approximately, 'to sweet talk'. The metaphor, coming from the culture of the dancehall, generalises the singer's skill with lyrics into any kind of verbal skill. The DJ Lloyd Lovindeer notes the importance of mastering the language of seduction: 'So if you go to a girl in the dancehall and say, "Ah, may I have the pleasure of this dance?" she know right away that she don't really want to dance wid you. Because if you talk like that, more likely yu cya[a]n wine. And in the dancehall is bubbling and wining. The regular three-step business don't work.' 'Women in Dancehall', *Jamaica Journal* 23.1 (1990): p. 52 (transcribed and edited by Carolyn Allen).

17 Maureen Rowe, 'The Woman in Rastafari', *Caribbean Quarterly* 26.4 (1980): p. 14.

18 Quoted in Stephen Davis, 1983, p. 207.

19 Revelation 18: 2–3.

CHAPTER 8 Slackness hiding from culture: erotic play in the dancehall

The lyrics of the DJs define the furthest extreme of the scribal/oral literary continuum in Jamaica. Unmediated by a middle-class, scribal sensibility DJ oracy articulates a distinctly urbanised folk ethos.[1] The literariness of this *massive*,[2] popular cultural form is marginalised by its context of performance: the dancehall. The primary function of the DJ's art is to *ram dancehall an cork party*.[3] Decontextualised, the lyrics often become decidedly limp. To the uninitiated much of the 'noise' that emanates from the DJs is absolutely unintelligible. The insistent sing-song of fixed rhythmic structures conspires to obscure meaning; individual words become submerged in a wash of sound. But if you permit your ears to become attuned to this border-line sound and allow for the free play of the intellect, then patterns of meaning cohere and a framework of analysis both socio-linguistic and literary may be constructed.

As Jamaican becomes appropriated by the official culture (for example as 'folk heritage'; or for 'authenticity' in the advertising industry); and as the use of Jamaican in the scribal literary tradition becomes acceptable and conventional, then the rude impulse of the language, formerly manifested in 'backward' folk culture, can be seen to now reassert itself in contemporary forms of verbal maroonage such as the lyrics of the DJs. This downtown, purely oral art-form can be both differentiated from, and situated within the broader context of the work of *oraliterate* writers like Louise Bennett, Vic Reid and Erna Brodber, for example, who are substantially uptown folk easily commanding the full breadth of the scribal/oral literary continuum. With the DJs there is no presumption of an essentially 'scribal' literary tradition as the context of performance.

The DJs' lyrics interrogate other song traditions – for example, Jamaican folk songs and African–American rhythm 'n' blues – with comic (and often ironic) effect. For example Higgs and Twins' 'Jump Up Time' is a dancehall update of a 'folk' song, 'Evening Time', written by Barbara Ferland in the fifties:

Jump an spread out time
Come everybody better form a line!
Wi da wuk from mornin,

Da wuk from mornin,
Da wuk from nine til five.
Mek wi rock up fi wi body line
Mek wi dance an sing,
Do wi owna ting
Inna dancehall style.

The tune of Red Dragon's 'Love Oonu' is that of a children's ring game, 'There's a Brown Girl in the Ring'. The song's derogatory reference to Shaka Zulu modulates, somewhat ironically, into minstrelsy:

If yu no favour Shaka Zulu
Se, tra-la-la-la-la
If yu no ugly lakka patu
Se, tra-la-la-la-la
An if yu know yu smile pretty
Se, tra-la-la-la-la
An if yu know yu teet white
Se, tra-la-la-la-la

Yellowman's 'Waan Mi Virgin' employs the melody of a Revival song for satirical purposes: 'Mi alone, mi alone ina di wilderness/Forty days an forty nights ina di wilderness', becomes 'Mi no waan, mi no waan we di man dem nyam an lef/Di man dem walk a mile an a half ina yu gungo walk.' The repeated 'walk' encodes subtly different meanings; 'walk' as both the act of sexual intercourse and the place where it occurs. The primary sex/food metaphor is extended in the identification of the woman's body with both the lush fertility of a bed of gungo peas and the distastefulness of left-over food.[4] Further, 'walk' as fowl-run and/or the place in which a game-cock is kept widens the sexual allusiveness of the song. Undomesticated, brazen female sexuality is both desirable (to many men) and threatening (to some), so the ambivalent DJ seeks a virgin. 'Waan Mi Virgin' also echoes an earlier Mento song, 'Mi no waan, mi no waan we Matty Walla lef/Matty run a mile an a half eena gungo walk', thus suggesting that sexual innuendo is not at all peculiar to the much maligned lyrics of the DJs, but is firmly established in Jamaican popular culture. Indeed, a loaded line of the Mento song, 'Ol lady run a mile an a half an shi tumble down', evokes the evasive/complicit sexuality of the cunning, experienced old woman, a theme that is brilliantly developed in Lovindeer's 'Granny Two-Teet'.

The sustained narrative and metrical line of Lovindeer's artful compositions, and especially his sensitive handling of double-entendre (*pun/aani*),[5] are evidence of his sheer genius and mastery of form. His penchant for *picong* – that Trinidadian art of wicked wit – suggests that he is schooled in the calypso idiom. For example, his signature tune, 'Panty Man', parodies Sammy Davis Junior's 'The Candy Man':

> Who cyan rock di party?
> Who cyan mek it ram?
> Mek all of di uman kick up an raise de han?
> Di panty man cyan.

Lovindeer's lyrics illustrate not only his personal genius, but the shaping influence of literacy on a predominantly oral verbal art form. Lovindeer composes his lyrics somewhat like Mikey Smith did – responding to vivid expressions heard on the street and then incorporating them into a carefully developed artistic statement. Lovindeer keeps a notebook of ideas to which he refers when he begins to formally compose. The sequential narrative line of his compositions, as distinct from the repetitive, formulaic structures of a Shabba Ranks, for example, seems to be possible only with self-conscious literacy. A comparison of Shabba Ranks' 'Trailerload a Girls' and Lovindeer's response, 'Customs Officer' clearly illustrates these structural differences. This pair of songs also illustrates the general 'intertextuality' of dancehall songs. Here the continuity is thematic: Shabba needs a Customs Officer to clear a trailerload of girls he has imported; Lovindeer is the officer who will do the job, determining appropriate duty based on the cc rating of the engine, the nature of the front-end, bumper and general shock-absorbing capacities of the trailer's contents. Lovindeer's sustained use of mechanical imagery to define female anatomy again illustrates his formal training in scribal literature. The intertextuality of dancehall songs is usually rhythmic and melodic, the same basic format being used for a number of songs. Indeed, music is far less important than lyrics in this genre. What is often dismissed as the limiting repetitiveness of dancehall music is more the shaping metrical foundation on which formulaic phrases are constructed.

Further, the DJ's verbal art originates in an inclusivist neo-African folk aesthetic – a carnivalesque fusion of word, music and movement around the centre pole, and on the common ground of the dance floor. The DJ's original function of *livelyin up* dance sessions made him a kind of praise poet for his sound system. His status was enhanced by his control of lyrics that *cyaan done.* [6] Dick Hebdige, in 'Reggae, Rastas and Rudies', accurately traces the development of the genre, after making the sweepingly wrong generalisation that '[b]efore "ska" (the forerunner of reggae) Jamaica had little distinctive music of its own':

> in the 1950s, in West Kingston, R. and B., imported from America, began to attract attention. Men like Duke Reid were quick to recognise the potential for profit and launched themselves as disc-

> jockeys forming the flamboyant aristocracy of the shantytown slums; the era of the sound system began. Survival in the highly competitive world of the backyard discos, where rival disc-jockeys vied for the title of the 'boss-sound', demanded alertness, ingenuity and enterprise; and, as American R. and B. began to lose its original impetus in the late fifties, a new expedient was tried by the more ambitious d-j's (sic), who branched out into record production themselves. Usually, an instrumental recording was all that was necessary, and the d-j would improvise the lyrics (usually simple and formulaic: 'work-it-out, work-it out', etc.) during 'live' performances.[7]

Over time, DJing evolved from primarily functional talk subject to an economic imperative – *drawin crowd* – to talk as an entertaining end in itself. The DJ is now the star performer, no longer a mere functionary in the sound system business. But in performance the DJs, conscious of lineage, and needing to sell themselves efficiently in an increasingly competitive market, elaborately declare their mastery of the field. For example, Super Cyat:

> An anywe mi go,
> Mi a di mike magician
> Mr Cyat on a style an fashion
> An mi come ina di place
> An hol di mike ina mi hand
> Come ina di place an talk,
> An den di session hafi ram
> . . .
> Cau mi se dis is di Cyat
> Jah man im jus passin t(h)rough
> An anywe mi go
> Mi nice up yu revenue.

The literariness of the DJ's art is thus subsumed in the totalising function of the dance. By contrast, the origins of the work of a neo-oral writer like Louise Bennett, whose poetry seems close in spirit to the pure orality of DJ performance, can be traced to both oral and scribal literary forms. Bennett's creolising of the inherited ballad form is, initially, an act of conscious literary modelling. Aware of conventional poetic forms that provided a sense of historical context, Bennett becomes a Creole practitioner within an established (English) literary tradition. The poem 'Bans a Killin' makes this clear. Jamaican is one of a number of regional dialects of English that must be preserved; Bennett's dialect poems are legitimate regional verse of good pedigree: Chaucer, Burns, Lady Grizelle and Shakespeare:

> Dah language weh yuh proud a
> Weh yuh honour an respec –
> Po Mas Charlie, yuh no know seh
> Dat it spring from dialect!
> . . .
> Yuh wi haffi kill de Lancashire,
> De Yorkshire, de Cockney,
> De broad Scotch and de Irish brogue
> Before yuh start kill me!
>
> Yuh wi haffi get de Oxford Book
> A English Verse, an tear
> Out Chaucer, Burns, Lady Grizelle
> An plenty a Shakespeare![8]

This contextualisation of Bennett's work is not intended to detract from the distinctiveness of her accomplishment – inscribing Afro-Jamaican folk culture on the literary imagination – but to underscore its paradoxical conservatism. In a paper entitled 'The Decay of Neo-Colonial Official Language Policies. The Case of the English-lexicon Creoles of the Commonwealth Caribbean', Hubert Devonish argues that the firm opposition to the early *literary* Creole experiments of Bennett in Jamaica and Wordsworth McAndrew in Guyana 'forced . . . [them] to take a rather defensive position concerning the Creole language question':

> They ended up stressing the need for the *preservation* of Creole in its existing roles and functions. There was, at least, a tacit acceptance on their part that, in spite of the expressiveness and efficiency of Creole as a medium of communication, the role of English as the sole official language could not be challenged. This defensive position made it easy, after independence, for the new political elite who had inherited political power to co-opt the work and positions of people like Bennett and McAndrew. In the quest for national symbols to place alongside those of the flag and national anthem, the new political elite occasionally find it necessary to refer to the special place which the 'folk' speech plays as a mark of national identity. But, at best, when the existence of Creole is at all recognised by those who hold political power, this recognition is granted to a symbol and nothing more.[9]

The Creole of the DJs is not preserved 'folk' speech' appropriated by the political/cultural elite. It is a language on the make: *trash an ready*.[10] But if the language of the DJs has not attracted co-optation by the state the themes of the 1980s recordings nevertheless are characterised by their apparent political conservatism and an overwhelming preoccupation with 'slackness'. In his study of the cultural politics of race and nation in Britain, *There Ain't No Black in the Union Jack*, Paul Gilroy argues that:

> Jamaica's DJs steered the dance-hall side of roots culture away from political and historical themes and towards 'slackness': crude and often insulting wordplay pronouncing on sexuality and sexual antagonism. I am not suggesting a simple polarity in which all toasters were agents of reaction and all singers troubadours of revolution. The Jamaican DJ tradition had been as involved in the spread of Rastafari during the late 1960s and early 1970s as recorded *song*. The two aspects of reggae culture interacted and combined in complex fashion. Even as slackness achieved ascendancy there remained popular toasters like Peter Metro and Brigadier Jerry who fought to maintain rhymes with a social content in the dances. However, the role and content of reggae changed markedly after 1980. This shift related to the consolidation of Seaga's regime and the consequent militarization of ghetto life. Both were also expressed in roots music and in the social relations of sound system sub-culture where guns became an increasingly important aspect of the rituals through which the crowd communicated its pleasure to the DJs.[11]

Yet, paradoxically, though DJ slackness as critiqued by Gilroy is conceived as politically conservative, it can be seen to represent in part a radical, underground confrontation with the patriarchal gender ideology and the pious morality of fundamentalist Jamaican society. In its invariant coupling with Culture, Slackness is potentially a politics of subversion. For Slackness is not mere sexual looseness – though it certainly is that. Slackness is a metaphorical revolt against law and order; an undermining of consensual standards of decency. It is the antithesis of Culture. To quote Josey Wales: 'Slackness in di backyard hidin, hidin from Culture.' Slackness as an (h)ideology of escape from the authority of omniscient Culture is negotiated in a coded langage of evasive *double-entendre*. Gilroy himself notes, but does not fully explore at the level of politics, 'the subversive potential in the ability to switch between the languages of oppressor and oppressed':

> The aesthetics of sound system culture had from its inception been built around the pleasures of using exclusive or specialized language in cryptic coded ways which amused and entertained as

> well as informed the dancing audience. For example, highly ritualized exchanges between the DJs and the crowd that conveyed appreciation of a particular rhythm (record) or style (sequence of rhymes) frequently involved the systematic corruption of ordinary innocent English words into new forms of public speech. 'Massive', 'Safe', 'Settle', and 'Worries' are all words which were playfully endowed with meanings unrelated to those invested in them within the dominant discourse.[12]

Particularly in reference to the oppositional values Slackness/Culture, we should add 'wicked', which signifies massive approval of the subject thus dubbed. Linguistic innocence in the dancehall is not a virtue.

Eschewing respectability, the DJs operate subversively at the low end of the scale of accepted social propriety. Their privileged subjects are DJing itself, and sexuality. Heterosexuality most often requires a precise listing of body parts, almost exclusively female, and an elaboration of their mechanical function. Homosexuality is gloriously vilified in graphic excremental imagery. Supremacy in DJing is ritually contested, as in Lecturer's 'Well, if a DJ waan fi tes mi, tell im fi come'. Verbal and sexual skill are often indistinguishable. Lyrics that *cyaan done* and rough riding rhythms become symbols of sustained sexual potency, as in Beenie Don's 'Look (h)ow mi slim, but mi (h)ealthy an (s)trong/Keep pon dem ridim like a dyam stallion.' It is not size but technique that determines staying power. Recurring horse-racing imagery connotes not only sexual power, but also the verbal skill of sports commentators on horse-racing, who are able to sustain intelligibility despite an extremely fast-paced delivery that enacts the speed and excitement of the race itself. This kind of skill, as much as the old-fashioned radio DJs' rhymes – 'the cool fool with the live jive' – provides models for the DJs' tongue-twisting, ear-bending lines.

The core of the data base for this study is the Derrick's One Stop record shop (Kingston, Jamaica) two-volume collection of 35 'Latest Reggae '88'; this is supplemented by Lovindeer's *Panty Man* album and his hit 'Wil(d) Gilbert', Yellowman's 'Waan Mi Virgin' and 'Titty Jump', and Josey Wales' 'Culture a Lick' and 'Slackness Done.'[13] These songs can be grouped thematically into five broad categories: (1) songs that celebrate DJing itself; (2) dance songs that vigorously invite participants to *wain an push iin*; (3) songs of social commentary on a variety of issues, for example, ghetto violence and hunger; (4) songs that focus on sexual/gender relations – by far the largest number in the sample. Some of the songs in this group are clearly inflammatory in intent; Lovindeer and Yellowman are the chief perpetrators. But others, and not just those sung by the female DJs, celebrate the economic and sexual independence of women, thus challenging the conservative gender ideology that is at the heart of both pornographic and fundamentalist conceptions of woman as commodity, virgin and whore. (5) Songs which directly confront the Slackness/Culture dialectic.

Of the three songs in group five, 'Slackness Done' by Josey Wales is the least ambiguous. The opening frame, with its militaristic motif, defines the terms of the DJ's heroic and presumably suicidal mission – cleaning up the dance-hall. Many of the DJ songs have an opening frame that is spoken, not sung. This is indicated in italics.

> Colonel Josey Wales!'
> Yes, Commissioner.'
> 'I would like yu to go into di dance-hall an clean up
> all dose slack DJ who is spoilin di kids of today'.

(Note the Creole interference in the Commissioner's reported English. 'Order' is already breaking down as linguistic Slackness disarticulates Culture.) But the Commissioner is not being parodied. The DJ, faced with two mutually hostile orders of responsibility – that of the *massive* who require out-of-order lyrics, and that of the Commissioner of Police, the voice of official morality and social order – simply bows to the censorial authority of state power.

But the sluggish rhythm of the song and the dispirited tone of the reverberating, inebriated first verse suggest that not only Slackness but the DJ himself has been done in:

> An yu ever ina dancehall drinkin stout,
> A stout, a stout, a stout,
> Yu dip ina di crate,
> Put di bockle a yu mout,
> Yu mout, yu mout, yu mout,
> An all of a sudden yu bredrin a shout,
> A shout, a shout, a shout,
> Se di Colonel Josey Wale im de ya,
> Im de bout, de bout, de bout, de bout.

After this rather half-hearted start, the Colonel, attempting to carry out the Commissioner's directive, launches his attack:

> A talkin to di DJ from di street,
> Di street, di street
> Di people in di community cyaan sleep, Lawd.
> Wi goin on like wi live on di rubbish heap
> Life is pretty,
> Wi shoulda tek it more smoothly,
> Tek it more sweet.

Believe mi, A tell yu
Becau slackness done,
An mi no waan none
Slackness hafi done,
Cau mi no waan none.

The 'rubbish heap' image is an accurate representation of how *nice an decent people* [14] in Jamaica view DJ Slackness. The *Daily Gleaner* of Friday, 13 January 1989 dedicated its page 9 'Letters to the Editor' column to six letters with the following headlines: '"Respect due" to reggae music'; 'Unprofessionalism in local music'; 'Stop, stop, now!'; 'No!, no! to slackness'; 'To spurn indecency'; 'Stance against slackness'. The letter from the Chief Executive Director of King of Kings Promotions, who claims to have 'suffered greatly' as a 'consciousness' promoter 'because the public has gotten so used to reading and hearing about the antics of the slackness merchants', (antics/monkey/jungle/Africa/savage), characterises the offending DJs as 'gutter louts'. The event which precipitated this public outcry was the Sting '88 stage show, attended by an audience of over 25 000, some of whom, apparently anxious to have the DJs Flourgon and Ninja Man come on stage, pelted off two 'singers'.

The singer/DJ tension seems rooted in a basic contradiction between the generally sentimental lyrics of the singers and the more earthy particulars of the DJs. Several of the songs in the sample exploit the disparity between the two sensibilities. African–American hip-hop, which has clear affinities with DJing, articulates a similar disengagement from the rhetoric of R & B. In an *Essence* magazine article, Harry Allen characterises hip-hop thus:

> It exhibits none of the creative listlessness with which much of R & B is currently burdened. Nor does it have the hands-off, gloves-on reverence with which jazz often finds itself draped. Rather than pretending to bourgeois standards of style, or attempting musically to evoke a time dead and gone, as many jazz and R & B artists are wont to do, rappers instead sling the rawest, most realistic insights at your ear. Deejays take your favorite records, cut 'em up, mix 'em around and serve 'em to you on a record platter. Meanwhile their crowds move and shake their bodies in ways that Grandmother once said would definitely get you pregnant or arrested. It all comes together in a whole: funky. Youknowhumsayin?[15]

With this frame of reference, it is not surprising to note that Josey Wales offers the sweet, smooth 'life is pretty' line as the alternative to Slackness on the rubbish heap: 'Come my man, tell yu, leave aaf di street/ Talk about some lovin an huggin mi frien(d)/Dis Slackness business comin to a en(d)'. Conversely, Admiral Bailey's 'Waini-Waini' energetically denounces 'huggin up':

> Mi se huggin up is agains di law
> Hi bwoy!
> Wi doan dance like dat anymore
> Mama!
> If yu cyaan do di waini-waini dance
> Hi bwoy!
> Step aside an gi di bubbler a chance.

Waini-waini is to hugging up as DJing is to singing: the bottom versus the top end of the market. Indeed, when Ninja Man and Flourgon came on stage at the infamous Sting stage show the bottom dropped out of the market.

In his impassioned report of the event in the *Daily Gleaner* of Friday, 30 December 1988, page 6, Howard McGowan, the Entertainment columnist, after decrying the 'stoning' of the two singers, though conceding that one of them was 'just not up to standard singing so badly off key that the deaf would have had a problem', proceeds to savage the DJs:

> But perhaps the single most distasteful situation came during the clash of male DJs when the worst squalor was presented on stage for lyrics by Ninja Man and Flourgon, ironically two of the leading candidates for the DJ of the Year title, something I will address at another time.
>
> So vulgar was this section that the plug was rightly pulled on them saving the ears of the people from the assault on their decency launched by these individuals.

Presumably not all members of the audience were equally grateful for having their ears saved from the 'assault'; but the fine distinction drawn between 'the people' and 'these individuals' reinforces the alienation of the scapegoated DJs from the common fold of humanity. In his 'On the Record' column in the *Sunday Gleaner* of 1 January 1989, page 5, McGowan, in his promised elaboration on the problem of indecent lyrics, proposes a sweeping solution:

> Against this background ON THE RECORD will not be selecting a male or female DJ of the year this year and I have had verbal support from the programmes managers of both RJR and JBC. Further, I have been given the assurance that when the JAMI Nomination Committee meets this week, this body could also consider dropping these categories this year. Rockers say they are

> willing to go along with the moral majority who spurn indecency, and will therefore not support any DJ awards.

The headline of the piece, 'Time for a stand against "dirty lyrics"', is deliciously suggestive to the dirty-minded deconstructionist, especially when compounded with the following question: 'Why, you may ask, the sudden decision to come down so hard on "dirty lyrics"' . . .? The traitorous signifier at play: *vive la différance*! Harry Allen objects to the fact that

> White music critics and cultural historians are talking about hip-hop and find themselves tossing long, funny words into the air to describe it. Words like *deconstruction, appropriation, iconography* and *recontextualization.* But those words have little to do with the way African-American people live or make music, and hip-hop is no more or less than Black life on black vinyl. Whatever one finds in the community, they'll find in the records. This has a lot to do with why it's so attractive to some people and repulsive to others.[16]

Ethnophallogocentricity!

'Culture a Lick', also by Josey Wales, suggests more ironic possibilities than the straightforward 'Slackness Done'. Iconography is appropriated, deconstructed and recontextualised. In the opening frame, personified Slackness is addressed in terms that evoke a judge handing down a prison sentence. But the 'punishment' is a highly-valued commodity – an exit visa: 'Now Slackness, I am givin you a indefinite multiple to leave Jamaica.' Many Jamaicans routinely sweat for a visa, as illustrated in Edward Baugh's wicked 'Nigger Sweat'. Edward Baugh is not a DJ;[17] but the spirit (and language) of his poem is that of peasant revolt against the magisterial dismissiveness of foreign embassies. The epigraph to 'Nigger Sweat' is drily ironic:

> Please have your passport and all documents out and
> ready for your interview. Kindly keep them dry.
> (Notice in the waiting-room of the U.S. Embassy,
> Visa Section, Kingston, Jamaica, 1982.)[18]

Slackness's multiple entry visa allows easy access in and out; it means temporary displacement, not total banishment. And in any case, since the DJs sing of their vaunted successes in Miami, Toronto and London (for they too have multiple entry visas), it is only Jamaica that will suffer the loss of Slackness.

The DJ's signalled intention in the first verse of 'Culture a Lick' seems honourable despite the fact that it is an implied Other, not the Colonel himself, who now castigates the slack DJ:

> O! Tell dem DJ dis
> Tell dem fi stop all di Slackness
> Slackness business big ina Jamaica
> Spoil di youtman an granfader
> All di yout dem a criticize di daughter
> Mus remember wi comin from a modder

But the chorus has multiple resonances that invert the dominant/sub-dominant relationship of Culture to Slackness: 'Slackness in di backyard hidin, hidin, hidin/ Slackness in di backyard hidin, hidin from Culture'. The repetition of 'hidin' suggests dalliance, Slackness seductively lay *waitin* Culture; but conversely, it also suggests the cowering posture of threatened victim, not predatory villain: Culture, the Senex, the respectable dirty old man, in pursuit of youthful, female Slackness; or Slackness, the Don Juan, entrapping virginal, female Culture. Further, in melody and parallelism of form, this chorus is identical to a Revival song, 'Adam in di garden hidin, hidin, hidin/ Adam in di garden hidin, hide imself from God', and also to a children's ring game, 'Bread in di oven bakin, bakin, bakin/ Bread in di oven bakin, bakin til a mornin.'

The ring game seems to encode rituals of sexual initiation, for the bread baking in the oven becomes in the second verse a sleeping little sister who must be shaken, and then awakened in the third verse. The *OED* cites a 1753 slang usage of 'bread-basket' as the stomach. Rising bread is thus an analogue of pregnancy, as in African–American folk speech – 'she's got a bun in the oven' – and contemporary British slang usage. Adam, soon to be cast into the backyard, is hiding in the garden because he knows that he is naked. And although he has no bread to rise – unlike Eve who has seduced him into slackness and is edited out of the text – his goose is definitely cooked. The fall from grace is supremely tragic for Adam, but absurdly comic to Eve. For she's the fall guy in the routine and doesn't even blame Adam. Walter Redfern, in his 'Introduction' to *Puns,* cites Baudelaire on 'the comic sense engendered by the Fall of Man [that] must be exploited in the fight-back towards wholeness. The artist, he said . . . "is an artist only so long as he is double and faces up to all the implications of his double nature."'[19] Similarly, Herbert Marcuse in *Eros and Civilization* summarises the existential dilemma in Freudian terms:

> The categories in which philosophy has comprehended the human existence have retained the connection between reason and suppression: whatever belongs to the sphere of sensuousness, pleasure, impulse has the connotation of being antagonistic to reason –

> something that has to be subjugated, constrained. Everyday language has preserved this evaluation: the words which apply to this sphere carry the sound of the sermon or of obscenity.[20]

Henry Louis Gates Jr's signifying monkey, which is clearly related to that other trickster Anansi, provides a West African model of 'wholeness' that transcends the polarities (en)gendered in Western cultures:

> Esu is figured as paired male and female statues, which his/her devotees carry while dancing, or as one bisexual figure. Often she holds her breasts in the female figures. Even Esu's sexuality is indeterminate, if unsatiable.[21]

Gates thus privileges Esu as hermeneutic icon, the ambivalent signifier of non-sexist critical discourse:

> Metaphysically and hermeneutically, at least, Fon and Yoruba discourse is truly genderless, offering feminist literary critics a unique opportunity to examine a field of texts, a discursive universe, that escaped the trap of sexism inherent in Western discourse. This is not to attempt to argue that African men and women are not sexist, but to argue that the Yoruba discursive and hermeneutical universes are not. The Fon and the Yoruba escape the Western version of discursive sexism through the action of doubling the double; the number 4 and its multiples are sacred in Yoruba metaphysics. Esu's two sides 'disclose a hidden wholeness'; rather than closing off unity, through the opposition, they signify the passage from one to the other as sections of a subsumed whole. Esu stands as the sign of this wholeness.[22]

These far-reaching correspondences make it clear that the Culture/Slackness antinomy extends beyond the domain of the half-heartedly suppressed 'vulgarity' of the DJ. Its culturally specific manifestations in Jamaica suggest not only the continuity of West African ideological traditions in the diaspora, but also the conflict between those traditions and the official Christian morality of the Garden of Eden in which both the suppression of sexuality and the secondariness of woman are institutionalised: Adam (and Eve) hiding from God; versus Esu as the gateway to God.

Chaka Demus's 'Back Out' is the most clearly subversive of the three songs in the Culture/Slackness grouping. It is Slackness pure and simple masquerading as Culture:

> *Now all slack it DJ, A waan unu fi run, yu know, cau Culture come fi mek unu run like unu hear news. Now hear dis. Heh, heh, heh! It name*

Some man a talk bout dem waan punaani,
Some man a talk bout dem waan puninash,
Some man a talk bout punaani too sweet,
Dem mosi lick it wid dem tongue,
Dem mosi bite it wid dem teet
Is ow dem get fi know
Se dat punaani too sweet.
Mi se unu fi back out,
Unu fi back out
All Slackness DJ,
Mi se unu fi back out.

The playful lingering over the juicy details of 'punaani' and 'puninash' suggests that the DJ speaks with a forked tongue. Further, the covert reference to homosexuality – backing out as inverted withdrawal – and again:

Becau Culture come fus
An Slackness come las
Bwoy, ass is ass
And class is class.
Come lisn Chaka Demus
Ina A1 class
Wen mi siddown pon di ridim,
Rasta know mi a di boss

intimates that there are hierarchies of slackness: heterosexuality, however indulgent its excesses, is infinitely superior to its homosexual variant. Heterosexuality is culture and class; homosexuality is slackness and ass.

In the cluster of songs that focus on sexual/gender relations, there is a small subgroup in which the homophobic thrust of Jamaican style machismo is evident in derogatory references to homosexuality and cross-dressing. In Jamaica, cross-dressing is a clear sign of other crosses: taking sleep to mark death. For example, Shabba Ranks's defensively mocking line in 'Get Up, Stan(d) Up': 'Man ina pants an shirt, no man no hitch up inna frock' ('hitch up' implying a posture of embarrassment); and much more extensively in Lovindeer's 'Mad Puss Tonic' and 'Bump Up'. The latter, wallowing in the messy details of anal intercourse, protests (perhaps too much) against the double standard of Howard McGowan's 'moral majority', who manifest no public outrage at a homosexual beauty contest, but lambast the DJ for publicly displaying his fetishistic trademark, a spectacularly oversize red panty almost as wide as Lovindeer is tall: a clear parody of cross-dressing and a simultaneous glorification of what the garment withholds. Note the balancing of 'up' and 'down' in the first two lines, and the mischievous understatement of line 6:

Now mi did hol up a panty on TV
An half a Jamaica come down pon mi
De write letter to newspaper daily
De call radio an complain bout mi
Se mi corruptin di youts of di country
An all because of a red panty.
Now dese same people se nutin to di press
About dis dyam batty man contes.
De will fin(d) demselves in a hell ev a mess
If dem support dis kin(d) of slackness.

Alliteration bears the full weight of the DJ's contempt: 'Ladies and Gentlemen! The Winner of the Mr Gay Mobay is that bouncing batty bwoy from backso, bumpy batty Bombo!' Lovindeer makes no apology for any offence that his scurrilous lyrics may incite. In 'Mad Puss Tonic', which also reports at second hand, of course, on the contest, he simply declares that clean ends justify dirty means: '*Yu know se my lyrics dem lick hot. Mi a go step pon nuff man corn, but mi no business. Nasty business call fi nasty lyrics.*' In an ironic reversal of roles, the DJ becomes the lone prophetic voice in a wilderness of moral woe, crying out against defaulting homosexuals who let the side down, and to neglected women whom the DJ himself is chivalrously moved to service:

Come! Some girls will have to wait in line
Bow! Cause a real man is so hard to fin(d)
(Like me)
Everyday I tell them doan ben(d) down
But they doan listen to my soun(d)
I sing an preach to them a lot
They doan remember they forgot, forgot, forgot.[23]

The sweetly sentimental melody and unsyncopated rhythm of the ironically detached verses that describe, in English, the homosexual happening are counterpointed with the characteristic DJ styling of those verses in Jamaican that deride it:

Some will say that it is their right
To do whatever they like
But if we really should let them
How do we explain it to the children
When they enquire innocently
'Why is that man wearing a brassiere and a panty?'
Come! Mi se, no put it on,
Doan put it on
. . .

Im offer yu di panty
Doan put it on
Brassiere an di dress
Doan put it on
Di wig an di perfume
Doan put it on
High heel shoes
Doan put it on

Peter Tosh, in a 1984 *Pulse* interview, criticising the management of local radio stations for the high percentage of foreign music aired in comparison to reggae, makes a revealing connection between the imported 'huggin up' lyrics of popular R & B love songs and male cross-dressing:

> I hear one, two, three, four, five already pon the charts is foreign music. And even if it was even fifty per cent foreign, is still too much. If it was even twenty-five. Me go to America and certain places out there man, fe months you wait fe hear all one reggae, and when them play is like them sorry fe you. Ina my country me haffi a bow fe hear dem foolishness when we hear fe so long? Me hear them things too much and them not saying nothing more than 'Darling I love you. I swim the ocean and climb the mountains!' Madness! Ah them things make Merican man wear pantie.'[24]

This kind of sentiment that decries the conventions of both heterosexual 'romance' and sexual 'deviance' as non-indigenous, seems to illuminate not only Lovindeer's parodic strategies in 'Mad Puss Tonic', but also the ironic framing devices used in several of the songs in the sample that satirise the aberrant 'madness' of romantic love. For example, Professor Grizzy and Little Lenny join forces in the combination Sing-J style to caution men against brutalising women. But the ironic disparity between the two modes – the ethereal sentimentality of the R & B song and the violent specifics of the DJ's lyrics – seems to make a mockery of the entire enterprise:

> *Now yu, doan brutalize your girl dem way de man! Yu must treat ar good. Now step up!*
> I'll be your guidin star
> My darlin cross my (h)eart
> I'll never leave you in the dark
> Oh, oh, and I'll be your light
> On top of the hill
> Love you little darlin, I will never leave you
> I'll stay.
> . . .
> Treat yu lover bad, treat yu lover bad.

Bad, bad, bad, bad, bad, bad
Yu no fi treat yu lover bad
Doan beat ar wid no stick
Doan brutalize ar wid no kick
Shi is someone to ave an to (h)old
Doan kick ar like no ball in no goal
Whisper in my ear then I ear you tell the world
Let me tell you darlin,
You just got to be the lady of my life
Come follow mi now!
So doan give ar no cut
Doan give ar no gun butt.

There is also the unfortunate hesitation – 'Treat yu lover bad' – which does not make it immediately clear that it is the *not* treating bad of the lover that is being affirmed.

'Heartbreaker', by Lady Junie and Tristan Palmer, employs a similar technique of inversion, but here the woman, having once fallen for the smooth lines of the con-man singer, is now immunised and offers consolation to similarly-seduced women. Lady Junie relates a cautionary tale of distress, within which is embedded an ironic love song. The pattern is repeated in the parable of Devon and Sharon:

Mi a go tell yu bout dis con man we dem call Devon
Bout dis sexy chick an wa dem call Miss Sharon.
Tell ar ow much im ave cyar, (h)ouse an lan
When shi check im out, yes, im doan own a dyam
Im se:
'Honey, honey, girl I really, really, really, really love you.
Honey, honey, I wana take care of you
We've been kissin an touchin
An burnin t(h)rough an t(h)rough
Kissin an touchin really turns you on
Let me make love to you' (*rep.*)
Ear ar now, ear ar now, ear ar now:
'No bodder mek love to mi, no mek love to mi
No mek love to mi, an yu no mean i. (*rep.*)
Cause if yu waan fi lef mi, mi se set mi free
No ask mi fi stay an den mi live in misery.
After all ina mi face it naa grow no tree'

But the potential for irony is not fully developed. Lady Junie's practical advice on basic survival strategies – 'So don't yu go mad, no bodder go crazy/Anodder ting doan cry mek im see'; and 'Go outa street an get anodder smadi' – also reinforces patterns of economic dependency: 'Mek sure yu get one we ave a degree/Im gi yu nuf money mek yu feel irie.'

In Sugar Minott and Lady G's 'Whole Heap a Man', Sugar's seductive lines are trivialised by Lady G's derisive interjections:

> Your frien(d)s all say dat you mus(t) dance with me
> (Fi wa Sugar?)
> An darlin, why won't you let it be?
> (It's dat a fac(t)?)

Unmoved by Sugar's sweet talk, Lady G declares her fixed position:

> Mi se mi name is Lady G, an mi no tek brivery (sic)
> From mi a no willin man, so let it be.
> I am a different uman, I doan check fi folly
> Yu no bodder tink yu cyan come an hypmotise (sic) mi.

Her advice to other women, unlike Lady Junie's somewhat exploitative speculations, affirms a measure of independence:

> Mi a go tell yu di trut(h), mi naa go tell yu no lie
> No bodder follow dem ya man, dem full up a samfie.
> Dem wi bruk yu (h)eart an mek yu cry
> No bodder give dem di chance fi get no more blai.[25]

'No more blai' alludes to a long history of female complicity with male *samfie-ness,* from which Lady G carefully distances herself. But there is also an element of coy seductiveness in her flaunted awareness of her desirability; she asserts the woman's right to choose, even if the confusing multiplicity of options inhibits choice. Her teasing indecision is underscored in the following rhymes:

> Yes, I'm sorry Sugar Minott, I'm not in di mood
> Whole heap a man ina mi life, mi haffi pick an choose.
> So man, doan get mi wrong, doan tink I'm rude
> Too much man ina mi life fi get mi confuse.

Johnny P's 'Gyal Man' and Shelley Thunder's 'Yu Man a Rush Mi' approach the problem of *samfie* men from clearly opposing perspectives. Whereas Johnny P simply blames the duplicitous woman for abducting her friend's innocent man – 'Now dis one dedicated to all di girl dem we a go roun an tek dem frien(d) man. So young girls, if yu waan to know yu frien(d), introduce ar to yu man, an yu wi know if a yu frien(d)' – Shelly Thunder firmly allocates blame to the compliant, and more often actively seductive man. Her song opens to a chorus of taunting male voices: 'Run, gyal, run, di owner fi di man a come!'; which, suggestively, parallels the sentiment and form of Chaka Demus's line, 'Mi se run, Slackness, run, an mi se Culture it a come!' The fleeing 'outside' woman is Slackness; the 'owner' is Culture; the man is commodified: The rigid, proprietorial respectability of marriage versus the looseness of more fluid sexual arrangements. But Shelly's retort puts both legal and extra-legal affairs in perspective: 'Well, no girl suppose fi mek a nex girl hafi run. Cau if it wasn fi your man, yu wouldn get burn!' Seeming to subversively contest the otherness of the 'other woman', she narrates a tale that indigenises the eternal female rivalries replayed in the dilatory drama of the soap opera:

> Hear dis ya drama:
> Ina mi (h)ouse mi, an mi son an mi daughter
> Was two o'clock so mi a watch soap opera
> Telephone ring an it mi go answer
> Pon di odder en a gyal a scream an a oller
> 'Mek mi chat to di gyal Shelly Thunder!'
> I said, 'Who is this?'
> Shi se, 'Tell ar Sandra'.
> I said, 'Could you tell me in reference to what?'
> Shi se, 'Shi de wid mi baby fader!
> Ow yu mean if a wa?
> In im telephone book mi fin(d) ar phone number'.
> I said, 'This is Shelly. Who is yu baby fader?'
> Shi se, 'Yu de wid a man we name Peter
> Im no really want yu, a t(h)rough yu a entertainer.
> Im love mi bad, bad, bad, mi im a mad over
> Im jus buy mi a (h)ouse an a criss Mazda.
> Im se a business, but im a no Producer
> A gwine bruk up yu – if yu no lef mi lover!'
> A se, 'Dibi-dibi gyal, ear ow yu vulgar!
> Come aaf a mi phone, an mek mi prosper.
> Becau yu man a rush mi, yu man a rush mi
> Yu man a rush mi, so yu cyaan blame Shelly.'

This is no simple sisterly solidarity against delinquent males. There is a smug superiority and malicious wit in Shelley's contempt for her self-deluding rival. (Note the distancing English initially assumed by the aggrieved Shelly to put the 'dibi-dibi gyal' in her place; in the open hostility of the verbal battle the Thunder grandly descends to Jamaican). Her description of the physical deficiencies of yet another 'unfeminine', would-be competitor is full of disdain: 'Her foot dem tough like shi did a dig yam/Her muscle dem huge, look big an (s)trong/Like shi use to fling hog pon truck a Portland.' For the female DJ, as much as for the male, sexual prowess is an essential element of the kudos of the entertainer. But female sexuality is imaged in terms of the male gaze:[26] 'A bwoy stop mi an start a conversation/ Im se mi look nice ave a sexy bottom/Im get goose bump when im see mi ina session.' Shelly Thunder's female *persona* is clearly a voiced subjectivity, despite being the object of the male gaze. She approvingly views herself in the flattering light of that gaze while simultaneously voicing her independence of male scrutiny: she reserves the right to choose.

In Johnny P's 'Gyal Man,' a man is perceived as just one of a number of valuable possessions that successful women display as signs of prosperity. He is a kind of essential accessory for the fashionable woman, somewhat like a handbag[27]:

> Yu mus always ave fi yu own man
> No mek nobody come a fight up fi no man
> Come a talk bout yu a tek fi dem man.
> Yu jus hol up yu han, gyal, a no one frock yu ave!
> Jump up, gyal, yu no ave no one frock!
> Lif up yu foot, gyal, yu no ave no one shoes!
> Hol up yu head, yu no ave one hairstyle!

An instructive sub-text of Johnny P's song is his respect for the upward social mobility of enterprising women like those cunning characters celebrated by Louise Bennett – ex-domestic servants, perhaps turned higglers, who have ambitiously extricated themselves from traditional drudgery: 'Hol up yu head, cau yu naa scour people pot/Hol up yu head cau yu ave ambition/Jump about cau yu full of protential (sic).' These women's attention to matters of personal hygiene is one of the social graces that is particularly appreciated in the intimacy of the dance:

> Hol up yu han cause yu arm smell good.
> Jump up, gyal, yu no frowsy, jump up!
> Bounce a gyal we a frowsy!
> Hol up ar han an scent start come up
> Dem de gyal de, yu know yu cyaan stomach.
> Dem de gyal, dem no bathe, dem wipe up
> An come a dancehall, an dem a jump up
> An dem a wain up, and dem sweat up
> An den di frowsy scent it start come up

The dancehall is the social space in which the smell of female power is exuded in the extravagant display of flashy jewellery, expensive clothes, elaborate hairstyles and rigidly attendant men that altogether represent substantial wealth. In the words of Higgs and Twins's 'Jump Up Time':

Lovers hand in hand, single man an uman
Pretty pretty hairdo, nuff style an fashion
Mini skirt, belly skin girls a champion
Di French cut acid dem a se one.
Dem a bounce, spread out an shake bottom
Di man dem stan up at attention.
Tcho! Six to six an di dance still ram
Five nights a week, everybody a jam.

Inevitably, in a culture of multiple possessions, some women will have more than one man. So there are songs of female inconstancy. Ninja Man's 'Tell Me' employs in part the wistful melody and somewhat modified lyrics of a folk song, 'Liza Gyal', to sing about lost love and, simultaneously, his skill 'roun di microphone':

Everytime mi member fi mi gyal frien(d) Adina
Water come a mi eye
Becau mi love ar to mi (h)eart and mi love ar to mi soul
Mi love ar to mi min(d) an dat, a dat mi control
Roun di microphone mi come fi rackle yu soul
An dis is wat mi givin to di young an di ol
Mi waan yu tell mi, tell mi, tell mi gyal, tell mi
Tell mi why yu love mi an leave mi
Run gone wid di dyam glibiti, glamiti?

The answer could be that provided in Shabba Ranks's 'Cyaan do Di Wuk':

Some man cyan only give yu collaterals
But where di international work is concern
Tcho! Sof soap dat.[28]
Ear mi now girls!
Yu jus jump aroun if yu man cyan wuk
Oller out if yu man cyan wuk
Wain up yu body if yu cyan tek di wuk
Some man a let aaf di money
An dem cyaan do di wuk.

This ability to 'do di wuk' and 'tek di wuk', which separates the men from the boys and the girls from the women, is the heart of Slackness. And it is the sexuality of women, much more so than that of men, which is both celebrated and devalued in the culture of the dancehall. The songs in the sample that are simply about *wainin* often appeal exclusively to women for approval, using the yardstick of their response as the measure of the song's success. For example, Shabba Ranks's 'Get Up, Stan(d) Up': 'I'm not goin to a circus, I'm not goin to a fair/If is di stage show or di dancehall Shabba Rankin will be dere/Tcho! Time for lyrics di girls waan to hear.' Women's enjoyment of sexual and economic independence, as demonstrated in their uninhibited solo *wainin* on the dance floor, is most clearly illustrated in Flourgon's 'Fret an Worry'. The DJ, unintimidated by the women's show of strength, is absolutely confident of his own abilities. He is therefore in a favourable position from which to mock his less fortunate rivals:

> Some a fret an worry, dem a fret an worry
> Se dem a mad over di girl dem body
> All dem a spen, mi se dem cyaan get i
> Cau di girls dem nowadays a dem no liki-liki.
> Some a fret an worry, dem a fret an worry
> Becau dem cyaan get di girls dem body
> Sexy body Pam an di one Audrey
> Look ow dem a shock out in di party!
> Mi se some a dem slim, an some a dem fat
> Look ow di girls dem sexy an trash!
> None a dem no live pon no yeye top
> So yu gwaan blink none a dem naa go drop.

The erotic wink has been devalued by the women's superior currency – their own. So they can afford to brazenly out-gaze the aspiring man and put him firmly in his place:

> 'Wi cyaan come a dance come beg nobody
> An wi naa come a dance come fa nobody
> So who waan chat, an mi se, mek dem chat chat
> All dem a chat, Lawd wi still hot
> Mek dem gwaan quint, wi naa drop
> None a wi no live pon no eye top.
> Cau, ina mi ouse, it haffi trash
> Cau mi colour TV mi siddown an watch
> Ina one corner yu fin(d) mi wat-not
> An mi figurine dem mi cock up on dat
> Mi se two lickle hen an one big cock
> Pon di wall a di granfader clock.
> Easy Flourgon, dem know se yu hot
> Entime yu come a dance it haffi block'.

The 'mi cock up' *double-entendre* is wickedly accurate: women made doubly cocky by economic independence, assuming traditionally male privileges of selection, while retaining the conventional woman's right to pick and choose. If we attribute the ambiguous last two lines above not to the self-validating DJ, but to the women, then it seems that they themselves accept that their only match is the DJ, whose sexual/lyrical prowess is imaged in the tableau on the what-not.

Lovindeer's 'No Pussy Tes(t)', excellent feminist polemics, asserts the woman's right to sexual pleasure as an essential constituent of total health. The song starts off as simple Slackness, but gradually develops into a critique of the Public Service and health care systems in Jamaica:

> Patsy complainin day an night
> Se her pussy doan ha no appetite
> Shi use to be so lively an fat
> Now shi is jus a lickle mawga cyat.
> Well, personally, mi love di lickle pet
> So mi tell Patsy fi tek ar to di vet.

The doctor's preliminary investigation raises a number of questions, one of which is about health insurance. Satisfied that the puss is covered, he proceeds with the examination. But before he can 'look into' the problem fully the lights go out. In a frustrated orgiastic scene the puss eludes the gaze, to the distress of the owner, the doctor and the DJ:

> Di doctor se, 'Lady I'm sorry to say
> Yu have to come back anodder day.
> Doan blame mi, blame JPS
> Dem lock off di light, so no pussy tes(t)'.

The song also subversively suggests that the pets of the middle-class are likely to have access to much better health care than the vast majority of poor people in Jamaica who have no 'health insurance', and are forced to depend on the vagaries of the notoriously inadequate clinic system.

Age is no barrier to sexual pleasure for women. 'Granny Two-Teet', also by Lovindeer, is a witty tale of callow Youth versus cunning Experience:

> Mi know a young man dem call Don Juan
> Cau when it come to love im a di champion.
> Im check every uman, im no partial
> Im love ol foot, an im love young gyal.
> Now las week-en im go check Beverly
> Who live a Shortwood wid ar two-teet granny.
> Im drink off a whole quart bottle of sherry
> An lickle after dat im get tipsy.
> Im se, 'Roses are red and violets are blue,
> A gwine mek love to di both a yu.'

Beverly se, 'Du wat yu want wid mi
But please doan trouble mi two-teet granny.
Shi ol an feeble an very sickly
So don't yu come come hackle ar body.
Shi ave only two teet in ar mout
Too much hacklin a go mek dem drop out'.
Granny jump up se, 'Hush yu mout
Yu doan know wat yu talkin about.
Di man se di two a wi mus get it.
Come out a mi love life, doan romp wid it.
Come Don Juan, no pay ar no min(d)
Come mek mi show yu se Granny cyan wain.
Nowadays gyal only have so-so mout
Mi experience, de cyaan get mi out.
Mi got mi two teet, mi two teet, mi two teet (*rep.*)
Mi temperature jus start to rise
Come mek mi show yu mi panty size.
I know yu will be surprise to see
Mi still ave my glamity.
By the way, one question:
Yu is a Shortwood man?
A doan want yu go de an feel too shame
Cause I like di man dem from Long Lane'.

Granny, having risen to the counter-challenge of the omnivorous Don Juan:

'It seems to mii
Yu tek your lovin seriously
Well I gwine love yu tender an hot
For any amount of teet dat yu got.'

is prepared to do whatever is necessary to prolong sexual pleasure:

Don se, 'Cool off, yu too hot!
Yu figet se a only two teet yu got?
So done mi done, an mi ready to go'.
Granny se, 'Wait! Yu cyaan leave so!
Don Juan mi bwoi, yu mek love sweet,
Hol(d) on lickle mek mi fin(d) more teet.
Mi got two lickle one down in mi jaw corner,
Dentures in mi bureau top drawer
An if yu waan fi come back tomorrow
Mi cousin ave teet mi cyan borrow.
Teet we mi tief from Sister Mary

Teet we mi ugly fader dead lef mi
Teet we drop out from mi was a baby
Teet we mi tump outa mash mout Daisy
Teet we mi Aunty sen from foreign
Teet we mi get from mi dentist bredrin.'

Don Juan's anxiety about Granny's voracious sexuality (all those teeth!), has its counterpart in the DJ's comical distress, recorded in 'Panty Man', after his inadequate confrontation with Miss Fatty, 'a big panty gyal'. He sheepishly confesses: 'water come a mi eyes'; coming at an obviously inappropriate point:

Mi know a big panty gyal dem call Miss Fatty
An long a long time di gyal after mi.
But, t(h)rough mi know my limitation
Bow! Mi no tek on no big panty gyal.
Now one night, mi no know wa get ina mi
Bow! Ow mi decide fi check Miss Fatty.
Shi fling up a piece a wain under mi
Di gyal rackle every bone ina mi body.
Well! Shi will always be mi good frien(d)
But! Intimately? Never again.

Size, size, I have to look mi size
Shi hackle mi body til water come a mi eyes
If de had a competition
Yu would win di prize
For di girl wid di biggest panty size.

The melody of the 'size' coda, with its hymn-like resonance, underscores the wit of the irreverent lyrics. Miss Fatty's rackling, cutting rather close to the bone, ruffles the cock's feathers. The DJ's hackles are raised in self-defence. What is truly delightful about Lovindeer's wicked compositions is the variable male/female point of view which he assumes. His songs cannot be reduced to simple gynaephobia. For even when he appears to be deriding aggressive female sexuality he simultaneously affirms its compelling potency: 'mi no know wa get ina mi'. The man, out of his depth, may fear that the supernatural has been invoked to overwhelm him. But there is also a sense of conquest in having tested his limitations and surviving to tell the tale.

Women who enjoy the humour and innocuous slackness of songs such as these – and their less subtle variants – are subject to censure under the terms of the prevailing double standard. Thus, Mr McGowan, again:

> Let us not fool ourselves, however (sic) the fault is not entirely that of the DJs but it lies with a certain section of our society. If females can dance and shout when men stand on stage and give details of sexual exploits with women, then something is very wrong.[29]

And a censorial male letter-writer to the *Daily Gleaner* of Friday, 13 January 1989, page 9, on the subject of the Sting stage show:

> A good show, until two DJs . . . displayed their vulgarity, and certain females, if I must call them so, jumped and shouted to their delight to hear certain sections of their body being described most disgracefully. The DJs were urged on by these women who had on the most outrageous outfits that can ever be worn on the face of this earth. Something is definitely wrong. Could it be illiteracy or stupidity?

Explicit in that final question is the slackness/illiteracy equation. A similarly denunciatory letter to the *Daily Gleaner* from a young woman inadvertently highlights the contradictions of these simplistic moral generalisations: 'The women who dance to this filth do not know better and need to be taught. Many of these women go to church and put on their choir robes and sing Christian hymns.'[30] In the conservative discourse of fundamentalist ideology, Slackness is thus feminised and censured. Undomesticated female sexuality – erotic maroonage – must be repudiated: it has the smell of prostitution.

Lovindeer's complex 'Doan Mess Wid My Pum-Pum' is an excellent example of a feminist-sounding song about women's sexual independence, that seems to quickly degenerate into the old-fashioned rhetoric that tries to keep women in their subservient place as sex objects, available at a fixed market price:

> Well I've been out of crotch now for a long, long time
> So I take an ol frien(d) for a little grin(d).
> Shi said, 'I can help yu if yu want to come
> But yu, yu gotta pay mi, freeness days are done.
> Strictly cash I deal with, I doan trus(t) no man
> They are only out to get everything they can.'
> The price that shi told mi was very high
> I said, 'I only wanna rent it, I doan wanna buy.'

But the loaded 'trus(t)' – 'I doan trus(t) no man' – with its divergent commercial and emotional resonances puts the woman's dilemma clearly into focus. The song is much more than just a mocking deflation of the woman's value/price. It is a disturbing comment on the grim economic conditions in Jamaica that force some women of all social classes to commodify their sexuality: 'Shi se "I'm a working girl, I doan have a lot/ Pum-pum is the only thing of value that I got."' And the price of the commodity has to continually escalate to keep up with the rising cost of living. Note the brisk rhythm of the repeated third line, with its sequence of stressed syllables, that enacts the upward march of prices. Sexuality becomes a taxing issue:

> Mi check a lickle daughter fi buy a lickle jook
> Shi tell mi se mi money cyan only buy a look.
> Mi se pum-pum price gone up
> Tell yu se di pum-pum price gone up.
> An mi se tings an times dem a get so tight
> Up-town girls haffi work at night
> Workin to survive
> Tell yu se di pum-pum a keep dem alive.
> De taxin dis an de taxin dat
> De taxin every lickle ting dat wi got
> Jook dem wid di pum-pum tax
> Im soon jook dem wid di pum-pum tax.
> Yu doan have to pay if yu give it free
> But if yu use it commercially
> Get ready fi di pum-pum tax. (*rep.*)
> Except at certain time a di month
> Pum-pum taxes pay up front
> Batty man haffi pay back tax. (*rep.*)

There's the inevitable stab at the homosexual who is doubly taxed. Menstruation, as universal taboo, turns the woman's natural bodily functions inside out and back to front. 'At certain time a di month' woman becomes devaginated, a symbolic batty man, facilitating the 'straight' man's working out of homophobic anxieties. Widened beyond the immediate context of prostitution, the taxing jook becomes a provocative metaphor for Government's rapacious desire to muscle in on all forms of small-scale economic activity in the 'non-formal' sector: Bureaucratic Culture seeking to control enterprising Slackness.

There *are* a few songs in the sample in which the commodification of women's sexuality by men assumes truly vulgar proportions: Yellowman's 'Waan Mi Virgin' and 'Titty Jump'. Gilroy identifies Yellowman as the clearest example of the 'decline of radical reggae':[31]

> After two explicitly political sides chronicling the rise of authoritarian statism in Jamaica – 'Soldier Take Over' and 'Operation

> Eradication' (the latter a particularly effective version of The Itals' heavy 'Ina Disya Time' rhythm), he opted for the safety of nursery rhymes, animal noises and anti-woman jive talk.[32]

'Titty Jump' is the kind of song that draws down the wrath of the righteous and the disdain of the feminist alike. Woman is reduced to a collection of body parts which seem to function independent of her will. This is the crucial difference between 'Titty Jump' and, for example, Johnny P's 'Wain an Push Iin'. In the latter, the woman is a whole being actively enjoying her own sexuality. In the former, one part of her anatomy is isolated, and despite its jumping, is a passive, abused object of pleasure for a lecherous voyeur:

> Girls, yu cyan do wat di guys do yu know an still be a lady
> Titty jump, titty jump, mek mi see yu titty jump!
> Some gyal titty stiff like elephant trunk
> Some gyal titty stiff like any tree stump
> Some gyal titty jump like any bull frog
> Wen di brassiere come aaf it favour tread bag.

The tread/money-bag image (which includes the transferred meaning of bag as udder), is particularly deflating. Women's sexuality is negatively imaged in terms of the market place. The fact that women, and not only higglers, sometimes secrete money in their bosom (a complex symbol of private space where women exercise absolute control of material and sexual resources) is demeaningly extended as the ultimate comic image of woman reduced to undignified, bare essentials. Economic power is the antithesis of sexual power: the money-bag is no substitute for the real flesh and blood thing. But the fractured first line of the song can be read ironically: 'Girls, yu cyan do wat di guys do yu know' – go through the motions, 'an still be a lady' – remain untouched. The 'sexual liberation' of woman, her commodification for the pleasure of man, is pure pornography[33] in the most literal sense of the word: 'description of life, manners, etc. of prostitutes and their patrons' (*OED*).

'Waan Mi Virgin' is not quite as damning as its inflammatory title would suggest. Indeed, read subversively, the song deconstructs itself. It begins: 'All special request to di cyat name Audrey, an di cyat call Sandra, an di cyat call Jacqueline, an di cyat call Susie, OK?' These 'special' requests, going indiscriminately to the feline posse, cannot by their very inclusivity be deemed special. But, perhaps, this is the essential difference in the way that men and women understand the language of mating. Women assume that 'special' means 'exclusive'; men know that 'special' simply means, well, special. Yellowman states his preference for a virgin and proceeds to describe his meeting with a prospective candidate:

Know a gyal from St Elizabeth.
Ask ar we shi name, an shi name Paulette.
Shi se, 'Mi ave supn we no man never get'.
Mi se, 'Gi mi di virgin, waan di maiden
Gi mi di virgin, waan di virgin
Gi mi di virgin an A gwe tek di maiden
Gi mi di virgin, waan
Mi no waan, mi no waan, we di man dem nyam an lef'.

The elided 'di virgin' in the penultimate line, which syntactically compresses what is wanted and what is not, foregrounds the image of woman as object of conflicting desire. Woman is valued for her fleeting virginity and, simultaneously, for her willingness to give it up. Unlike Lovindeer's engulfing Big Panty Gyal, or his lascivious Granny Two-Teet who, Anansi-like, bares her many hidden teeth only when she has securely grabbed a piece of the action, Yellowman's sought-after Virgin is innocently non-threatening.[34] Paulette, herself, in her unsolicited advertisement, seems to passively accede to the commodification of her sexuality, marketing her alleged virginity as scarce goods which she is hoarding until the right buyer comes along. But in the second cycle of the song when the meeting with Paulette is again described (we assume that it is the same Paulette and not another interchangeable virgin of the same name), a somewhat different scenario unfolds. Self-assertive Paulette not only dismisses Yellowman's desperate suit but declares her unwillingness to give in to the man she 'de wid' until she has been appropriately and lengthily wooed.

Becau meet up a gyal las week Satiday
Mi ask ar we shi name, shi name Paulette.
Mi se if shi love mi, di gyal se, 'Gu we!
Cool Yellowman, mi an yu bredrin de.
But di someting we mi ave, im never get
Di bwoy waan come mek love right away.'

Paulette knows the rituals of romance, and/or is simply holding out for a higher price in a seller's market. What is important is that it is she who calls the shots. The frustrated Yellowman continues on his quest; desire, unlike virginity, is a renewable resource.

But even Yellowman's narrow sexism can be viewed somewhat expansively, especially by feminists who theorise the conjunction of gender, class and race, as a 'small man' revolt against the institutionalisation of working-class female domestic rule and middle/upper-class male dominance in Jamaican society. For as I suggest in the analysis of representations of female sensibility in the poetry of Louise Bennett, disempowered working-class men cannot be simply stigmatised and dismissed as unqualified 'oppressors' of women. Their own oppression by gender-blind classism and notions of matriarchy itself motivates their attempted oppression of women. For example Super Cyat's need to 'control' a number of women both locally and internationally:

Cau mi se dis is di Cyat it
An im a di wil(d) Apache
An every we a we mi go,
An dem a fight over mi.
Ave girl ina yard,
An girl ina broad,
An ina Miami
Ragamuffin Mr Cyat,
Im a di wil(d) Apache.

Cowboys fighting Indians fighting women fighting each other: a chain of disempowerment. The raw sexism of some DJs can thus be seen as an expression of a diminished masculinity seeking to assert itself at the most basic, and often the only level where it is allowed free play.

Further, the relatively low status of the DJ himself in the mercurial business of record production that is ultimately controlled by the monied producer (as in *The Harder They Come*), can account in part for much of the self-aggrandising bravado displayed in those songs that celebrate DJing. For example, Lecturer makes the extravagant claim, as befits his sobriquet, that he is a pen-and-paper DJ:

Daddy Lecturer one di lyrical tongue
An DJ come, an mi naa go run
Pon di groun mi sit down
Wid mi pen an mi paper
Mi write mi lyrics down.
An mi study it, an ina dancehall
Mi fling it down.

The confrontational, throwing-down-the-gauntlet rhetoric of the DJ, imaged in the flinging-down of lyrics, suggests not only the DJ's aggressive readiness to defend his honour, but also the disposable quality of his throwaway lines.

It is also Lecturer who in 'DJ A Look Fi Mi' attempts to put the female DJ in her proper domestic place – away from the male-dominated dancehall. Women should have no business in the dancehall save as ardent fans. The female DJ should become a sleeping beauty, safely resting at home, awaiting the kiss of Don Gorgon Prince Charming:

'Charmaine, wa mek yu vex
When mi tell yu se "go sleep!"
A woman fi sleep
Fi tek out wrinkle an pleat.'

Vexed Sister Charmaine is clearly not compliant. Lecturer's attempt to lay the female DJ to rest is clearly an impotent male fantasy given the powerful presence of women in the dancehall as active agents – whether as DJs, disdainful, inaccessible sexual beings or as 'fans'. Pinchers' account in 'Ardent Fan' of the eager response of a female autograph-hunter and her admiring friends similarly voices the DJ's desperate need to lionise himself:

So her friends dat stand up,
Dey also did feel di vibe
An upon their faces I saw
The glee an welcome in their eyes.
Dey told mi some come to trill,
But dey ave the confidence
I come to reign.
Cause when I'm in my dancehall style
Is worries, agony an pain.
They're listenin to my voice
An also feelin my melody
Dat also bring a strong belief
Dat I'm a legend to be.

Shabba Ranks's 'No Bodder Dis(respec) Mi' challenges rival DJs to test their skill against his own, recognising that it is the music itself that gives the socially outcast DJ a measure of respectability:

No bodder dis, Mr Sophistic
Soun(d) a soun(d), ol pan a ol pan
Wi no kill champion, wi raise champion
A di music we wi play wi gain recognition
An mi bomb up a dance ina Englan.
If it come to Canada,
Yu know se dat done ram
No bodder dis, doan bodder dis,
I'm tellin yu

Lorna Goodison's 'Jah Music', '(for Michael Cooper)' similarly celebrates the healing power of the underground music that bestows recognition on its creators:

The sound bubbled up

through a cistern one night
and piped its way into
the atmosphere
and decent people wanted
to know
'What kind of ole nayga music is that
playing on the Government's radio?'
But this red and yellow and dark green
sound
stained from travelling underground
smelling of poor people's dinners
from a yard dense as Belgium
has the healing
more than weed and white rum healing
more than bush tea and fever grass cooling
and it pulses without a symphony conductor
all it need is a dub organiser.[35]

Like Shabba's 'No Bodder Dis', 'Min(d) Yu Disrespec Mi' by Gregory Isaacs and Josey Wales confirms the DJs' need for both respect and respectability, the latter a commodity that is often so splendidly devalued and sardonically deferred to in DJ culture. Indeed, this song validates Culture in the old-fashioned, non-elitist sense of the word. It employs biblical injunction – 'Honour yu modder, honour yu fader/ Dat yu days may be longer' – and proverb – 'Wat yu pickin up A put down already/ Young bird doan know storm' – to recall a whole way of life, a vanishing rural past in which a folk culture of ritualistic deference to elders is affirmed in the language of proverbial wisdom.

Of the small group of songs classified as (non-sexual) 'social commentary', Flourgon and Thriller U's 'Peace' is the only one that deals explicitly with political issues. It begins to the accompaniment of simulated gunshots: '*Salute di Peace! Cau yu know se widout peace tings no right.*' Employing the familiar contrast between the sentimental optimism of the love song and the brutal reality of ghetto life, 'Peace' calls judgement on the politicisation of violence in Jamaican society:

Ear dem a talk bout love
Mi no see no lovin a gwan
Ear dem a talk bout peace
Mi no see no peace a gwan.
. . .
Laad, mi se a pure gunshot,
A pure lootin

Ina one corner
A pure screamin
Up di road, Jahman,
A pure people runnin
Everybody runnin
An hear dem shoutin
'Wi want love, Laad',
Everyone screamin
A pure gunshot bad bwoy firin
Ear dem a talk bout love

Similarly illustrating that upright folk piety that can co-exist unselfconsciously with Slackness in the dancehall, Lady G's 'No Bad Mind' conflates two biblical references in its plea to 'all a di people dem fi live right': 'A fool despiseth his father's instruction; but he that regardeth reproof is prudent', Proverbs 15: 5; and 'Thy word is a lamp unto my feet and a light unto my path', Psalm 119, verse 105:

Becau nuf wickedness mi se inna mankind
Some a tek fi dem daughter to be fi dem wife
Some a go outa street an a tek people life.
Come now, lisn dis a lyrics people if yu wise
Commandment is a lamp an a lamp is a light
Reproof of instruction is di way of life
So done away wid hatred, an done away wid strife
An mek wi pray to di Father day an night.

Papa San's 'Watch Mi a Watch Dem', warning against the folly of interfering in other people's business to the detriment of one's own, values the covert wisdom of Anansi:

Yu fi see an blind, yu fi hear an deaf
An no watch people business, a it yu fi lef
An ina fi yu own yu naa put no interes
A fi yu own a spoil t(h)rough yu careless.

He offers a humorous, literal-minded solution to the problem of 'watching':

Becau if yu watch man, Poopa San im ave a plan
Jus open yu ears an understan:
Mi a go put dem ina suit like a military man
Buy dem a baton fi cyarry ina dem han
Mek dem walk wid a alstatian (sic)
So yu a watchman yu fi dress like one.

Clement Irie's 'Hungry No Laugh' makes a serious social statement, employing the dissonant imagery of play: 'See food de! Mi no romp wid it, romp wid i.' Personified hunger is a formidable enemy:

> *Now request to all di people dem who feel hungry an know wat is hungry. Yu no know, a lot of people don't know wat is hungry, man, cau dey don't feel it. Now who feels it, know it. Watch it! Laad a mercy! It name*
> Hungry no laugh, an Hungry no talk, mi frien(d).
> Now ina yu belly bottom Hungry a walk.
> . . .
> Becau Hungry is a ting no respec(t) no body
> Hungry no partial, modder, neither pikni
> So mi sorry for di people who cyan hardly afford it.
> Hungry no romp, Hungry no skin
> Hungry is a ting we mash up yu system.
> Yes, no frien(d) im too much an mek im get too lovin
> Now else im a go tek over yu body system
> Mash up yu organ an yu intestine
> Yes, yu cyannot see Hungry, but yu only feel im.
> Now Hungry mek yu do some very dangerous ting
> Like bruk people (h)ouse, shop an kitchen.

'Hungry No Laugh' is an excellent example of the use of metaphor in Jamaican to embody abstraction. Humourless, uncommunicative *screwface* Hungry assumes the emaciated form of his victims.

Lovindeer's brilliant 'Wil(d) Gilbert' is the classic in this grouping of songs of social commentary, if not in the entire sample. In the opening frame, the hurricane's power – elemental Slackness on a grand scale – is acknowledged in the DJ's caution to address Gilbert only in his absence: '*Well Gilbert, yu gaan! Aha! Now wi cyan chat behin(d) yu back.*' This is the cunning of Anansi who can feign great bravery when it is least likely to be challenged. In the opening verse, Lovindeer evokes the bizarre atmosphere of the hurricane in the clever fusion of the real and the surreal:

> Water come iina mi room
> Mi sweep out some wid di broom
> Di lickle daag laugh to see such fun
> An di dish run away wid di spoon.

The nursery-rhyme dish becomes the satellite dish, bearer of imported, prepackaged, instant culture. Its alien, flying-saucer values, like the strange English nursery-rhymes of childhood, are made familiar in the two-way flow of human and media migration: 'Dish tek aaf like flying saucer/Di roof migrate widout a visa.'

Natural disaster reinforces old barriers of privilege; the wealthy are able to recover much more quickly than the poor. With *their* visas they can fly to Miami for generators and other essential commodities. Not so the exploited DJ, spokesman for the discontented *massive*:

> Mi iina di dark, no light no on ya
> An t(h)rough mi no ave no generator
> Mi se, one col(d) beer cos(t) ten dollar.
> Mi fish an mi meat spoil in di freezer
> A pure bully beef full up mi structure.

But opportunist, looting youth quickly recognise the catastrophe as an act of divine providence. In the spirit of 'Hungry No Laugh', *dem doan mek fun fi tief people tings:*

> Mi a look somewe safe, dry an warm
> Di yout dem a loot in di ragin storm.
> Wi tank di Laad wi never get hurt
> Dem se, 'Tank yu, Laad, fa Mr Gilbert.
> Cause, yu see mi fridge?
> Gilbert gi mi.
> Yu see mi colour TV?
> Gilbert gi mi.
> Yu see mi new stereo?
> Gilbert gi mi
> Yu see mi new video?
> Gilbert gi mi'.

The video is the next best thing to the satellite dish.

The inset tale of Knotty Dreadlocks and Mr Chin wittily counterpoints basic Jamaican stereotypes: the Rastaman, emblem of the renunciation of worldly goods; the Chineyman, symbol of acumen in commercial affairs. Gilbert temporarily levels both:

> Knotty Dreadlocks siddown inside
> A look ow Gilbert a gwan outside.
> When breeze lik down Mr Chin restaurant
> Knotty Dread jump up an chant:
> 'Lik dem Jah, gwan go dwiit,
> A dem did gi di Dread pork fi eat.
> Juk dem Jah wid storm an tunder
> Tear aaf dem roof an bruk dem window.'
> . . .

Likle aafa dat Gilbert turn back
Lif(t) aaf di roof aaf a Knotty Dread shack
Im se, 'Blouse an skirt, Jah mosa never know
Se I-an-I live right yasso.'

Naturally, in all of this social commentary, Lovindeer must indulge in a little low-key Slackness. 'Blouse an skirt', old-fashioned, euphemistic swear words, is one of a few references to clothing – 'Mi save mi brief, but mi lose mi shirt' – that suggest the inadequacy of the DJ's undergarments to protect his unmentionable private parts from a thorough soaking during the storm: '"Water wet up mi wat's it not."/"Yu mean yu wat-not!"/"No, mi wat's it not!"'. The Slackness theme is full-blown in Lovindeer's other Gilbert song, 'Hell of a Blow-job.'

The Culture/Slackness antithesis that is mediated in the dancehall is one manifestation of a fundamental antagonism in Jamaican society between uptown and down-town, between high culture and low, between literacy and oracy. That the lyrics of the DJs should be identified as an appropriate subject for literary analysis is itself evidence that Culture is in hot pursuit of fleet-footed Slackness: subjection to analysis is yet another form of containment. But the equivocations of pursuit and capture are transacted in the metathesis 'Culture hiding from Slackness'. For marginalised oral discourse, penetrating the rigid boundary of the hegemonic, scribal canon, requires that it yield to accommodate the full Creole/English, oral/scribal range of verbal creativity in Jamaica. The literariness of DJ oracy thus declares itself somewhat ambiguously in the loose language of Creole Slackness.

Notes

1 The notable exception is the auspicously named Lloyd Lovindeer (not a sobriquet), who used to teach English language and literature at Kingston College; a clear case of Slackness seducing Culture.

2 DJ term for people in a party, as in Beenie Don's 'all a di massive unu get up an dance!', perhaps a folk etymological amelioration of the somewhat pejorative 'masses', but also see Gilroy below.

3 DJ's ritual claim that denotes verbal skill.

4 The *Dictionary of Jamaican English* entry on *nyam* notes that 'The source is multiple: both verb (*eat*) and noun (*food*, or specific foods) existed in a number of W Afr languages, and many were brought to Ja. . . . The resulting multiplicity has in the course of time become sorted out so that, in general, NYAM is the verb, NINYAM a noun (food), and NYAAMS a specific food (YAM).' The dictionary notes the negative connotations of the verb: 'To eat, esp roughly or voraciously.' For an extended analysis of the sex/food homology in another Caribbean popular song tradition see Gordon Rohlehr, 'Images of Men and Women, in the 1930s Calypsoes: The Sociology of Food Acquisition in a

Context of Survivalism', in Patricia Mohammed and Catherine Shepherd, (eds), *Gender in Caribbean Development* (Jamaica, Trinidad and Tobago, Barbados: The University of the West Indies Women and Development Studies Project, 1988), pp. 232–306.

5 *Punaani, puninash, glibiti* and *glamiti*, all words for female genitalia in DJ culture.

6 See note 2 to Chapter 1.

7 Dick Hebdige, 'Reggae, Rastas and Rudies', in Stuart Hall and Tony Jefferson (eds), *Resistance through Rituals* (London: Hutchinson, 1975), p. 142.

8 Louise Bennett, *Selected Poems*, ed. Mervyn Morris (Kingston, Jamaica: Sangster's 1982), pp. 4–5.

9 Hubert Devonish, 'The Decay of Neo-Colonial Official Language Policies. The Case of the English-lexicon Creoles of the Commonwealth Caribbean', in Manfred Gorlach and John A. Holm (eds), *Focus on the Caribbean* (Amsterdam/Philadelphia: John Benjamins Publishing Co., 1986), pp. 23–4.

10 Jamaican slang meaning, approximately, 'fit and ready' – for consumption, not disposal.

11 Paul Gilroy, *There Ain't No Black in the Union Jack* (London: Hutchinson, 1987), p. 188.

12 Ibid.

13 Thanks to John Thomas for supplying DJ tapes and commenting on my argument at an early stage of its development. Thomas, who does gardening in the University community where I live, usually works to the accompaniment of dancehall music. After enforced hearing of these songs over several months I decided to give the lyrics more serious attention.

14 Phrase frequently used by the DJ in reference to the audience, as in Red Dragon's 'Love Unu': 'Now dis one dedicated to all nice an decent people.' Read in opposition to the moral majority's contempt for 'indecent' lyrics, this phrase encodes divergent decencies.

15 Harry Allen, 'Hip-hop Madness', *Essence*, April 1989, pp. 78–9. See also Michael Gonzalez and Havelock Nelson, *Bring the Noise: A Guide to Rap Music and Hip-Hop Culture* (New York: Random House, 1991).

16 Harry Allen, p. 114.

17 He is Professor of English and University Orator, University of the West Indies, Mona, Jamaica.

18 Edward Baugh, *A Tale of the Rain Forest* (Kingston, Jamaica: Sandberry Press, 1988), p. 50.

19 Walter Redfern, *Puns* (Oxford: Basil Blackwell, 1984), p. 4.

20 Herbert Marcuse, *Eros and Civilization*, 1955; rpt (Boston: Beacon Press, 1966), p. 159.

21 Henry Louis Gates, Jr, *The Signifying Monkey* (New York: Oxford University Press, 1988), p. 29. Compare with reports of women at dancehalls in Jamaica engaging in acts of self-pleasuring on the dance floor.

22 Ibid., p. 30.

23 'Forgot' becomes 'faggot', slang for homosexual.

24 Peter Tosh, interview by Carolyn Cooper, *Pulse*, June 1984, p. 15. R & B 'Romance' becomes Rastafarian 'Ras-mance' and, ultimately, DJ 'Rass-mance'.

25 *Samfie* means 'cunning', *blai* 'breaks'.

26 For a revisionist, feminist reading of the 'male gaze' see Maggie Humm, 'Is the Gaze Feminist?', in Gary Day and Clive Bloom, eds, *Perspectives on Pornog-*

raphy: Sexuality in Film and Literature (London: Macmillan, 1988), p. 70: 'But the problem with the concept of the "gaze" hinges, paradoxically, on feminists' expert attention to representation and the male spectator. Feminist criticism has not, as yet, explored the ways in which the representation of sexuality denies women a sexual voice as well as sexual subjectivity.' Humm argues that in some film instances '[t]he voices of fascinating and independent women (however problematically presented) won out over the visual construction of spectator relations', p. 71.

27 I am indebted to Erna Brodber, in conversation, for this analogy.

28 Compare with the proverb 'Oman an hood never quarrel'; 'hood', Jamaican for 'wood' as erect penis. Firmness is clearly at a premium. The inverse relationship between economic and sexual power suggests the compensatory nature of sexual prowess for the economically under-endowed man.

29 *Sunday Gleaner*, 1 January 1989, p. 5

30 *Daily Gleaner*, 13 January 1989, p. 9.

31 Gilroy, p. 188.

32 Ibid., pp. 188–9.

33 Despite the notorious problems of definition – what exactly is the difference between pornography and 'erotica'? – I use the term because of its decidedly negative connotations. But I am aware of subversive readings of the feminist arguments against commodified sexuality. For example, Gary Day argues in his 'Introduction' to *Perspectives on Pornography* that '[f]eminist attacks on the presentation of sex without love, or sex where women are treated as objects, may perhaps be regarded, at least in part, as an unconscious attempt by feminists to preserve and defend one of the most important sites of subjectivity for women. If this is the case, then there is something profoundly conservative about feminist writing on pornography, for it is implicitly accepting that sex and love are privileged sites for female subjectivity, and the intensity of some feminist attacks on pornography could be said to reflect an unconscious acquiescence in patriarchy's distribution of subject positions. . . . Perhaps the shock of feminism embracing pornography would create a greater potential for radical change than feminism's criticism of it', p. 4.

34 For a comparable calypso version of 'woman as devourer of male sexuality', see Rohlehr, op. cit., especially pp. 252–3: 'beneath the condemnation of prostitution lies the fear of castration or emasculation, which is itself a rationalization of male sexual inadequacy', p. 252; and 'If the precocious young woman was regarded with a mixture of moralizing anxiety, dread and the eager anticipation of the rake on the prowl, the libidinous old woman was regarded with positive horror', p. 253.

35 Lorna Goodison, *I Am Becoming My Mother* (London: New Beacon Books, 1986), p. 36.

CHAPTER 9 From 'centre' to 'margin': turning history upside-down

The history of ideas in the 'anglophone' Caribbean has conventionally been defined as a one-way flow of knowledge from the centred 'Mother Country' to the peripheral colonies. Though the patriarchal mother has long given her illegitimate children flag-independence, the superstition that upper-case Culture is intrinsically foreign does persist. Conversely, the womanist project of these essays – 'Me Know No Law, Me Know No Sin' – is to reproduce a body of subversive knowledge that originates in the centres of consciousness of the historically dehumanised peoples of the region. This 'culture an' tradition an' birthright' is being refined in the revisionist work of native Caribbean intellectuals – both 'folk' and 'academic' – who are remapping the boundaries of 'margin' and 'centre'.

In attempting to retheorise marginality and power, these essays begin with primary texts, centring the ideological narrative on close readings of the texts themselves. This repositioning of the displaced 'primary' text at the centre of the theorising project is itself a subversive act. Instead of imposing polysyllabic, imported theories of cultural production on these localised Jamaican texts, I have attempted to discover what the texts themselves can be made to tell us about the nature of cultural production in our centres of learning.

In this concluding chapter, I also argue that this transgressive blood knowledge, moving from the Jamaican 'centre' outwards, may be related to similar processes of subversive cultural production in other contexts of marginalisation and recentring within the Caribbean, and beyond – for example, as evidenced in the work of Jamaica Kincaid and George Lamming. Indeed, to appropriate the uncontested, fixed discourse of 'centre' and 'margin' is to run the risk of reducing the knowledge that originates in our small place to mere illustration of some totalising, neo-imperialist theory: making our *parole* the mimicking of some other culture's *langue*.

The burden of British colonial education was to make us the 'monkey see, monkey do' bearers of the *langue* of Empire, both literally and tropologically. But the emergence of counter-colonising Caribbean languages that africanise English, French, Spanish, Dutch and Portuguese, confirms our humanity as proactive bearers of culture, not mere zombies – passive receptacles of the will of the enslaving other. If Britannia once ruled the waves, and Britons never, never, never should have been slaves, then the perverse, schizophrenic logic of Empire produces, for example, a George Lamming from Little England/Barbados who creates within the castle of his skin alter/native structures of political consciousness. The G/Trumper ideological split in Lamming's first novel seems to be the exteriorisation of the conflict within the writer from a colonial society who must claim the makeshift castle of his elitist education as well as the vulnerable shelters of the self that the migrant labourer from the Caribbean takes, tortoise-like, to the centres of Euro-American empire. With communal support, the cunning tortoise often out-distances the lone hare in the fabulated aerodynamics of folk-tale.

Louise Bennett's satirical poem, 'Colonization in Reverse', written in response to the waves of Caribbean migration to the United Kingdom in the 1950s, gleefully celebrates the transforming power of Jamaican culture as it implants itself on British soil in a parodic gesture of 'colonization'. History is turned upside down as the 'margins' move to the 'centre' and irreparably dislocate that centre:

> What a joyful news, Miss Mattie;
> Ah feel like me heart gwine burs –
> Jamaica people colonizin
> Englan in reverse.
>
> By de hundred, by de tousan,
> From country an from town,
> By de ship-load, by de plane-load,
> Jamaica is Englan boun.
>
> Dem a pour out a Jamaica;
> Everybody future plan
> Is fi get a big-time job
> An settle in de motherlan.
>
> What a islan! What a people!
> Man an woman, ole an young
> Jussa pack dem bag an baggage
> An tun history upside dung![1]

The cultural 'bag an baggage' of the migrants had to be accommodated within the reluctant host society. But settling in is not an easy passage. The lines '[e]verybody future plan/Is fi get a big-time job/An settle in de motherlan' (p. 106) seem deliberately ambiguous. The placement of 'plan' at the end of a line that optimistically asserts the anticipated benefits of migration – everbody's future is planned – seems conclusively to confirm the almost proverbial certainty of expected success. But the reading of 'plan' as active verb is immediately revised in the next line which turns 'plan' into a somewhat more passive noun of intention.[2] These reassuring plans for a secure future depend on the migrant's getting a 'big-time job' as a prerequisite for happy settling; settling down might require settling for less than what one had expected.

The 'joyful news' of the secular gospel of upward and outward social mobility requires a global redistribution of the world's wealth. Indeed, it is the common poverty of British subjects in the Commonwealth that precipates the mass reverse colonisation process.[3] Forced to seek economic refugee status in the very bosom of the appropriated motherland, the outside children of Mother England demand their natural inheritance as free citizens of the Empire, however far removed from the imperial centre. In a lovely bit of mischief worthy of Jamaica Kincaid's Lucy, Velma Pollard suggests the promiscuity of Victorian Mother England in peopling the multi-coloured Empire: 'Thinking about it now, we must have had different fathers. And I would have regarded that as perfectly natural given the examples in the district around me.'[4] In this parodic reversal, prim and proper Mother England becomes a very loose woman indeed, just like all those other unbecoming daughters of Empire.

'Colonization in Reverse' continues somewhat wryly to assert that if no suitably dignified jobs are forthcoming, the role-playing, Anansi-like migrant will learn how to beat the system by getting on the dole. For centuries, the English in the Caribbean have boxed the bread out of the natives' mouth. Now, the tables appear to be turned. But few migrants could find work to suit their dignity; they are forced to do the dirty work that the English natives, themselves, consider beneath their dignity:

Oonoo se (sic) how life is funny,
Oonoo see de tunabout?
Jamaica live fi box bread
Out a English people mout.

For when dem catch a Englan
An start play dem different role
Some will settle down to work
An some will settle fi de dole.

Jane seh de dole is not too bad
Because dey payin she
Two pounds a week fi seek a job
Dat suit her dignity.

Me seh Jane will never fine work
At de rate she dah look

For all day she stay pon Aunt Fan couch
An read love-story book.

What a devilment a Englan!
Dem face war an brave de worse;
But ah wonderin how dem gwine stan
Colonizin in reverse (p. 107)

Like the 'love-story book' that Jane reads instead of looking for work, the romantic fiction of Empire that the native has a home in the motherland makes the settling in process deceptively easy.

But Bennett's parodic representation of the cunning, reverse-colonising Jamaican abroad, and at large, is not entirely deflating; it raises suspicions of a perverse pride in counter-conquest. Three complementary poems, 'Independence Dignity', 'Independance' (sic) and 'Jamaica Elevate', suggest quite humorously that Jamaicans are, indeed, larger than the speck on 'worl-map' would suggest.[5] Physical size is no absolute determinant of real power, or of a people's sense of their proper place in world history, as evidenced in Miss Mattie's self-satisfied speech in 'Independance':

She hope dem caution worl-map
Fi stop draw Jamaica small,
For de lickle speck cyaan show
We independantness at all!

Moresomever we must tell map dat
We don't like we position –
Please kindly teck we out a sea
An draw we in de ocean. (p. 118)

The personification of 'worl-map' – an excellent example of the way in which predominantly oral Jamaicans conceptualise abstraction – brilliantly underscores the arbitrary nature of the cartography of geo-political power. 'Worl-map' is just like any other out-of-order individual that you can reprimand, if you don't like the way he (?) chooses to position you in the larger scheme of things. Miss Mattie, who advocates the cautioning of 'worl-map', intuitively recognises that maps are not absolutely fixed representations of some divinely orchestrated ecosystem; maps delineate the geopolitics of the times. To study the history of the maps of the world is to understand the shifts of power among those who still claim the (natural) right to define the boundaries of their own world, and other people's.[6]

A revisionist reading of the global history of map-making leads to the discovery of 'lost' cartographers, like the fourteenth-century explorers and map-makers of Mali, who have been marginalised in the eurocentric maps of conquest. As part of this project of reconstruction, the 'Columbus in Chains' episode in Jamaica Kincaid's *Annie John* celebrates the paralysis of patriarchy, and the liberalism of disinterested explorers. Annie John maps an ingenuously amusing African–Caribbean geography of exploration that does not require the genocide of the discovered as the price of mutual curiosity:

> I was sure that if our ancestors had gone from Africa to Europe and come upon the people living there, they would have taken a proper interest in the Europeans on first seeing them, and said, 'How nice,' and then gone home to tell their friends about it.[7]

In Bennett's parodic geo-politics, the song and dance of 'Independance' may lead self-aggrandising Jamaicans like Miss Mattie up the garden path. In the opening verse of the poem the speaker questions the nation's preparedness for the rigours of independence:

> Independance wid a vengeance!
> Independance raisin Cain!
> Jamaica start grow beard, ah hope
> We chin can stan de strain! (p. 117)

Wittily contrasting the ordinary Jamaican's sense of self-importance with the Government's newly-acquired status as independent nation, Bennett emphasises the disparity between official conceptions of the nation state and the everyday, small-scale politics of individual empowerment:

> Independence is we nature
> Born an bred in all we do,
> An she glad fi see dat Government
> Tun independant to. (p. 118)

From Miss Mattie's perspective, personified Government, usually dismissed as an irrelevant abstraction, belatedly comes to discover the independence that individual Jamaicans have always assumed, naturally:

> Mattie seh it mean we facety,
> Stan up pon we dignity,
> An we don't allow nobody
> Fi teck liberty wid we. (p. 118)

But Bennett's primary speaker in this ambivalent poem is not quite as confident as Miss Mattie, whose comments she merely reports. She concludes, somewhat derisively, that independence requires a capacity for self-sacrifice which she is not sure that big-chat Jamaicans like Miss Mattie are ready to demonstrate. The jackass rope of the final stanza is more than the tobacco that the premature smoker will use; independence becomes the symbolic rope that the proverbial fool uses to hang himself:

> No easy-come by freeness tings,
> Nuff labour, some privation,
> Not much of dis an less of dat
> An plenty studiration.
>
> Independance wid a vengeance!
> Wonder how we gwine to cope?
> Jamaica start smoke pipe, ah hope
> We got nuff jackass rope! (p. 119)

'Independence Dignity' is no less satirical. The speaker who is addressing a Jamaican away from home, suggests in the very first verse that Independence is an act of capture, not one of release:

> Dear Cousin Min, yuh miss sinting,
> Yuh should be over yah
> Fi see Independence Celebration
> Capture Jamaica. (p. 116)

In his gloss on the poem, Mervyn Morris notes that 'capture [is] ironic, as though Jamaica is being captured again, as by the Spanish in 1494, and the English in 1655. The word also carries a resonance from Rastafarian usage: to "capture" land is to occupy it illegally.'[8] Morris elaborates:

> The Independence Celebrations 'capture' Jamaica, and all the people are on their best behaviour. In the parody of 'The Burial of Sir John Moore at Corunna', a British piece much recited by Jamaican schoolchildren in the colonial period, it is as if the colonizer is being buried while a new nation is born. But the poem is also aware of elements of Jamaica which may be problems in independence: the arrant commercialization, the many pretences which cannot be expected to last beyond Independence time. The dignity might prove temporary. 'De behaviour was gran', transforming people for a time; but the mention of the unruly and ill-mannered, the lazy, the disunited, the feeble, serves to remind us that the good behaviour might not long survive the occasion to which everybody has risen. The unpleasing reality is set ironically against the hopes embodied in the national anthem. The poem seems to welcome the celebrations but, in its unillusioned irony, allows for the struggles that may have to follow.[9]

Morris cites stanzas one and four of the Wolfe original:

Not a drum was heard, not a funeral note
As his corse to the rampart we hurried;
Not a soldier discharged his farewell shot
O'er the grave where our hero we buried.
. . .
Few and short were the prayers we said,
And we spoke not a word of sorrow;
But we steadfastly gazed on the face of the dead,
And we bitterly thought of the morrow.

The Bennett parody reads thus:

Not a stone was fling, not a samfie sting,
Not a soul gwan bad an lowrated;
Not a fight bruck out, not a bad-wud shout
As Independence was celebrated. (p. 116)

Even if one does not recognise the specific poem that Bennett parodies, one nevertheless senses a satirical intention in the mock-English grammar and syntax, and the military precision of the rhythms of the verse. The parody extends beyond precise verbal echoes. The catalogue of negative events that do not occur seems somewhat more weighty than the actual decorous celebrations. The heartfelt, soulful celebration of independence seems to mask the conspiratorial, hand-in-glove thickness of thieves. The imperial image of the gloved hand as a sign of the ceremonial nature of the occasion is colonised in a deft parodic turn.

Teet an tongue was all united,
Heart an soul was hans an glove,
Fenky-fenky voice gain vigour
Pon 'Jamaica, land we love'. (p. 117)

Further, independence is in prime '[f]i de whole long mont a Augus' (p. 116) – and just that. The fact that Independence Day, 6 August was made to supersede Emancipation Day, 1 August, in the official calendar of social progress, confirms the ambivalence about the meaning of our history as a slave society that our politicians often have. Just as Government gets independence late in the day, opportunist Government also quickly forgets the long history of the people's struggle for emancipation. Independence is a gift horse into whose mouth Government should definitely have looked. There can be no 'independence' without emancipation. Indeed, freedom that is not earned the hard way, has very little value.

In 'Jamaica Elevate' the speaker writes to yet another Jamaican abroad, singing the praises of the new state of independence. But the speed with which Independence is dropped on Jamaica leaves the letter-writer giddy.

She appears to reel under the collective weight of the buff-biff-baps of Referendum, Election and sudden Independence. At the root of the poem is the cautionary Jamaican proverb, 'The higher monkey climb, the more him expose himself.' This presumptuous elevation of Jamaica to a scanty army, an unformed navy, consuls and ambassadors dipping their mouth in heavy world affairs, is clear evidence of the pride that goes before the fall:

We tun Independent Nation
In de Commonwealth of Nations
An we get congratulation
From de folks of high careers;

We got Consuls and Ambassadors
An Ministers and Senators
Dah rub shoulder an dip mout
Eena heavy world affairs.

We sen we Delegation
Over to United nation
An we meck O.A.S. know dat
We gwine join dem.

We tell Russia we don't like dem,
We tell Englan we naw beg dem,
An we meck Merica know
We is behine dem.

For doah we Army scanty
An we Navy don't form yet,
Any nation dat we side wid
Woulda never need to fret;

We defence is not defenceless
For we got we half a brick,
We got we broken bottle
An we coocoomacca stick;

But we willin to put down we arms
In Peace and Freedom's name
An we call upon de nations
Of de worl to do de same. (p. 114)

The make-do armaments of the newly-independent nation – 'half a brick', 'broken bottle' and 'coocoomacca stick' – are remarkably similar to the stones that are not flung during the period of Independence Dignity: the more things change, the more they remain the same.

Most amusing of all is the case of mistaken identity that Independence occasions. The new, native Governor-General resembles a family member. The immediate response to his picture in the newspaper humorously defines the usual circumstances in which a black person would be deemed newsworthy in the media politics of the times: 'Something bad happen to John!' (p. 115) He is too old to have passed exams; he is not likely to have bought a winning sweepstake ticket; it must be a calamity.

These parodic poems on Jamaica's independence, mocking the forms of English verse and the politics of (neo)colonialism, illustrate the mobility of the definition of parody which Linda Hutcheon proposes: 'a method of inscribing continuity while permitting critical distance. It can, indeed, function as a conservative force in both retaining and mocking other aesthetic forms, but it is also capable of transformative power in creating new syntheses. . . .'[10]

One new synthesis that Bennett seems to be affirming is the interdependence of Caribbean nations that might have been possible with the West Indian Federation. Mocking the nation's lack of preparedness for independence, while simultaneously asserting the sense of cultural autonomy of individual Jamaicans, Bennett claims the transformative power of parody beyond mere mockery. The alternative to premature independence is not simply the return to colonial relations of dependency on Mother England. The West Indian Federation was a viable option.

In his gloss on Bennett's 'Dear Departed Federation', Rex Nettleford cites the Jamaica Labour Party's 1961 election slogan, 'Jamaica, yes, Federation, no,' which in its opportunistic binarism set up a false conflict between Jamaican nationalism and Caribbean regional integration. This deceptively simple slogan, like Eric Williams' mathematics – 1 from 10 leave 0 – undermines the fragile Federation. As Bennett prophetically notes in the last six lines of the poem, if the shared suffering of Caribbean small states is prolonged, the murdered Federation might yet need to be resurrected. The personification of Federation, for whom the poem is a mock elegy, again reinforces the sense of the intimate scale of politics in small societies:

Dear Departed Federation,
Referendum murderation
Bounce you eena outa space
Hope you fine a restin place.
Is a heavy blow we gi yuh
An we know de fault noh fe yuh
For we see you operate
Over continent an state.

But de heap o' boderation
Eena fe we lickle nation
From de start o' yuh duration
Meck we frighten an frustrate.
A noh tief meck yuh departed
A noh lie meck yuh departed
But a fearful meck we careful
How we let yuh tru we gate.
Fearful bout de big confusion
Bout de final constitution
An Jamaica contribution
All we spirit aggrivate.
An we memba self-protection
All we [y]ears of preparation!
Referendum Mutilation
Quashie start to contemplate!
Beg yuh pardon Federation
Fe de sudden separation
If we sufferin' survive
We acquaintance might revive.
Dear Departed Federation
Beg you beg dem tarra nation
Who done quarrel and unite
Pray fe po' West Indies plight.[11]

It is in the mass movement out of Jamaica that Jamaicans came to fully understand, in a practical way, 'po' West Indies plight' – the regional politics of marginalisation. The shared experience of migration to Britain created the conditions in which separate small islanders all found their common West Indian identity away from home. In *The Pleasures of Exile* Lamming confirms the cultural significance of the discovery of West Indianness in Britain, and the later need he felt to extend the borders of affiliation to the wider, multi-lingual Caribbean: the Caricom sensibility.

> It is here that one sees a discovery actually taking shape. No Barbadian, no Trinidadian, no St. Lucian, no islander from the West Indies sees himself as a West Indian until he encounters another islander in foreign territory. It was only when the Barbadian childhood corresponded with the Grenadian or the Guianese childhood in important details of folklore, that the wider identification was arrived at. In this sense, most West Indians of my generation were born in England. The category West Indian, formerly understood as a geographical term, now assumes cul-

> tural significance. . . . Today, . . . I find that I refrain from saying that I am from the West Indies, for it implies a British colonial limitation. I say, rather, I am from the Caribbean, hoping the picture of French and Spanish West Indies will be taken for granted. So the discovery had taken place, partly due to the folklore, and partly to the singing, and especially to the kind of banter which goes between islander and islander.[12]

Lamming, in emphasising the role of folklore, singing and banter in the discovery of West Indianness in Britain, provides yet another example of the transformative movement of parody beyond mere mockery. The expectancy of Bennett's Anansi-like Jamaicans, bent on colonising England in reverse, is shared by the writers. The 'illiterate' Caribbean peasant and displaced urban labourer is not reduced to an object of ridicule, as, for example, in the fiction of a DeLisser or a Naipaul. The Caribbean intellectual and the Caribbean folk, sharing equally in that moment of discovery of the ridiculousness of their mutual displacement in the Mother Country, become one. The bearers of the bag and baggage of Caribbean popular cultural forms reassert their humanity in this new centre. They recognise a common heritage: language, music and the reassuring intimacy of blood knowledge.

Lamming's description of the moment of arrival, at the end of the long sea-change, brings together the voices of the writer, his fictional other selves (the stowaway) and, somewhat reluctantly, with cold comfort, his reluctant host:

> The voyage was over. The captain would soon turn the stowaways over to the police. England lay before us, not a place, or a people but as a promise and an expectation. Sam and I had left home for the same reasons. We had come to England to be writers. And now we were about to be anchored at Southampton, we realised that we had no return ticket. We had no experience in crime. Moreover, our colonial status condemned us fortunately to the rights of full citizenship. In no circumstances could we qualify for deportation. There was no going back. All the gaiety of reprieve which we felt on our departure had now turned to apprehension. Like one of the many characters which he has since created, Sam said on the deck: 'Is who send we up in this place?' For it was a punishing wind which drove us from looking at the landscape. An English voice said that it was the worst spring he had known in fifty years. We believed him, but it seemed very cold comfort for people in our circumstances.

That Sam Selvon is depicted by Lamming in the humorous terms of the bewildered fictional characters he has created, illustrates the new intimacy between the Caribbean writer and the natives of his person. Selvon's *The Lonely Londoners* revises the boundaries between the oral and the scribal literary traditions, between popular culture and culture proper, between the vulgar and the refined. It is the experience of migration that forces Selvon to experiment with narrative voice, making the language of the omniscient narrator identical with that of the characters. Issues of language and national/regional identity are clearly crucial in the migration experience. That fundamental question – 'Is who send we up in this place?' – encodes a whole history of expectations beyond individual volition. The amusing anonymity of that 'who' implies yet another enforced middle-passage to another kind of indentured labour for the Caribbean writer in exile.

For Lamming, it is in the experiments with the form of the novel that the Caribbean intellectual rediscovers his peasant origins:

> Unlike the previous governments and departments of educators, unlike the business man importing commodities, the West Indian novelist did not look out across the sea to another source. He looked in and down at what had traditionally been ignored. For the first time the West Indian peasant became other than a cheap source of labour. He became, through the novelist's eye, a living existence, living in silence and joy and fear, involved in riot and carnival. It is the West Indian novel that has restored the West Indian peasant to his true and original status of personality.[13]

The canonical texts of West Indian literature, however androcentric, did create openings in the Great Tradition of English literature, that allowed the much later entry of more vagrant texts. No matter how English the language of narration, the novelist had to experiment with the language of the *massive* for authenticity of voice, not mere local colour.

But Lamming's well-intentioned claims for the restorative power of the West Indian novel are somewhat presumptuous: the Caribbean peasant has never been in doubt of his/her own humanity, as the popular culture tradition so eloquently illustrates: '"I dont know much 'bout book, but I tell you what me fren, I is a man wid a terrible long head, I can tell you, and de man dat want fe mek me a fool, mek him come."' The intellectual in his castle might have been educated into anxiety; the ignorant folk have the proverbial reassurance that 'where ignorance is bliss, 'tis folly to be wise'. In Jamaican, 'ignorant' means more than it does in English. To 'get ignorant' is to become angry, to consciously assume an attitude, especially in combative circumstances where the dignity of the ignorant is in question. The *Dictionary of Jamaican English* defines 'ignorant' as: 'evid[ently] a malapropism for indignant, though the regular sense is sometimes mingled in'. Samuel

Johnson's definition of 'indignant', cited in the *OED* – 'inflamed at once with anger and disdain' – captures the Jamaican sense of 'ignorant'.

Lamming himself seems to recognise the exemplary wisdom of this disdainful ignorance in his description of the movement of the middle-class intellectuals to the common meeting-ground of Port-of-Spain's Woodford Square. The new inter/nationalism espoused in that egalitarian street university, challenges the colonial logic that defined education purely in terms of limitation of access. Knowledge that was local and popular, and thus in good supply, was, by its very nature, of little value – to capitalise on Lamming's metaphor of commodified knowledge as scarce imported goods.

Three decades after the publication of Lamming's *The Pleasures of Exile*, this historically devalued Caribbean popular culture has now become part of the fiction of multi-cultural Britain. The 1991 issue of *The Oxford Literary Review* on 'Neocolonialism' opens with a terse statement by Robert Young, entitled 'Neocolonial Times', which, even if it does not quite concede that history has been turned upside-down, nevertheless acknowledges that colonisation in the present requires a reappraisal of history itself. It confirms the complexity of the cultural accommodations within the Mother Country that reverse-colonisation requires:

> We are talking, with neocolonialism, about the legacies of history, not as textual archive, but as the continued productivity of history in the present. Nowhere is this marked more trenchantly than in the urban centres of the West where local culture has become hybridized by once migrant groups, and where assimilation, still often assumed to be a one-way process, has developed a form of diasporic internationalism, undoing the ideology of race and nation in a new epoch in our cities. The exotic no longer beckons in the East but has become a part of the everyday of the West. This complicates not only the traditions of contemporary culture but also those paradigms of our political heritage, from the privilege of class to the liberalism whose tolerance is strictly limited to other relativisms – which is not to forget the presence of the direct survivals of colonial ideology, of racism, inequality and injustice.[14]

It is these direct survivals of the ideology of race and nation that Jamaica Kincaid critiques so bitingly in *A Small Place*. In an act of transgressive straight-talking, Kincaid abandons the mask of fiction to speak politics directly. She examines the tourist industry in Antigua, and, by extension, in the Caribbean and beyond as another version of assimilationist, diasporic internationalism, this time on the migrant's exoticised native soil. With savage, Swiftian satire (or the *picong* of the calypsonian), Kincaid exposes the grotesque body of the ugly tourist as a legible sign of the diseased body politic from which s/he issues.

But Kincaid also undermines the fixity of constructs like 'visitor' and 'native', 'centre' and 'margin':

> That the native does not like the tourist is not hard to explain. For every native of every place is a potential tourist, and every tourist is a native of somewhere. Every native everywhere lives a life of overwhelming and crushing banality and boredom and desperation and depression, and every deed, good and bad, is an attempt to forget this. Every native would like a rest, every native would like a tour. But some natives – most natives in the world – cannot go anywhere. They are too poor. They are too poor to go anywhere. They are too poor to escape the reality of their lives; and they are too poor to live properly in the place where they live, which is the very place you, the tourist, want to go – so when the natives see you, the tourist, they envy you, they envy your ability to leave your own banality and boredom, they envy your ability to turn their own banality and boredom into a source of pleasure for yourself.[15]

In her 1990 novel, *Lucy*, a transatlantic repositioning of the earlier *Annie John*, and a womanist up-dating of Sam Selvon's *The Lonely Londoners*, Kincaid allows her native to take a tour.

Somewhat like Moses, Selvon's stowaway novelist, Lucy, the frustrated artist as *au pair*, learns that pictures of reality are much more satisfying than reality itself. The fictions created in the castle of the skin redefine the power relations that are formed in the small place of her island of origin. The angry question that Lucy silently keeps on asking of her smug employer, Mariah – '[h]ow does a person get to be that way?'[16] – effectively turns the native's banality and boredom into a source of pleasure for the visitor. The photographic still that Lucy creates out of the chaos of the party that Mariah designs to distract her, turns the natives into flat, monochromatic, cardboard cutouts. The imported catalogue that encodes the signs of good taste for her fashionable father, shapes Lucy's own signifying on her urbane natives. In this extended passage from the novel, Kincaid brings together several of the themes of *A Small Place*:

> One of my pastimes at home, my old home, had been to sit and look through a catalogue from which, each year, my father ordered a new felt hat and a pair of dress shoes. In the catalogue were pictures of clothes on mannequins, but the mannequins had

> no heads or limbs, only torsos. I used to wonder what face would fit on the torso I was looking at, how such a face would look as it broke out in a smile, how it would look back at me if suddenly we were introduced. Now I knew, for these people, all standing there, holding drinks in their hands, reminded me of the catalogue; their clothes, their features, the manner in which they carried themselves were the example all the world should copy. They had names like Peters, Smith, Jones and Richards – names that were easy on the tongue, names that made the world spin. They had somehow all been to the islands – by that, they meant the place where I was from – and had fun there. I decided not to like them just on that basis; I wished once again that I came from a place where no one wanted to go, a place that was filled with slag and unexpectedly erupting volcanoes, or where a visitor was turned into a pebble on setting foot there; somehow it made me ashamed to come from a place where the only thing to be said about it was 'I had fun when I was there.' Dinah came with her husband and her brother, and it was her brother that Mariah had really wanted me to meet. She had said that he was three years older than I was, that he had just returned from a year of travelling in Africa and Asia, and that he was awfully worldly and smart. She did not say he was handsome, and when I first saw him I couldn't tell, either; but when we were introduced, the first thing he said to me was 'Where in the West Indies are you from?' and that is how I came to like him in an important way.[17]

Lucy's holiday romance with Hugh is possible because he does not assume that the West Indies is a chain of indistinguishable islands. He does not assume the *persona* of visitor, just as he does not make Lucy his discoverable native. He is not the Rochester of Charlotte Brontë's *Jane Eyre*, nor is he the deliberately unnamed husband of Jean Rhys's revisionist *Wide Sargasso Sea*. Kincaid, like Rhys, turns history upside down, placing her Caribbean native-as-anthropologist in the privileged position of critical observer of the strange customs and manners of fractured mannequins. Like so many foreign experts in the Caribbean, Lucy knows her natives. Of Paul, a later lover, she anthropologises:

> I knew him better than he realized. He loved ruins; he loved the past but only if it had ended on a sad note, from a lofty beginning to a gradual, rotten decline; he loved things that came from far away and had a mysterious history. I could have told him that I had sized him up, but it was not as if he were going to matter to me for years and years to come.[18]

The reduction of the islands to mere places of degenerate fun, that exist primarily for the distraction of the bored visitor, makes Lucy ignorant. But the process of becoming a tourist is also a transgressive playing out of a repressed identification with, and desire for, the native, as illustrated in Lucy's own dreams, and in the complicated sexual contracts that are negotiated on Caribbean beaches. The social, racial and gender border-crossings that are not permissible at home become possible when one enters the temporary fiction of tourist.

For example, even a rudimentary study of the sociology of the Reggae Sunsplash Festival in Jamaica, which was originally developed as a tourist product for the low-occupancy summer season, discloses the promiscuous coming together of native and visitor. The border-crossing between Jamaica and home that the visitor makes is analogous to the crossing of social class barriers within Jamaican society itself. The otherness of uptown and downtown is temporarily effaced in a carnival of displacement somewhat like the Trinidad original, which is itself being imported into Jamaica as an experiment in intra-regional cross-fertilisation.

But ideological tensions between the predominantly up-town Jamaica Carnival and the largely downtown Sunsplash, around the public representations of sexuality, reproduce the social class conflicts that only appear to be mediated by these ritual events. In carnival, downtown 'slackness' becomes permissive uptown 'licence'. The freedom of the middle-class to parade its nakedness in the streets is a symbolic acting-out of its usual position of social superiority, literally at centre-stage. Indeed, the increasing cost of participation in Jamaica Carnival reduces working-class aspirants to the role of mere spectators who find themselves on the periphery of a new decentring drama of social dominance.

For Jamaica Carnival '91, I happened to be in the first band that crossed the official judging stage. After prancing on stage we were quickly whisked away to the Police Officers' Club where the main fete would take place. As I waited just outside the entrance to the Club for my co-revellers in another band, I overheard a conversation between a woman and her children. I regret that I do not know this woman's name, for I want to give her full credit for her anger and her insight. She was righteously ignorant because the price of entrance to the fete had not been advertised, and she could not pay her way into the 'real' event. But this was her consolation: she understood why she was marginalised. She told her children that she knew why the entrance fee was so high. Her collective employers – she was a helper – did not want her to be able to mingle with them and see them acting so slack: Dem no waan wi fi si dem a gwaan so bad. Wi naa go av no rispek fi dem. Respectful envy is the only proper posture for the native in relation to both foreign and local visitors on the loose.

Attempts by the organisers of Jamaica Carnival to incorporate reggae into the predominantly calypso/soca entertainment package are akin to the Reggae Sunsplash 'bowing' to calypso in 1991, with the addition of a Caribbean (calypso) night to the week-long festival programme. The uneasy liason between calypso and reggae in these commercial ventures does not arise from any basic incompatibility between these two Caribbean musical forms. Both calypso and reggae are potentially subversive in their own context, as Gordon Rohlehr's work on the Trinidad calypso so eloquently illustrates, and as I have tried to demonstrate in the analysis of the lyrics of Bob Marley and the DJs. Conflicts arise from the nature of the ownership of the processes of production in the music industry in Jamaica. Both Jamaica Carnival and Reggae Sunsplash are 'owned' by middle-class Jamaicans. Both are marketed as tourist products. Entertaining the natives is a happy accident, a by-product of more clearly commercial motivations.

An early Louise Bennett poem, 'Free Movement', celebrating the 1955 visit to Jamaica of Beryl McBurnie's Little Carib Dancers, acknowledges the perennial Jamaican receptivity to carnival, while making a sly crack at the Trinidad Government's objection to unrestricted freedom of movement between the federated Caribbean islands:

Excitement up a airport
Wen de Trinidadians lan',
Jamaica gather roun' fe kiss
An greet an shake up han!

Ah sey skoo yah! But tap tap!
Wat a sinting! Po me gal!
Koo how Trinidad come teck
Jamaica meck Carnival.

Calypso dance an Shango dance
Drum-beatin'! Se yah mah,
Wat a dickens Trinidad a-kick up
Eena Jamaica!

Dem dress like Lord an Lady, birds
An beas, wile animal,
Dem leggo line an kick up shine
An call it Carnival!

An wen dem do so ping, pong, pung,
An strike up de steel ban',
Yuh wan' hear de sweet music dem
Get outa ole tin-pan!

Dem dance de Tambo Bamboo, an
De Bacanal dem prance,
Me never see movement more free
Dan Trinidadian dance.

Me watch Trinidad carrins awns
An baps me understan
How dem teck 'freedom of movement'
An confuse federation.

Me sey Massi me Massa
Trinidad noh ordinary,
Dem chat gains 'Freedom of Movement'
But a so dem movement free!

But Trinidadian deed gwine fine dem out
As sure as fate,
Wen McBurnie dancin movement
Meck West Indies federate.[19]

Like Lamming, Bennett recognises that the term 'West Indies' assumes cultural significance beyond the difficult politics of constitutional federation. The Governments of the region may not be federated, but the people of the Caribbean share a common capacity to make sweet music out of the industrial waste of our societies. The calypsonians, reggae musicians, dub poets, craft workers, barbers, hairstylists, auto-mechanics of the Caribbean – the devalued, 'low culture' artistes and artisans – create out of the garbage of the material conditions of our times popular art and appropriate technology that first service local needs, but increasingly cater to the international mass market in exoticised 'world culture', as the present study of Jamaican popular culture so clearly confirms.

The reverse colonising power of this exported culture, as it spreads internationally through communities of migrants, is a compelling trope of the liberating potential of a transgressive poetics of marginality. History is turned upside-down in a process of hierarchy-inversion that challenges the pretensions to absolute authority of the old and new colonialisms. In the words of Stallybrass and White in their 'Introduction' to *The Politics and Poetics of Transgression*:

> When we talk of high discourses – literature, philosophy, statecraft, the languages of the Church and the University – and contrast them to the low discourses of a peasantry, the urban poor, subcultures, marginals, the lumpenproletariat, colonized peoples, we already have two 'highs' and two 'lows'. History seen from

> above and history seen from below are irreducibly different and they consequently impose radically different perspectives on the question of hierarchy.[20]

All the texts examined in this account of oral/sexual discourse in Jamaican popular culture – performance poetry, auto/biographical narrative, film and popular song – illustrate a deep-rooted understanding of the history of exploitation and marginalisation of afrocentric culture in the Caribbean that is replicated internationally in the devaluation of the currency and the cultural traditions of the impoverished two-thirds world beyond the North Atlantic.[21]

Jamaicans, as consumers of the remaindered goods and over-priced services of the dysfunctionally overdeveloped one-third world, are indeed economically poor, and made poorer with each round of 'negotiation' with the International Monetary Fund[22] and the World Bank. But as culture bearers, Jamaicans are not 'undeveloped'. The international development industry, the modern equivalent of the old missionary societies, needs to take into account broadly cultural, not only economic, determinants of 'development' and productivity. The British-based DJ, Macka B, at the 28 December 1991 'Best of White River Reggae Bash' concert in Ocho Rios, recognised the achievements of world-famous Jamaicans who 'big-up' the nation:

> *Now yu see Jamaica, Jamaica is so famous all over di world. Jamaica have so much don and donette is unbelievable. All over di world dem rispek Jamaicans, seen, so hear dis now! A capella!*
>
> Fi such a small island in the Caribbean
> Yu produce whole heap a don man and woman
> In Jamaica, Ina Jamaica,
> Listen mi now!
> We yu get dem from, Jamaica?
> We yu get dem from?
> Yu mosi mek dem in a factory pon di island (*rep.*)
> Marcus Garvey, im was a great man
> Born ina Jamaica, ina St Ann.
> Tek Black consciousness to di American,
> Show black people which part im come from.
> Bob Marley im was a next one,
> Tek reggae music go a every nation
> Im big-up Jamaica, big-up Rastaman

Contesting the dominance of the ideology of Euro-American cultural imperialism – the CNN/Eurovision synoptic worldview – the cultural products of the small island state of Jamaica, particularly reggae music, articulate a profound sense of self-centredness and cultural autonomy. But the international transmission of this message of 'autonomy' through multinational recording/distributing companies, must itself be problematised as part of a global network of capitalist economics. Local structures of ownership of the music industry in Jamaica are replicated internationally.

Nevertheless, despite the contradiction that the subversive message of low culture reggae music is appropriated by the media-colonisation economics of high-tech high culture, the international superstar status of D.J. Shabba Ranks, needs to be analysed as yet another instance of colonisation in reverse. The language of the beat is universal and thus immediately consumable by non-Jamaicans. But the language of Shabba Ranks's lyrics needs to be translated, even for some Jamaicans; that process of translating redefines the powerful and the powerless, the 'centre' and the 'margins'. Potential receivers of Shabba Ranks's lyrics, who have limited competence in Jamaican, become peripheralised in a hierarchy-inverting discourse that defines them, however temporarily, as ignorant. They become dependent on mediators.

My own decision *not* to translate into English all of the Jamaican texts analysed in this study is part of this reverse colonisation project. For non-Jamaicans, the apparent inscrutability of these texts is an invitation to engage in the rehumanising act of learning a new language. For Jamaicans, these texts present an opportunity to extend the knowledge of the noises in the blood beyond immediate family. Translating becomes not so much an act of colonisation as a mutually liberating process of discovery. The ending of the project is, by its very nature, deferred.

Thus, the Third World Band's description of themselves as 'reggae ambassadors' aptly defines the role of culture-broking Jamaican musicians who help maintain links between Jamaicans at home and abroad, between Jamaicans and their host communities and between Jamaica and other countries in which there is no significant Jamaican residential population. In the spirit of Louise Bennett's 'Jamaica Elevate', the somewhat parodic notion of 'reggae ambassador' undermines the authority of the official Jamaican ambassadors who, despite their disposition to 'rub shoulder an dip mout/ Eena heavy world affairs', often do not have the reach of the reggae musician. There is a story, perhaps apocryphal, of a Jamaican ambassador who when asked about Marley, mistakenly assumed the enquiry to be about (Prime Minister) Manley.[23] This is yet another example of the subversive power of the low to transform the more usual power relations between the high and the low.

The authority of Jamaica's reggae ambassadors was unequivocally demonstrated during the twelve-hour musical tribute to Winnie and Nelson Mandela that was held in the national stadium in Kingston, Jamaica in July,

1991. That free public concert was an excellent example of the internationalisation of political consciousness that is a powerful stream in Jamaican popular culture. As we danced in the stadium, which was rammed to capacity with 32 000 Jamaicans and others joined in a primal celebration of the simple justness of the African National Congress struggle for liberation from the stranglehold of white racism in South Africa, I marvelled at how many anti-apartheid songs had originated in Jamaica. I also remembered that Bob Marley had been invited by the Government of Zimbabwe to sing redemption songs for their Independence celebrations.

It is a significant statement on the high seriousness of the occasion that the one singer who attempted to introduce the 'slackness' theme into the proceedings was loudly booed and prevented by the crowd from singing his entirely inappropriate song about body odour. The crowd as collective censor made it abundantly clear that within the consciousness of the people themselves there operate principles of propriety and social decorum that are often presumed to be beyond them. To quote the DJ Lovindeer: 'When we talk about slackness . . . there's a time and place for everything.'[24] In his elaboration of this truism as it applies to dancehall culture Lovindeer acknowleges the relative autonomy of contextually determined moral codes:

> what is wrong with the slackness is that it is exposed outside of the dancehall. Inside the dancehall it is OK. (sic) because you have consenting adults there who want to hear those kinds of things, and it's OK with them. But outside you have children, Christians and other people who don't want to hear those kinds of things. It turns them off. What is wrong with the slackness is that it is exposed to people who don't want to hear it.[25]

The not entirely innocent juxtapositioning of children and Christians raises a host of subversive possibilities.

At the Mandela Day concert, Macka B performed his brilliant 'Devil Dance'. In a wicked inversion of the moral majority's usual demonising of the dancehall, Macka B's anti-apartheid lyrics define the dancehall itself as the contested sacred space over which the devil, as promoter, seeks to extend his control. Ronald Reagan becomes a rapper; Margaret Thatcher is a DJ and Pik Botha is the operator of the Apartheid High Power sound system:

> *Now Lucifer di devil, he don't like to see when di righteous a keep*
> *dance. So him se to imself, 'Who? Mi a go hold a dance to.'*
> *Hear di devil dance ya now!*

Chorus:
Se mi naa go, heh-heh, ina dis session, no way
Se mi naa go ina dis ya dance. (*rep.*)
Devil dance, Satan a keep a session (*rep.* × 3)

Well Lucifer di devil was di promoter
An di dance did-a keep ina South Africa.
Im print invitation, im print poster,
Anybody want a ticket dem fi check Lucifer.
Well di rate at di gate was a pound or dollar
Give Lucifer yu soul, den yu can enter.
Di Sound which a play, Apartheid High Power
Wid di bwai Botha as di operator.
Im invite Mussolini, im invite Hitler,
Di Klu Klux Klan an di Boston 'trangler.
Im invite rapist an mass murderer,
An anybody who support apartheid in Africa.
Well outside di dance some black informer
A beg Lucifer fi mek dem enter.
Lucifer se, 'ow yu mean? Unu come iin, Suupa!
If it wasn fi unu, mi wouldn get so broad!'

Chorus:
Devil dance, Satan a keep a session (*rep.* × 3)
Watch ya!

Fi add a little spice to di wicked session
Satan decide to hold a competition
Fi all di world leaders, man an woman
Fi see who get di prize as di wickedest one.
Well first pon di stage, dat a Ronald Reagan
Im start rap like an American:
'Hi, I'm Ron, I'm a son of a gun,
When I was in, poor people didn have no fun.
I never help the black people in America
Not once did I ever chant down Botha.'
Next pon di stage Margaret Thatcher
Shi start dj like shi a Suupa.
'Come!
Well a mi name Maggie, di iron Lady, eh eh!
Mi no like black people, an dem don't like mi, mi mi.
Mi mek di poor poorer, gi di rich more wealth
Mi smash di Unions and di National Health!'

Next pon di stage a di bwai Botha
Start chat, di place ketch a fire:
'Mi a Bad, Bad, Bad Botha!
Mi a Ba Ba Bad, Ba Ba Bad, Bad Botha!
Mi have di black people gold, mi have dem silver
Mi got dem ina jail, like di one Mandela.
Emergency laws have dem under pressure,
Mi still a deal wid England an America.'
Crowd gone wild, Satan se, 'Yu big!
How yu so bad? So, how yu so wicked?
Yu win first prize, an di prize mi a go give
Is a 666, put it pon yu forehead!'

Jimmy Cliff's 'Many Rivers To Cross', one of the most heartrending of the songs from the movie *The Harder They Come*, was transposed from its culture-specific Jamaican context to become a praise song for the Free Azania movement. Like the Atlantic ocean, the many rivers that must be crossed are not only barriers, but routes of cultural exchange. Revisionist readings of the geography of suffering that was mapped in this hemisphere in the age of European enlightened discovery, reposition Africans as explorers, if not *conquistadores*. They did come before Columbus, but apparently had no heart for the imperial enterprise. There is a burden of cultural arrogance at the core of the discovery project that assumes the centre of the world to be the point at which one begins. But the crossing and recrossing of rivers does not necessarily require the decimation of the discovered, as Jamaica Kincaid's Annie John imaginatively reminds us.

In 'Many Rivers to Cross', the micro image of domestic disharmony – the man abandoned by his woman – engenders yet another level of intimacy in the macro-economics of global suffering. Winnie Mandela publicly affirmed that the songs of Jamaican musicians energised her in the loneliness of political fighting; Nelson Mandela described Man-de-Ya[26] day in Jamaica as the happiest day of his life. No mere hyperbole, but a generous acceptance of the outpouring of creativity that the day inspired.

At the Bureau of Women's Affairs tribute to Mrs Mandela, Lorna Goodison chanted her 'Bedspread' poem. That moving affirmation of the telepathetic communication which sustained Nelson and Winnie Mandela over the long, lonely rivers of years, employs images of domesticity – the simple intimacy of a shared bedspread; the slender, capable hands of nurturing women – to connote political affiliation:

Sometimes in the still
unchanging afternoons
when the memories crowded
hot and hopeless against
her brow
she would seek its cool colours
and signal him to lie down
in his cell.
It is three in the afternoon Nelson
let us rest here together
upon this bank draped in freedom
colour.
It was woven by women with slender
capable hands
accustomed to binding wounds
hands that closed the eyes of
dead children,
that fought for the right to
speak in their own tongues
in their own land
in their own schools.
They wove the bedspread
and knotted notes of hope
in each strand
and selvedged the edges with
ancient blessings
older than any white man's coming.
So in the afternoons lying on this
bright bank of blessing
Nelson my husband I meet you in dreams
my beloved much of the world is
asleep blind to the tyranny and evil
devouring our people.
But, Mandela, you are rock on this sand
harder than any metal
mined in the bowels of this land
you are purer than any
gold tempered by fire
shall we lie here wrapped
in the colours of our free Azania?
They arrested the bedspread.
They and their friends are working

to arrest the dreams in our heads
and the women, accustomed to closing
the eyes of the dead
are weaving cloths still brighter
to drape us in glory in a Free
Azania.[27]

These women weavers of Azania, like Goodison herself, and all the cunning fabricators whose work is the subject of this study – the performance poets, singers, DJs, oral/print/electronic historians – are recreating the upful texts of an obeah/myal poetics of hierarchy inversion: chanting down Babylon. The etymological origins of textuality in the craft of weaving, restoring the primacy of the tactile presence of the body of the text, invert the high art/low craft-scribal/oral hierarchy of spell-bound literates. Popular culture, low culture, mass culture, the vulgar discourses of the feminised native body, pronounce the ancient blessings of the word made flesh: noises in the blood; echoes in the bone.

Notes

1 Louise Bennett, *Selected Poems* (Kingston: Sangster's, 1982); rpt 1983, p. 106. Subsequent references cited in text.
2 In Jamaican there is no grammatical marker of the passive voice; the context of use determines voice.
3 See Diana Brydon's signifying on 'Commonwealth' in her essay 'Commonwealth or Common Poverty?: the New Literatures in English and the New Discourse of Marginality', *Kunapipi*, Vol. xi, no. 1, 1989, pp. 1–16.
4 Forthcoming in *Unbecoming Daughters of the Empire* (Aarhus, Denmark: Dangaroo Press).
5 Note, for example, the popularity in dancehall culture of notions of 'big', 'broad', 'large', 'massive', that suggest the high self-concept of Jamaicans. The disparaging references that Jamaicans often make to the 'small-islanders' of the Eastern Caribbean is part of this culture of 'largeness'.
6 See, for example, Graham Huggan, 'Decolonizing the Map: Post-Colonialism, Post-Structuralism and the Cartographic Connection', in Ian Adam and Helen Tiffin (eds), *Past the Last Post: Theorizing Post-Colonialism and Post-Modernism* (Calgary: University of Calgary Press, 1990), pp. 125–38.
7 Jamaica Kincaid, *Annie John* (New York: Farrar, Straus, Giroux, 1985), p. 76.
8 Mervyn Morris (ed.), Louise Bennett, *Selected Poems*, p. 161.
9 Ibid., pp. 159–60.
10 Linda Hutcheon, *A Theory of Parody* (New York: Methuen, 1985), p. 20.
11 Louise Bennett, *Jamaica Labrish* (Kingston: Sangster's, 1966); rpt 1975, pp. 168–9. The rhythm of this rap which is structured around the repetition of 'tion' is reminiscent of Jamaican children's ring games and the lyrics of the DJs.
12 George Lamming, *The Pleasures of Exile*, 1960; rpt (London: Allison & Busby, 1984), pp. 214–15.

13 Ibid., pp. 38–9.
14 Robert Young, 'Neocolonial Times', *The Oxford Literary Review*, 13.1–2 (1991): pp. 2–3.
15 Jamaica Kincaid, *A Small Place*, (New York: Farrar, Straus, Giroux, 1988), pp. 18–19.
16 Jamaica Kincaid, *Lucy* (New York: Farrar, Straus, Giroux, 1990), p. 17.
17 Ibid., pp. 64–5.
18 Ibid., p. 156.
19 Louise Bennett, *Jamaica Labrish*, pp. 163–4.
20 Peter Stallybrass and Allon White, *The Politics and Poetics of Transgression* (Ithaca, New York: Cornell University Press, 1986), p. 4.
21 I am indebted to Rex Nettleford for this inversion of worlds, to which he referred in his speech as University Orator, at the Special Convocation Ceremony to confer the Honorary Degree of Doctor of Laws on Mr Nelson Mandela, held on 24 July 1991 at UWI, Mona, Jamaica.
22 Known in some irreverent circles as the International Mother Fucker.
23 I am indebted, again, to Erna Brodber for this lovely anecdote.
24 Lloyd Lovindeer, 'Women in Dancehall', *Jamaica Journal*, 23.1 (1990): p. 51.
25 Ibid., p. 52.
26 Translated 'Man-is-here', this pun, in Jamaican, on the name Mandela is yet another example of the inventiveness of collective street wit.
27 Lorna Goodison, *I am Becoming My Mother* (London: New Beacon Books, 1986), pp. 42–3.

APPENDIX I: Proverbs from Louise Bennett's *Jamaica Labrish* and *Selected Poems*

I. Animal

Dog a sweat but long hair hide i.
But 'posen mawga dog don't dead? Crow haffe nyam green grass.
Every puppy got him flea.
Yuh play wid dawg dem lick yuh mout.
Yuh sleep wid dawg yuh ketch him flea.
When ashes cowl dawg sleep in deh.
When dawg marga him head big.
When kitchen dressa tumble dung, de mawga dog dem laugh.
Cock cyaan beat cock eena cock own yard.
Cockroach no bizniz a fowl yard.
Noh mock mawga cow, him a bull muma.
Donkey tink him cub a racehorse.
Jackass say de worl' noh level.
All fish nyam man, dah shark one get de blame.
When horse dead cow fat.
John Crow tink him pickney white.
Ef yuh fly wid John crow, yuh wi haffe nyam dead meat.
Monkey should know weh him gwine put him tail before him order trousiz.
Fire wan deh a Musmus tail him tink sey dah cool air.
Puss laugh when pear-tree fall.
When puss hungry him nose clean.

II. General

Back no know weh ole shut do fi i so tell ole shut tear off.
Bad luck wus an obeah.
Before me tumble down me hole macca.
Cook up yuh fat eena jesta pot, but no t'row weh yuh old bun-pan.
Coward man kip soun bone.

Ef yuh fe dead wid coco-bey gun-shot kean teck yuh life.
Ef yuh no go a man fire-side, yuh no know ow much fire-stick a bwile him pot.
Every seckeh got him jeggeh.
Every sidung-smaddy got dem tan-up day dah come.
Every sore foot got him blue-stone.
Everything wha shine no gole piece.
'Fore bickle pwile, meck belly bus.
Howdy an tenky bruk no square.
Kip yuh stick til yuh done climb hill.
Mout a laugh, but heart a leap.
No care how smaddy dah gwan bad sinting deh fi spokes him wheel.
Noh care how man sey dem bad, man kean badda dan Dead.
No cuss long man till yuh sure sey yuh done grow.
Oman luck deh a dungle.
Sidung-man kean look straight eena tan-up ooman y'eye.
Sweet mout fly follow coffin go a hole.
Time longer dan rope.
When trouble teck man, pickney boot fit him.
Yuh gwine reap what yuh sow.
Yuh shake man han but yuh no shake dem heart.
Wait no kill nobody.

Appendix II: Jamaican proverbs: a gender perspective

Sources:

Beckwith, Martha. *Jamaica Proverbs*, New York, 1925; rpt. 1970.

Cundall, Frank and Izett Anderson, *Jamaica Proverbs and Sayings,* London, 1910; revised 1927; rpt. 1972.

Female characteristics: (psychological and physiological)

Cunning better than strong.
De saby woman have eye but no ear.
Market house a woman court-house.
Cutacoo full, woman laugh.
When pocket full, and bankra full, woman laugh.
Woman and wood, and woman and water, and woman and money never quarrel. (B)
When guinea-hen cry him say, 'woman no fe play'.
Woman tongue, 'was-was' and tamarind tree, the three worse things.
Woman mout and fowl a one.
Perfect woman and white John Crow scarce.
Drizzle drizzle favour contentious woman.
Woman deceitful like star-apple leaf.
Handsome face woman not de bestest kind of woman.
Beautiful woman, beautiful trouble.
Obeah man daughter always pretty. (B)
Pretty face and pretty clothes no character. (B)
Woman no want to dance she say her frock short.
When man have trouble, woman take it make laugh.
Dog-flea tell him wife say, 'If man see me, lef dinner fe me; if woman see me, make me coffin.'
Snake say if him no hold up him head, female take him tie wood. (B)

When man drunk, him walk and stagger; when woman drunk, she sit down and consider.
Rum make woman sit down and consider, rum make man walk and stagger, and de man who refuse rum is a booby. (B)
A drinking dame a special shame.
Fool-fool gal him blush at everything.
Woman rains never done.

Old women

Trouble make old woman trot.
Callaloo a swear fe old woman, old woman a swear fe callaloo.
If you want to know if old woman tongue long you must pull her jigger hot.
Rub old woman back, she will make you taste her pepper pot.
If you follow old woman you will nyam pot bottom.
Go a cross pass, you see old woman, no trouble her.
Old woman did want to cry before, what you think when she get sore eye.
Old lady want cry, she say smoke burn her eye.
When you see old lady run, no ask what de matter, run too.
If old woman dey a fire side, ram-goat won't hang himself.

Women and children

If you kill pickney give mumma, mumma won't eat; but if you kill mumma give pickney, pickney will eat. (B)
Hen never mash fe her pickney too hard. (B)
When fowl gravel her chicken, she no tell hawk fe pick it up. (B)
Fowl will swear a fe her egg; she can't swear a fe her pickney.
Hen 'gree fe hatch duck egg, but she no 'gree fe take duck-pickney fe swim.
Send out pickney you foot rest, but you heart no rest. (B)
When cow can't get water fe wash her pickney face, she take her tongue. (B)
Last pickney always kill mumma. (B)
Pig ask him mumma say what make her mouth long so; she say, 'A no mind, me pickney; dat something make fe me long so, will make fe you long so too.' (B)
Where the goat go, the kid follow. (B)
Many a mauger cow you see a common, a bull mumma.

Women and men

Ant follow fat; woman follow man.
When man have coco-head in a barrel, him can go pick wife.
Man can't marry if him don't have cashew.
When money done, love done. (B)
A no one time monkey want wife.
Before you marry keep you two eye open: after you marry, shut one.
Marriage have teeth and bite hot.
Two dog fe one bone, two woman fe one house, never 'gree long.
Fowl bex with rooster, a whe' she sleep?
Marry fe love, work fe money.
Marry you daughter when you can, you son when you please.
Good wife better than estate wagon.
Man build house, but woman make the home.
If man did know, him would a never plant yam inna stranger woman ground. (B)
No man too old fe old maid.
Driver beat him wife first.
Drummer wife never keep goat skin.

Men and children

One daddy fe twenty pickney, but twenty pickney no fe one daddy.
Cock no know fe watch chicken, but him know how fe nyam corn.
Children suck dem modder when dem young, dem fader when dem ole.

Gender, class and colour

Brown man wife nyam cockroach a corner, save money fe buy silk dress.
Hard push make mulatto woman keep saddler shop.
When dainty lady live well, she take pin fe nyam pea.

Bibliography

Allen, Harry. 'Hip-hop Madness', *Essence* , April 1989, pp. 78–79, 114.

Alleyne, Mervyn. *Roots of Jamaican Culture* (London: Karia Press/Pluto Press, 1988).

Anderson, I. and F Cundall (eds). *Jamaican Proverbs*. (Kingston Institute of Jamaica, 1910; rpt, Shannon, Irish University Press, 1972).

Appiah, Kwame Anthony. 'Is the Post- in Postmodernism the Post- in Postcolonial?', *Critical Inquiry*, 17.2 (1991) : pp. 336–57.

Barber, Karin. 'Yoruba Oriki and Deconstructive Criticism', *Research in African Literatures,* Vol. 15, no. 4, Winter 1984, pp. 497–518.

Bartley, G. Fitz. 'Jamaican stars in "Marked for Death"'. *Jamaica Record*, [Kingston, Jamaica] Sunday, 28 October 1990, p. 1C.

Baugh, Edward. *A Tale of the Rain Forest*. (Kingston, Jamaica: Sandberry Press, 1988).

Beckwith, Martha. *Jamaica Proverbs* (1925; rpt. New York: Negro Universities Press, 1972).

'Bennett on Bennett', Louise Bennett interviewed by Dennis Scott, *Caribbean Quarterly* 14, 1–2 (1968), pp. 97–101.

Bennett, Louise. *Jamaica Labrish*, ed. Rex Nettleford (Kingston: Sangster's, 1966; rpt 1975).

——. *Selected Poems*, ed. Mervyn Morris (Kingston: Sangster's, 1982; rpt 1983).

Brathwaite, Edward. 'Creative Literature of the British West Indies during the period of Slavery', *Savacou* 1.1 (1970): pp. 46–80.

——. *History of the Voice* (London: New Beacon Books, 1984).

Breeze, Jean Binta. *Riddym Ravings and Other Poems*. ed. Mervyn Morris (London: Race Today Publications, 1988).

——. Interview by Andrea Stewart, *Marxism Today*, November 1988: pp. 44–5.

Brodber, Erna. *Jane and Louisa Will Soon Come Home* (London: New Beaçon Books, 1980).

——. *Myal* (London: New Beacon Books, 1988).

—— and J. E Green. 'Reggae and Cultural Identity in Jamaica', Working Papers on Caribbean Society, Sociology Department, University of the West Indies, St Augustine, Trinidad, Series C, No. 7, 1981.

Brown, Lloyd. *West Indian Poetry*, Twayne's World Authors Ser. 422 (Boston: Twayne, 1978).

Brown, Stewart. 'Dub Poetry: Selling Out', *Poetry Wales* 22.2 (1987), pp. 51-4.

——. 'Exiles and heartlands: new Caribbean poetry', *Third World Quarterly* 11.4 (1989), pp. 265–74.

——, Mervyn Morris and Gordon Rohlehr (eds), *Voiceprint* (London: Longman, 1989).

Brydon, Diana. 'Commonwealth or Common Poverty?: the New Literatures in

English and the New Discourse of Marginality', *Kunapipi*, xi.1 (1989), pp. 1–16.

Burnett, Paula (ed.). *The Penguin Book of Caribbean Verse in English* (Harmondsworth: Penguin, 1986).

Bush, Barbara. *Slave Women in Caribbean Society 1650–1838* (London: James Currey; Kingston: Heinemann; Bloomington: Indiana University Press, 1990).

Cargill, Morris. 'Corruption of Language is no Cultural Heritage', *Sunday Gleaner* [Kingston, Jamaica] 29 October 1989, p. 8A.

Cassidy, F. G. and R. B. LePage (eds), *Dictionary of Jamaican English* (Cambridge: Cambridge University Press, 1967; rpt 1980).

Castle, Terry. *Masquerade and Civilization: The Carnivalesque in Eighteenth–Century English Culture and Fiction* (Stanford, CA.: Stanford University Press, 1986).

Chang, Victor. 'Creole and the Jamaican Novelist: Redcam, DeLisser and V.S. Reid', Unpublished paper, Sixth Annual Conference on West Indian Literature, UWI, St Augustine, 1986, pp. 1–9.

——, Rev. of Christian Habekost (ed.), *Dub Poetry: 19 Poets from England and Jamaica, Jamaica Journal* 21.3 (1988), pp. 49–50.

Clarke, Sebastian. *Jah Music* (London: Heinemann, 1980).

Cobham-Sander, Rhonda. 'The Creative Writer and West Indian Society: Jamaica 1900–50', Dissertation, University of St Andrews, 1981 (Ann Arbor, UMI, 1984).

Cooper, Carolyn. 'Cho! Misa Cargill, Riispek Juu', *Sunday Gleaner* [Kingston, Jamaica], 5 November 1989, p. 8A.

D'Costa, Jean and Barbara Lalla (eds), *Voices in Exile: Jamaican Texts of the 18th and 19th Centuries* (Tuscaloosa: University of Alabama Press, 1989).

Davis, Stephen. *Bob Marley* (London: Panther/Granada, 1984; rpt of Arthur Barker Ltd).

Day, Gary and Clive Bloom (eds), *Perspectives on Pornography: Sexuality in Film and Literature* (London: Macmillan, 1988).

DeLisser, Herbert. *Jane's Career* (1914; rpt. London: Heinemann, 1981).

Devonish, Hubert. 'The Decay of Neo-Colonial Official Language Policies. The Case of the English-lexicon Creoles of the Commonwealth Caribbean', Manfred Gorlach and John A. Holm (eds), *Focus on the Caribbean* (Amsterdam/Philadelphia: John Benjamins Publishing Co., 1986), pp. 23–51.

——. *Language and Liberation* (London: Karia Press, 1986).

Edwards, Bryan. *The History, Civil and Commercial of the British Colonies in the West Indies*, London, 1801 (5 vols).

Finnegan, Ruth. *Oral Literature in Africa* (Oxford: Oxford University Press, 1970).

Gates, Jr. Henry Louis (ed.). *'Race,' Writing and Difference* (Chicago: University of Chicago Press, 1985, 1986).

——. *Figures in Black: Words, Signs, and the 'Racial' Self* (Oxford: Oxford University Press, 1987; rpt 1989).

——. *The Signifying Monkey* (New York: Oxford University Press, 1988).

Gilroy, Paul. *There Ain't No Black in the Union Jack* (London: Hutchinson, 1987).

Glissant, Edouard. *Caribbean Discourse*, 1981; trans. J. Michael Dash (Charlottesville: University of Virginia, 1989).

Gonzalez, Michael and Havelock Nelson. *Bring the Noise: A Guide to Rap Music and Hip-Hop Culture* (New York: Random House, 1991).

Goodison, Lorna. *I Am Becoming My Mother* (London: New Beacon Books, 1986).

——. *Heartease* (London: New Beacon Books, 1988).
Hall, Douglas (ed.) *In Miserable Slavery: Thomas Thistlewood in Jamaica, 1750–86* (London: Macmillan, 1989).
Hall, Stuart and Tony Jefferson (eds), *Resistance through Rituals* (London: Hutchinson, 1975).
Hassan, Leila (ed.). *Women of the Word* (London: Creation for Liberation, 1988).
Hearne, John. 'Patois – a Barefoot Language', *Sunday Gleaner* [Kingston, Jamaica], 25 November 1990, p. 7A.
Huggan, Graham. 'Decolonizing the Map: Post-Colonialism, Post-Structuralism and the Cartographic Connection', in Ian Adam and Helen Tiffin (eds), *Past the Last Post: Theorizing Post-Colonialism and Post-Modernism* (Calgary: University of Calgary Press, 1990), pp. 125–38.
Huggins, Molly. *Too Much To Tell* (London: Heinemann, 1967).
Hurston, Zora Neale. *Their Eyes Were Watching God* (1937; rpt New York: Harcourt Brace Jovanovich, 1961).
Hussey, Dermott and Malika Lee Whitney. *Bob Marley: Reggae King of the World* (Kingston, Jamaica: Kingston Publishers, 1984).
Hutcheon, Linda. *A Theory of Parody* (New York: Methuen, 1985).
Irigaray, Luce. *This Sex Which is Not One* (1977; translation rpt Ithaca: Cornell University Press, 1985).
Jekyll, Walter (ed.). *Jamaican Song and Story* (1907; rpt New York: Dover, 1966).
Kennedy, Maev. 'Dark Horse in Poetry Contest Bridles at Sporting Metaphor', *Guardian* [London] 20 May 1989, p. 1.
Kincaid, Jamaica. *Annie John* (New York: Farrar Straus Giroux, 1985).
——. *A Small Place* (New York: Farrar Straus Giroux, 1988).
——. *Lucy* (New York: Farrar Straus Giroux, 1990).
Lamming, George. *The Pleasures of Exile* (1960; rpt London: Allison & Busby, 1984).
Long, Edward T*he History of Jamaica* (1774; rpt London: Frank Cass, 1970), Vol. II.
Lovelace Earl. *The Dragon Can't Dance* (1979; rpt London: Longman, 1985).
Lovindeer, Lloyd. 'Women in Dancehall', *Jamaica Journal* 23.1 (1990), pp. 51–2 (transcribed and edited by Carolyn Allen).
Marcuse, Herbert. *Eros and Civilization* (Boston: Beacon Press, 1955, 1966).
Mathurin, Lucille. *The Rebel Woman in the British West Indies During Slavery* (Kingston, Jamaica: Institute of Jamaica Publications, 1975).
McGowan, Howard. 'Sting 88: Pinchers Takes Round 2 From Sanchez; Singers "stoned"', *Daily Gleaner* [Kingston, Jamaica], 30 December 1988, p. 6.
——. 'Time for a Stand Against "Dirty Lyrics"; Suspend All DJ Awards This Year', *Sunday Gleaner* [Kingston, Jamaica], 1 January 1989, p. 5.
McKay, Claude. *Banana Bottom* (1933; rpt New York: Harcourt Brace Jovanovich, 1961).
McKenzie, Herman. Review of *Lionheart Gal, Jamaica Journal* 20.4, (1987–8): pp. 63–6.
Mohammed, Patricia and Catherine Shepherd (eds), *Gender in Caribbean Development* (Jamaica, Trinidad and Tobago, Barbados. The University of the West Indies Women and Development Studies Project, 1988).
Moreton J. B. *West India Customs and Manners,* 2d edn. (London: J. Parsons, 1793).
Morris, Mervyn (ed.). *Focus* (Kingston, Jamaica: Caribbean Authors, 1983).

——. 'Gender in Some Performance Poems', unpublished conference paper, Seminar on 'Gender in Caribbean Culture.' Women and Development Studies Project, UWI, Mona, June 1987, pp. 1–8.

——. 'Printing the Performance', *Jamaica Journal* 23.1 (1990): pp. 21–6.

Mugo, Micere. 'The Relationship between African and African–American Literature as Utilitarian Art: A Theoretical Formulation', in Joseph E. Harris (ed.), *Global Dimensions of the African Diaspora* (Washington, D.C.: Howard University Press, 1982), pp. 85–93.

Mutabaruka 'Dis Poem', poster, Kingston, Jamaica, lithographed by Stephenson's, n.d.

O'Callaghan, Evelyn, Rev. of *Lionheart Gal, Journal of West Indian Literature* 2.1 (1987): pp. 93–7.

Ong, Walter *Orality and Literacy* (New York: Methuen, 1982).

Parker, Patricia. *Literary Fat Ladies: Rhetoric, Gender, Property (*London: Methuen, 1987).

Patterson, Orlando. *The Children of Sisyphus* (London: New Authors, 1964).

Pollard, Velma. 'Dread Talk – The Speech of the Rastafarian in Jamaica', *Caribbean Quarterly* 26.4 (1980): pp. 32–41.

——. 'Figurative Language in Jamaican Creole', *Carib*, no. 3 (1983): pp. 24–36.

——. 'The Social History of Dread Talk', in Lawrence D. Carrington (ed.), *Studies in Caribbean Language* (School of Education, UWI, St Augustine, Trinidad, 1983) pp. 46–62.

Rashford, John. 'Plants, Spirits and the Meaning of "John" in Jamaica', *Jamaica Journal* 17.2 (1984): pp. 62–70.

Redfern, Walter. *Puns* (Oxford: Basil Blackwell, 1984).

Reid, Victor Stafford. *Nanny Town* (Kingston: Jamaica Publishing House, 1983).

Ross, Andrew. *Intellectuals and Popular Culture* (New York: Routledge, 1989).

Rowe, Maureen. 'The Woman in Rastafari', *Caribbean Quarterly* 26.4 (1980): pp. 13–21.

——. Telephone interview, February 1991.

S. M., Review of *The Harder They Come*, 'Rhygin . . . and now the book'. *Sunrays, Sunday Sun Magazine* [Kingston: Jamaica], 29 June 1980, p. 18.

Scott, Michael. *Tom Cringle's Log* (1838; rpt London: Everyman's Library, No. 710), 1938.

SISTREN with Honor Ford Smith, editor. *Lionheart Gal: Life Stories of Jamaican Women (*London: The Women's Press, 1986).

Slemon Stephen and Helen Tiffin (eds). *After Europe* (Mundelstrup, Denmark: Dangaroo Press, 1989).

Smith, Michael. *It A Come*, (ed.). Mervyn Morris (London: Race Today Publications, 1986).

Stallybrass, Peter and Allon White. *The Politics and Poetics of Transgression* (Ithaca, N.Y.: Cornell University Press, 1986).

Straw, Petrine Archer. 'Christopher Gonzalez's "Bob Marley Monument": Masterpieces from the National Gallery', Lecture No. 8, *Sunday Gleaner* [Kingston, Jamaica], 18 May 1986.

Tanna, Laura, 'Anansi – Jamaica's Trickster Hero', *Jamaica Journal* 16.2 (1983): pp. 20–30.

Thelwell, Michael. *The Harder They Come* (London: Pluto, 1980).

Tosh, Peter. Interview by Carolyn Cooper, *Pulse*, June 1984, pp. 12, 14–15, 32.

Walcott, Derek. 'What the Twilight Says: An Overture', in *Dream on Monkey Mountain and Other Plays* (New York: Farrar Straus and Giroux, 1970), pp. 3–40.
——. *Another Life* (London: Jonathan Cape, 1972; rpt 1973).
Walker, Alice. *The Color Purple* (New York: Washington Square Press, 1982; rpt 1983).
Warner-Lewis. 'Masks of the Devil: Caribbean Images of Perverse Energy', unpublished conference paper, UWI, St Augustine, 1991, pp. 1–21.
Weatherby, W. J. 'When Literary Worlds Collide'. *Guardian* [London] 28 May 1980.
White, Garth. *The Development of Jamaican Popular Music with Special Reference to Bob Marley: A Bibliography* (Kingston, Jamaica: African Caribbean Institute of Jamaica, 1982).
White, Timothy. *Catch a Fire* (New York: Holt, Rinehart and Winston, 1983).
Williams, Claudette. 'Images of Black and Mulatto Women in Spanish Caribbean Poetry: Discourse and Ideology', Dissertation, Stanford University, 1986.
Williams, Paulette. 'I Just Love The Carib', *Flair Magazine* (*Daily Gleaner*) [Kingston, Jamaica] 5 November 1990, p. 17.
Wilson, Basil and Herman Hall. 'Marley in His Own Words: A Memorable Interview', *Everybody's Magazine* [New York] 5.4 (1981): 23–6.
Young, Robert. 'Neocolonial Times', *Oxford Literary Review*, 13.1–2 (1991): pp. 2–3.

Discography

Bennett, Louise. *Yes M'Dear – Miss Lou Live*, Island Records, ICT 9740, 1983.
Breeze, Jean Binta. *Tracks*, LKJ, 1989.
Derrick's One Stop Record Shop Kingston, Jamaica. *Latest Reggae '88*, 1988.
Lovindeer, Lloyd. *Panty Man*, Prolific Productions, n.d.
——. *Wild Gilbert*, Stage Records, 1988.
Marley, Bob. *Burnin'*, Island Record, ILPS 9256, 1973
——. *Natty Dread*, Island Records, ILPS 9281, 1974.
——. *Rastaman Vibration*, Island Records, ILPS 9383, 1976.
——. *Exodus*, Island Records, ILPS 9498, 1977.
——. *Kaya*, Island Records, ILPS 9517, 1978.
——. *Survival*, Island Records, ILPS 9542, 1979.
——. *Uprising*, Island Records, ILPS 9596, 1980.
——. *Confrontation*, Island Records, ILPS, 1983.
Smith, Michael. *Me Cyaan Believe It*, Island Records, ILPS 9717, 1982.
Wales, Josey. *Culture a Lick*, Jammy's, 1988.
——. *Slackness Done*, Jammy's, 1988.
Yellowman. *Titty Jump*.
——. *Waan Mi Virgin*.

Index

Titles of books and albums are italicised, while individual songs and poems are in inverted commas.

afro-centric literature 14
Allen, Harry 144, 146
Alleyne, Mervyn 15
Anansi 47–8, 60–1, 102–3, 115, 168
Annie John (Kincaid) 178
Appiah, Kwame Anthony 15–16
archetypes, in film 97–8
'Ardent Fan' (Pincher) 166
audience, as interpreter 118
authorship/authority 4, 88, 89, 102
'Ava's Diary' (Sistren) 93

Babylon 9–11, 121, 131–2
'Babylon System' (Marley) 123
'Back Out' (Demus) 148–9
'Bad Card' (Marley) 5
bad words 98–9
Bailey, Admiral 145
'Bans O' Ooman' (Bennett) 52
Barber, Karin 84
Baugh, Edward 146
Beckwith, Martha 45
'Bedspread' (Goodison) 196–8

Bennett, Louise
  crafty women 9, 47–8
  disclaimers 103
  female sensibility 47–52, 57–66, 164–5
  Jamaican culture 175–7
  and literary tradition 139–40
  mother/child relationship 56, 57
  performance poetry 11
  persona 47–8
  proverbs 37–46
  West Indies 190–1
'Big Tings' (Bennett) 65
'Black Man's Lub Song, De' (anon.) 27–9
blai 153, 172 (n25)
Bob Marley: Reggae King of the World (Whitney) 121
Brathwaite, Edward 1, 4, 80, 99–100
Breeze, Jean Binta 4, 9, 68–9, 72–3, 81
Brer Nansi *see* Anansi
Brodber, Erna 3, 16, 120–1

Brown, Lloyd 47
Brown, Stewart 71
brutalisation 123, 151–2
'Bump Up' (Lovindeer) 149–50
Burnin' (Marley) 118, 121
Bush, Barbara 23, 27

calypso 138, 190
'Candy-Seller' (Bennett) 61–2
capitalism, and literature 102
Caribbean sensibility 183–5
Carmichael, Emma 27
Cassidy orthography 12–13, 91–5
Castle, Terry 24
Chang, Victor 90
'Chant Down Babylon' (Marley) 124–5
child-rearing 56, 57
Clarke, Sebastian 119–20
class, and language 90
class/gender, as power determinant 54
Cliff, Jimmy 196
collective values, and novel 103
colonialist discourse 100–1
'Colonization in Reverse' (Bennett) 175–7
Color Purple, The (Walker) 96
Confrontation (Marley) 118, 124–5
'Crazy Baldhead' (Marley) 122
Creole 12–13, 82, 90–5, 140–1
criticism, scribal 84, 100
cross-dressing 149–51
'Culture a Lick' (Wales) 146–7
Culture/Slackness 11–12, 141–2, 147–8, 154, 171
'Customs Officer' (Lovindeer) 138
'Cyaan do Di Wuk' (Shabba Ranks) 156

D'Costa, Jean 20, 22, 31, 33
Davis, Stephen 119
'Dead Man' (Bennett) 110–11
'Dear Departed Federation' (Bennett) 182–3
deconstructive criticism 84
DeLisser, Herbert 6
Demus, Chaka 148–9, 154

'Devil Dance' (Macka B) 194–6
Devonish, Hubert 140
dialect poetry 41
dialogic discourse 87, 91, 96
Dictionary of Jamaican English 31, 185
'Different Rage, A' (Cooper) 13
dirty lyrics 146
'Dis Poem' (Mutabaruka) 74
disclaimers 102–3
'Distinguish 'Merican' (Bennett) 65–6
'DJ A Look Fi Mi' (Lecturer) 165–6
DJs
  criticised 145–6
  cross-dressing 149–51
  double-entendre 137–8, 141, 157–8
  female 154–5
  intertextuality 138
  lyrics and folk ethos 136–9
  sexuality 142, 155, 158–60, 161–5
  and singers 144–5
  slackness 141, 144, 146, 148–9
  social commentary 167–71
'Doan Mess Wid My Pum-Pum' (Lovindeer) 161–2
double-entendre 68, 137–8, 141, 157–8
Dragon Can't Dance, The (Lovelace) 97–8
dub poetry 11, 17–18 (n10), 70–1, 80–1
'Dub Poetry: Selling Out' (Brown) 71
'Dubbed Out' (Breeze) 68

editorial *persona* 87, 88
education, and Rastafarianism 121, 122
Edwards, Bryan 23
'Eena Mi Corner' (Breeze) 76
'Ella' (Sistren) 94–5
Esu 148
Exodus (Marley) 118, 122–3, 127, 128, 129–30
exploitation 59–60

female sensibility 48–9, 164–5
fertility 69–70
'Figurative Language in Jamaican Creole' (Pollard) 38–9
film, 96, 102, 107
Finnegan, Ruth 45
folk aesthetic 89, 138
'Footworks' (Bennett) 64
'Forever Loving Jah' (Marley) 133–4
formulaic thought 120
'Free Movement' (Bennett) 190–1

Gates, Henry Louis 148
gender, and power 7, 20, 54
'Get Up, Stan(d) Up' (Shabba Ranks) 156
Gilroy, Paul 100–3, 141
'Give Me Little Dub Music' (Smith) 74–5
Glissant, Edouard 1, 2, 3
Goodison, Lorna 80, 166–7, 196–8
'Grandma's Estate' (Sistren) 87, 90, 93–4
'Granny Two-Teet' (Lovindeer) 137, 158–60
griot 4, 102
'Gyal Man' (Johnny P) 153, 155

Harder They Come, The (Thelwell) 9, 11, 96, 99–115
health care 158
'Heartbreaker' (Lady Junie and Tristan Palmer) 152–3
Hebdige, Dick 138–9
heterosexuality 142, 149
higglering 57, 61, 63
Higgs and Twins 136–7, 155–6
hip-hop 144, 146
History of the Voice (Brathwaite) 1, 80
'Holly' (Breeze) 76–7
homosexuality 142, 149, 162
'Hungry No Laugh' (Irie) 169
Hurston, Zora Neale 2, 7
Hutcheon, Linda 182

'I an I Alone' (Smith) 78–9
'I Shot the Sheriff' (Marley) 126–7
'I Sight Up Tacky' (Smith) 79–80
'If Me Want fe Go in a Ebo' 33–4
ignorance 185–6
'Independance' (Bennett) 177, 178–9
'Independence Dignity' (Bennett) 179–80
interpretation, and signification 118
intertextuality 2, 96, 138
Irie, Clement 169
'Is This Love?' (Marley) 127–8
Ivan, in *The Harder They Come* 102, 104–6, 107–113, 115

Jack Mandora 103
'Jah Music' (Goodison) 166–7
Jah Music (Clarke) 119–20
Jamaica Carnival 189–90
'Jamaica Elevate' (Bennett) 180–1, 193
'Jamaica Oman' (Bennett) 48–9
'Jamaica Philosophy' (Bennett) 37–8
Jamaican language 16–17 (n2)
  and English, compared 8, 89–90
  as language of scholarship 91–5
  legitimacy 40, 136
  orality 2–3, 9, 84
  orthography 12–13, 82
  see also Creole; oral/scribal discourse
Jamaican philosophy 117
Jamaican proverbs 45, 200–4

Jane's Career (DeLisser) 6
Jekyll, Walter 103–4
John Canoe 23–4, 25, 35 (n17)
Johnny P 153, 155
'Johnny Was' (Marley) 130
Jonkonnu song 23–4, 25, 35 (n17)
Journal of a West India Proprietor (Lewis) 32
'Jump Up Time' (Higgs and Twins) 136–7, 155–6

Kaya (Marley) 118, 122, 127
Kincaid, Jamaica 178, 186–7
knowledge 3–4, 186

Lady Junie 152–3
Lalla, Barbara 20, 22, 31, 33
Lamming, George 175, 183–4, 185–6
language
  and class 94–5
  DJs 140–1
  of massive 185
  of seduction 135 (n16)
  as subversion 121
  warding off evil 61
Lecturer 165–6
lesbianism 96–7
Lewis, Matthew G. 32, 33
liberation, internalised 123, 124
Lionheart Gal: Lifestories of Jamaican Women (Sistren Theatre Collective) 12, 87–95
literature, and politics 101
Little Lenny 151–2
Long, Edward 25–6, 27, 33
long head/book 1, 2, 3
'Love Unu' (Red Dragon) 137
Lovelace, Earl 97–8
'Lovin Wasn Easy' (Breeze) 77
Lovindeer, Lloyd 5, 135 (n16), 137–8, 149–50, 151, 158–60, 161–2, 169–71
Lucy (Kincaid) 187–9

Macka B 192, 194–6
'Mad Puss Tonic' (Lovindeer) 150
male/female relationships 51, 54, 92–3, 127, 160
  see also sexual politics
Mandela, Nelson and Winnie 194, 196
'Many Rivers to Cross' (Cliff) 196
map-making, revisionist 177–8
Marked for Death 97
Marley, Bob
  Babylon as whore 130–2
  ideology 121–6, 132–4
  language 5, 9–11, 117–18
  metaphor 126
  verbal play 118
  woman 127–30
  see also Rastafarianism
marronage 4, 136
Masquerade and Civilization (Castle) 24–5
'Mass Wedding' (Bennett) 53
McAndrew, Wordsworth 140
McGowan, Howard 145–6, 149, 160–1
McKenzie, Herman 88, 89
'Me and Annancy' (Bennett) 103
'Me Bredda' (Bennett) 58–9
'Me Cyaan Believe It' (Smith) 69
'Me know no law, me know no sin' 19–23, 29, 30–1
menstruation 98–9, 162
meta-dub poetry 68, 74
metaphor 37, 69, 126, 169
metonymy 69
migration to Britain 183–4, 193
'Min(d) Yu Disrespec Mi' (Isaacs and Wales) 167
mnemonics 38
Moreton, J. B. 20–2, 30
Morris, Mervyn 41, 42, 70, 73, 80, 179–80
mother/child relations 56, 57
'Mrs Govanah' (Bennett) 64–5
Mugo, Micere 14
Murray, H. G. 1, 2
Mutabaruka 71, 74
'My Dream' (Bennett) 60
Myal (Brodber) 3, 16

Nanny Town (Reid) 1, 3–4
native wit 115
Natty Dread (Marley) 118, 121–2, 125
'Nayga Yard' (Bennett) 41–2
naygacentric values 40–1
neocolonialism 186
Nettleford, Rex 39–40, 53, 61, 182–3
'New Govanah' (Bennett) 64–5
'New Scholar' (Bennett) 56
'Nigger Sweat' (Baugh) 146
Ninja Man 156
'No Bad Mind' (Lady G) 168
'No Bodder Dis(respec) Mi' (Shabba Ranks) 166
'No Pussy Tes(t)' (Lovindeer) 158
'No Woman No Cry' (Marley and The Wailers) 130

Ong, Walter 38, 120
Onuora, Oku 80–1
Oral Literature in Africa (Finnegan) 45
oral tradition 1, 2–3, 120

oral/scribal discourse
  Bennett 39–40
  continuum 6–7
  dialectics of 2, 174–5, 185
  dialogic 87, 94
  interwoven 82–4, 117
  orthography 12–13, 82–3
  proverbs 37–8, 200–4
  transitional forms 4, 120
  see also transcription problems
orality, and gender 20
Orality and Literacy (Ong) 38, 120
'Ordinary Mawning' (Breeze) 77–8
orthography 12–13, 82

Palmer, Tristan 152–3
'Panty Man' (Lovindeer) 138, 160
Parker, Patricia 10
parody 179–82, 184
'Peace' (Flourgon and Thriller U) 167–8
performance poetry 4, 11, 17–18 (n10), 68, 70–1, 80, 117
Perry, Lee 119
persona, Bennett 47–8
personal/political 87
picong 137–8, 187
'Pimper's Paradise' (Marley) 131–2
Pincher 166
Pleasures of Exile, The (Lamming) 183–4
politics 64–5, 87, 91–2, 101, 125–6
Politics and Poetics of Transgression, (Stallybrass and White) 26–7, 191–2
Pollard, Velma 38–9
pornography/erotica 173 (n33)
post-colonial literature 15
power talking 62
'Praises' (Bennett) 55
pregnancy 92
Professor Grizzy 151–2
proverbs
  African cultures 45
  collected 45, 200–4
  as framing technique 42–3
  gender perspective 202–4
  metaphorical 37–8
  as meta-text 105
  in oral tradition 2, 38
  and riddles 127
  sustained use 43–5
  work ethic 59–60
'Proverbs' (Bennett) 43–5

'Racket' (Bennett) 50–1
Rastafarianism 9–11, 106–7, 121, 122, 130–2
'Rastaman Chant' (Marley) 121
Rastaman Vibration (Marley) 118, 122, 127
Red Dragon 137
'Red Ibo' (Sistren) 93–4
'Redemption Song' (Marley) 123–4
'Reggae, Rastas and Rudies' (Hebdige) 138–9
'Reggae and Cultural Identity in Jamaica' (Brodber and Greene) 120–1
reggae music 4–5, 115, 117, 193–4
Reggae Sunsplash Festival 189
register, shifting 11–12
'Registration' (Bennett) 53–4
Reid, Vic 1, 3–4
reverse colonisation 183–4, 193
'Revolution' (Marley) 121–2
'Riddym Ravings' (Breeze) 68–9, 73, 74
'Rightful Way' (Bennett) 65
ring games 83, 247
Rohlehr, Gordon 70, 82, 190
role reversal 50
'Room dem a rent' (Smith) 83
Rowe, Maureen 10, 131
'Runaway, The' 32–3

'Sable Venus, The – An Ode' 23
samfie 153–4, 172 (n25)
scholarship, Jamaican as language of 91–5
Scott, Michael 20, 21, 23
scribal/oral continuum *see* oral/scribal discourse
seduction, language of 135 (n16)
'Seeking a Job' (Bennett) 57–8
sex/food metaphor 137
sexual love 127–8
sexual politics 27–8, 29, 70, 113
sexuality 76–7, 162–3
Shabba Ranks 138, 149, 156–7, 166, 193
signifier/signified 15
signifyin' 127
'Simple Tings' (Breeze) 75–6
singer/DJ tension 144
Sistren Theatre Collective 9, 12, 87–95

slackness
  and culture 11–12, 141–2, 147–8, 154, 171
  DJs 141, 144, 146, 148–9
  and illiteracy 161
  in oral discourse 40
  vs righteousness 127
  subversive 141–2
'Slackness Done' (Wales) 143–4
Slemon, Stephen 14
'Small Axe' (Marley) 119, 120
Small Place, A (Kincaid) 186–7
Smith, Honor Ford 87, 93

Smith, Mikey 9, 69–70, 73, 81, 82, 83
social commentary 167–71
'South Parade Peddler' (Bennett) 61, 62
speech/writing *see* oral/scribal discourse
Stallybrass, Peter 26–7, 191
Straw, Petrine Archer 126
subversion
  and dialogue 87
  feminist 87
  and knowledge 174
  and language 121
  in literature 22
  in relationships 29
  and slackness 141–2
'Sunday a Come' (Smith) 78
'Sunday' (Smith) 78
Super Cyat 139, 165
Survival (Marley) 118, 123
'Sweetie-Pie' (Bennett) 43

taboo-breaking 98–9, 162
'Tajo! My Mackey Massa!' 29–30
'Tan-Up Seat' (Bennett) 49–50
Tanna, Laura 60–1
taste 8, 9
'teck bad tings mek joke' 32, 45, 95
'Tell Me' (Ninja Man) 156
testimony 87, 94
Their Eyes Were Watching God (Hurston) 2, 7
Thelwell, Michael 9, 11, 96, 99–115
Theory of Parody, A (Hutcheon) 182
therapeutic masking 32, 45, 95
There Ain't No Black in the Union Jack (Gilroy) 141
Thunder, Shelley 153–4, 155
Tiffin, Helen 14
'Time Will Tell' (Marley) 122–3
'Titty Jump' (Yellowman) 163
Tom Cringle's Log (Scott) 20, 21, 23
Tosh, Peter 91, 99, 119, 151
tourism 186–7, 189–90
'Trailerload a Girls' (Shabba Ranks) 138

transcription problems 117–18, 120
  see also oral/scribal discourse
transgressive blood knowledge 22–3, 29, 32, 174
'Turn Your Lights Down Life' (Marley) 129–30

Uprising (Marley) 118, 123–4, 131–4
'Uriah Preach' (Bennett) 56–7

verbal creativity 117, 118, 142
verbal marronage 136
Voiceprint (Rohlehr) 82
vulgarity 8–9 *see also* slackness

'Waan Mi Virgin' (Yellowman) 137, 162, 163–4
Wailers, The 118–19
'Waiting in Vain' (Marley) 128–9
Walcott, Derek 13–14, 89
Wales, Josey 141, 143–4
Walker, Alice 96
'Warner' (Breeze) 83–4
'Watch Mi a Watch Dem' (Papa San) 168
'We and Them' (Marley) 132–3
Werner, Alice 103–4
West India Customs and Manners (Moreton) 20–2, 33–4
West Indian Federation 182
West Indian identity 183–4, 191
West Indian Poetry (Brown) 47
'Which One?' (Bennett) 65
White, Allon 26–7, 191–2
White, Garth 12
Whitney, M. L. 121
'Who the Cap Fit' (Marley) 127
'Whole Heap a Man' (Minott and Lady G) 153
'Wil(d) Gilbert' (Lovindeer) 169–71
Williams, Paulette 97, 98
'Winey-Winey' (Bailey) 145
'Woman in Rastafari, The' (Rowe) 131
women, status 27, 47–8, 66, 127, 131–2
women's federation movement 51–4
work/education 92
working-class occupations 57
'Writing Home' (Bennett) 56

Yellowman 137
'Yu Man a Rush Mi' (Thunder) 153–4

Zephaniah, Benjamin 71, 72

Carolyn Cooper is Senior Lecturer in English and a long-standing member of the Women and Development Group, University of the West Indies, Mona, Jamaica.

Library of Congress Cataloging-in-Publication Data
Cooper, Carolyn, 1950–
Noises in the blood : orality, gender, and the "vulgar" body of Jamaican popular culture / Carolyn Cooper. — 1st U.S. ed.
p. cm.
Originally published: New York : Macmillan, 1993.
Includes bibliographical references and index.
ISBN 0-8223-1580-7 (cloth : acid-free paper).—
ISBN 0-8223-1595-5 (pbk. : acid-free paper)
1. Popular culture—Jamaica. 2. English language—Jamaica. I. Title.
F1874.C66 1995 972.9206—dc20 CIP